Footprint Handbook

Honduras

RICHARD ARGHIRIS

This is
Honduras

Sliced, spliced and spread across a mountainous interior, Honduras is a pleasantly challenging surprise that has developed in curiously disconnected zones. In the heart of the mountains Tegucigalpa epitomizes the Latin city – a chaotic celebration of colonial architecture divided by steeply sloping cobbled streets. By contrast, the republic's second and more modern city, San Pedro Sula, on the coastal lowland plain, has a neat matrix of *calles* and *avenidas* that seem rather dull by comparison.

A world away, the Bay Islands bask under sunny skies. Utila thrives on a throw-it-together-and-see-if-it-works existence. It's easily the cheapest place to learn to dive in the western hemisphere.

Honduras is the second largest Central American republic after Nicaragua, but its population is smaller than that of neighbouring El Salvador, the smallest country. Bordered by Nicaragua, Guatemala, El Salvador and a narrow coastal Pacific strip, it is the northern Caribbean coast and beautiful Bay Islands that are a natural focus and a prime destination for visitors.

Inland, the mountainous terrain creates natural obstacles to easy, direct travel around the country. It also means that, for trekking and hiking, there are great swathes of beautiful hillside, much of which is dotted with small communities, largely disinterested in the comings and goings of the few travellers who venture so far off the beaten track.

Richard Arghiris

Best of
Honduras

❶ Gracias

Mighty Celaque, the country's highest peak, beckons intrepid hikers from the refreshing mountain town of Gracias. Once you've climbed its slopes and explored its cloudforests, you can descend to nearby hot springs and soak your weary limbs. Gracias is worth a visit for its fine colonial churches and restored fort. Page 42.

❷ Copán

The haunting ruins of Copán guard some of the Mayan world's most fascinating sculptures and statues including ornately carved stelae and sacrificial altars depicting the ruling dynasties, monuments dedicated to a pantheon of otherworldly gods and a hieroglyphic staircase that tells the remarkable history of the city. Page 63.

❸ Lago Yojoa

One of the largest natural lakes in
Honduras, Yojoa is a popular weekend
beauty spot, although you may be
tempted to stay longer than a day or two.
The verdant surroundings are filled with
rambling nature reserves and coffee fincas,
perfect country for hiking and wildlife
observation; don't miss the 42-m-high
Pulhpanazak waterfall. Page 67.

❹ Bay Islands

Honduras' fabled Bay Islands are a bastion
of tranquillity, best known for their
kaleidoscope of coral reefs and highly
affordable diving instruction. Explore the
underwater world of the Caribbean before
unwinding on the beach, kicking back to
calypso rhythms and sampling the local
rum. Page 85.

❺ Omoa

On the Bahía de Cortés, backed by jungle-
clad mountains, is this increasingly popular
beach and fishing village with an old fort.
There are good walks along the coast and
inland, and it makes for a handy stopover
on the way to Guatemala, with buses
to the border and boats to Livíngston.
Page 108.

❻ Around La Ceiba

The real attraction isn't the Caribbean
coast city of La Ceiba, but everything
that surrounds it, including culturally
fascinating Garífuna communities, tranquil
beaches and, in the Parque Nacional Pico
Bonito, tangled rainforests filled with
adrenalin-pumping whitewater rivers.
Offshore are the palm-fringed Cayos
Cochinos (Hog Islands). Page 115.

❼ Trujillo

A former banana port and the country's oldest town, Trujillo is now a laid-back place to visit. You can hike from town up the peaks in the Parque Nacional Capiro y Calentura, or visit the Isla de los Pájaros wildlife reserve by dug-out canoe. Strung along the mangrove-fringed coast nearby are a series of Garífuna villages, with attractive sandy beaches. Page 126.

❽ La Mosquitia

The Río Coco on the Nicaraguan border marks the spiritual heart of the Mosquitia, one of the most remote indigenous regions in Central America. Travel in this part of the country is as rewarding as it is challenging, a natural and cultural odyssey strictly for experienced adventurers. Page 135.

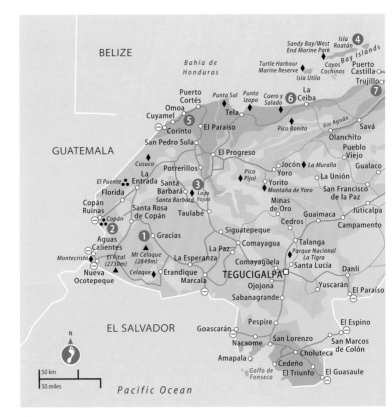

Isla Guanaja

Santa Rosa de Aguán   Limón   Iriona   Palacios   Cocobila

Capiro y Calentura   Río Sico   Sico   Río Plátano   Brus Laguna

Bonito Oriental   Las Marías

Río Paulaya   Reserva de la Biósfera Río Plátano   Puerto Lempira   Caratasca Lagoon

Río Patuca

Caribbean Sea

LA MOSQUITIA 8

Sierra de Agalta

San Esteban

Dulce Nombre de Culmi   Rus Rus   Leimus

Auasbila

Catacamas

Patuca

NICARAGUA

Iguana

Route
planner

With the popularity of the Bay Islands as a diving destination, mainland Honduras is often missed in the frenzied rush towards the sea. And, while the beauty of the islands cannot be overstated, picking a route that takes in some of the smaller towns of Honduras gives a far better understanding of the country as a whole.

One week

diving and Maya ruins

If you have just a week, you could use domestic flights to save time and visit just the must-see destinations of Honduras: Copán and the Bay Islands. West of Tegucigalpa, near the border with Guatemala, is Honduras' premier Maya archaeological site **Copán**, where new discoveries continue to be made, and some fine Maya art can be seen. A short distance from the site, the well-restored town of **Copán Ruinas** is a colonial gem and, nearby, the site of **El Puente** is beginning to reveal treasures hidden for centuries. Curving in an arc off the coast near La Ceiba, the **Bay Islands** of **Utila**, **Roatán** and **Guanaja**, plus the smaller **Hog Islands**, are some of Honduras' main tourist destinations. Travellers visiting just one part of Honduras often pick the islands. The diving is excellent and Utila is currently the cheapest dive centre in the Caribbean. The islands also have good beaches. Flights operate between the Bay Islands and La Ceiba and Tegucigalpa.

Three weeks or more

colonial towns and Garífuna villages

If you have ample time, you can travel a circular route around Honduras. Starting in the capital, **Tegucigalpa**, you could explore its old, colonial sector and a new section with modern hotels and shopping malls. Across the Río Choluteca is Tegucigalpa's twin city, **Comayagüela**, the working heart of the city with the markets and bus terminals. Around the capital, there are colonial villages, old mining towns, handicraft centres and good hiking areas, including **Parque Nacional La Tigra**, which will make ideal trips for a day or two.

Leaving Tegucigalpa, travel to the ruins of Copán, stopping at the colonial towns of Gracias and Santa Rosa de Copán on the way. There is lots of good hiking in the vicinity of Santa Rosa de Copán. A good way to explore this more traditional part of the country is to pick a route, travel in short distances and soak up the calm and tranquillity. From Copán ruins, it's a bus to San Pedro Sula, the second city of the republic and the country's main business centre, and a quick change for the **north coast**, which has a number of centres of interest. The main port is **Puerto Cortés**, while west of here is **Omoa**, a fishing village with a beach an old fort, and access to Guatemala. East of San Pedro Sula are **Tela**, a more established resort, and **La Ceiba**, a good base for visiting the nearby national parks of Pico Bonito and Cuero y Salado, whitewater rafting trips on the Río Cangrejal and departure point for the Bay Islands and La Mosquitia. Further east, **Trujillo**, sitting at the southern end of a palm-fringed bay, was once the country capital.

From La Ceiba, the ferry leaves for **Roatán** and **Utila**, the budget travellers' choice for diving, snorkelling and island life. Returning the capital, you can take an alternate route from San Pedro Sula through **Lago Yojoa** and **Comayagua**.

Visiting the **Mosquitia** takes extra planning and time – at least another week. It's most easily reached from La Ceiba, and is forested, swampy and very sparsely populated. Efforts are being made to promote sustainable development among the Miskito and the Pech. Small-scale ecotourism initiatives have been set up in some coastal communities and inland, making for adventurous and rewarding travel where the main ways of getting around are by boat, small plane or on foot.

When to go

... and when not to

Climate depends largely on altitude. In Tegucigalpa, at 1000 m, temperatures can be cold January to March but pleasantly hot April to May. On the Caribbean the dry season is from February to June, while the heaviest rains fall between August and December. Some of the central highland areas have a delightful climate, with a freshness that makes a pleasant contrast to the humidity and heat of the lowland zones.

Festivals

If the time and mood is right, there is little to beat a Latin American festival. Fine costumes, loud music, the sounds of firecrackers tipped off with the gentle wafting of specially prepared foods all (normally) with a drink or two. Whether you're seeking the carnival or happen to stumble across a celebration, the events – big or small – are memorable. Carnival is normally the week before the start of Lent. Semana Santa (Easter Week) is an understandably more spiritual affair. On 2 November is Día de los Muertos (Day of the Dead), when families visit cemeteries to honour the dead. Christmas and New Year result in celebrations of some kind, but not always public.

Other important local fiestas are also busy times; book ahead. Keep an eye out for patron saints of villages and towns. August is holiday time for Hondurans so accommodation can be scarce, especially in the smaller resorts.

Weather Tegucigalpa

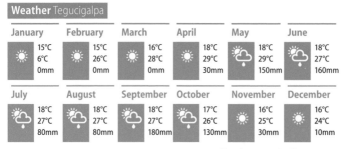

January	February	March	April	May	June
15°C	15°C	16°C	18°C	18°C	18°C
6°C	26°C	28°C	29°C	29°C	27°C
0mm	0mm	0mm	30mm	150mm	160mm

July	August	September	October	November	December
18°C	18°C	18°C	17°C	16°C	16°C
27°C	27°C	27°C	26°C	25°C	24°C
80mm	80mm	180mm	130mm	30mm	10mm

Public holidays lead to a complete shut-down in services. There are no banks, government offices and usually no shops open, and often far fewer restaurants and bars. It is worth keeping an eye on the calendar to avoid changing money or trying to make travel arrangements on public holidays.

Festivals and public holidays

Most Roman Catholic feast days are celebrated.

1 January **New Year's Day.**

1-4 February **Supaya**, southeast of Tegucigalpa, the most important shrine in Honduras with a tiny wooden image of the Virgen de Supaya.

14 April **Day of the Americas.**

March/April **Semana Santa** (Thursday, Friday and Saturday before Easter Sunday).

1 May **Labour Day.**

15 May **San Isidro**, La Ceiba's patrón saint, followed by a fortnight of celebrations. The highlight is a huge carnival on the third Sat in May.

15 September **Independence Day.**

3 October **Francisco Morazán.**

12 October **Columbus' arrival in America.**

21 October **Army Day.**

What to do

Adventure tourism

Mountain biking is increasingly popular as is horse riding around Copán. Hardcore adventure can be found in the swamp wetlands and tropical forests of Mosquitia, usually by taking an organized tour.

Archaeology and architecture

Western Honduras marked the eastern extent of Mayan civilization. The royal city of Copán is an exemplary beauty among Classic era sites, but there are no major ruins beyond it. The nation's colonial heritage dates from the 16th century and is far more widespread: the small cities of Gracias, Santa Rosa de Copán and Comayagua are all celebrated for their historical architecture, but there are also numerous smaller and well-preserved colonial settlements scattered throughout the mountains.

Birdwatching and wildlife observation

From lowland coastal mangroves to mountainous cloudforests, Honduras' diversity of ecosystems harbours a staggering variety of fauna. Scores of protected areas offer the prospect of wildlife observation (see Hiking below) with special highlights including manatees on the Caribbean coast, and jaguars, ocelots and tapirs in lowland forests, which are all quite tricky to spot. Monkeys, coati, opossums and sloths are far more common and fairly easy to encounter. Avian species in Honduras include notables such as the great green macaw, crested owl, great potoo, long-tailed manakin, harpy eagle and resplendent quetzal. Two highly reputable birding guides include former Peace Corp volunteer turned resident Robert Gallardo, www.birdsofhonduras.com; and Alexander Alvarado, who grew up in Copán Ruinas, www.honduranbirds. com. The national bird of Honduras is the scarlet macaw and these live in great numbers around the Mayan ruin of Copán.

Diving

Diving off the Bay Islands has long been the number one attraction in Honduras; the reefs and underwater pinnacles offer some of the best and most varied diving in Central America.

PADI courses are also among the cheapest in the world, with both Roatán and Utila drawings scores of scuba students. Snorkelling is excellent too.

Hiking

An extensive system of national parks and protected areas offers the chance to hike in some of the best scenery Honduras has to offer, much of it unspoilt and rarely visited. For mountainous terrain, head to western Honduras. Starting outside the capital, Parque Nacional La Tigra is a convenient cloudforest reserve with simple overnight accommodation. On the road to Copán, Las Trancas may reward with a glimpse of resplendent quetzals (if you're lucky). Further on, Parque Nacional Celaque is a definite highlight, as are the more remote and tricky to access reserves of Guisayote and Montecristo. On the road to San Pedro Sula, Parque Nacional Cerro Azul-Meámbar and Parque Nacional de Santa Bárbara are home to extensive waterfalls and karst scenery. Parque Nacional Cusuco, outside San Pedro itself, encompasses pine and cloudforests. The Caribbean coast tends to be flatter and steamier than the highlands but offers good potential for jungle treks. Options include Parque Nacional Punta Sal near Tela and the highly recommended Parque Nacional Pico Bonito near La Ceiba. The big reserves in the remote northeast are the Parque Nacional Sierra de Agalta and the Reserva de la Biósfera Río Plátano. Natural reserves continue to be established throughout the country.

Whitewater rafting

Rafting is growing steadily in Honduras with the hot spot being the River Cangrejal, close to La Ceiba, where Grade II, III and IV rapids test both the novice and experienced paddler. The sport is relatively new to Honduras and more sites are sure to be found in the coming years.

ON THE ROAD
Shopping

The best articles are those made of wood. Straw items, including woven ornaments, are also highly recommended. Leather is cheaper than in El Salvador and Nicaragua. As a single stopping point, the region around Santa Bárbara is one of the best places, with outlets selling handicrafts from nearby villages. In Copán Ruinas you can also get a wide range of products, including cigars and high-quality jewellery, as well as many Guatemalan handicrafts at similar prices. Alternatively you can explore the villages yourself and see the goods being made. Coffee is OK, but not great. Sales tax is 12%; 15% on alcohol and tobacco.

Where to stay

from business-style hotels to backpacker hostels

Accommodation in Honduras varies greatly. In Tegucigalpa and San Pedro Sula you will find the mix ranges from business-style hotels of international standards down to simple, but generally clean rooms. In popular tourist spots the focus is more on comfort and costs rise accordingly. Get off the beaten track and you'll find some of the cheapest and most basic accommodation in Central America; complete with accompanying insect life, it can be unbearable or a mind-broadening experience depending on your mood. There is a 4% extra tax on rooms in the better hotels.

Price codes

Where to stay	Restaurants
$$$$ over US$150	$$$ over US$12
$$$ US$66-150	$$ US$7-12
$$ US$30-65	$ US$6 and under
$ under US$30	

Price of a double room in high season, including taxes.

Prices for a two-course meal for one person, excluding drinks or service charge.

Food
& drink

prawn soup, fried plantain and pupusas

The cheapest meals are the *comida corriente*, or the sometimes better prepared and more expensive *comida típica*, which usually contain some of the following: beans, rice, meat, avocado, egg, cabbage salad, cheese, bananas, potatoes or yucca, and always tortillas. *Carne asada* is charcoal-roasted meat and served with grated cabbage between tortillas; it is good, although rarely prepared hygienically. Make sure that pork is properly cooked. *Tajadas* are crisp, fried *plátano* chips topped with grated cabbage and sometimes meat; *nacatamales* are ground, dry maize mixed with meat and seasoning, boiled in banana leaves. *Baleadas* are soft flour tortillas filled with beans and various combinations of butter, egg, cheese and cabbage. *Pupusas* are thick corn tortillas filled with *chicharrón* (pork scratchings), or cheese, served as snacks with beer. *Tapado* is a stew with meat or fish, plantain, yucca and coconut milk. *Pinchos* are meat, poultry, or shrimp kebabs. *Sopa de mondongo* (tripe soup) is very common.

Fish is sold on the beaches at Trujillo and Cedeño; also freshly fried at the roadside by the shore of Lago Yojoa. While on the north coast, look out for *pan de coco* (coconut bread) made by Garífuna (Black Carib) women, and *sopa de camarones* (prawn soup) prepared with coconut milk and lemon juice. Honduras is now a major producer of tilapia with exports to the US and fresh tilapia available in many restaurants.

Drink

Soft drinks are called *refrescos*, or *frescos* (the name also given to fresh fruit blended with water, make sure you check that bottled water is used as tap water is unsafe); *licuados* are fruit blended with milk. Bottled drinking water is available in most places. *Horchata* is morro seeds, rice water and cinnamon. Coffee is thick and sweet. The main brands of beer are Port Royal Export, Imperial, Nacional, Barena and Salva Vida (which is more malty than the others). Local rum is cheap, try Flor de Caña white, or seven-year-old amber. Twelve-year-old Flor de Caña Centenario is regarded as the best.

Essential Tegucigalpa

Finding your feet

The winding of streets in the city means that moving around in the first few days is as much about instinct as following any map. The Tegucigalpa section of the city uses both names and numbers for streets, but names are used more commonly. In Comayagüela, streets designated by number are the norm. Addresses tend not to be very precise, especially in the *colonias* around Boulevard Morazán east and south of the centre of Tegucigalpa.

Best places to stay

Humuya Inn, page 25
Minister Business Hotel, page 26
Nuevo Boston, page 26
Granada 2 and Granada 3, page 26

Getting around

There are cheap buses, but for safety it is better to use taxis.

Tip...

On arrival it is very much easier – and recommended for safety – to take a taxi to your hotel until you get to know the city.

Best restaurants

Hacienda Real, page 27
La Cumbre, page 27
Rojo, Verde y Ajo, page 27
El Patio, page 28
Don Pepe's Terraza, page 28

Safety

Generally speaking, Tegucigalpa is cleaner and safer (especially at night) than Comayagüela. If you have anything stolen, report it to **Dirección de Investigación Criminal (DGIC)**, 5 Avenida, 7-8 Calle (next to Edificio Palermo), T2237-4799.

Tip...

For good restaurants, take a walk down the pedestrianized stretch of Avenida Paz Barahona. In the evening, take a taxi to Boulevard Morazón.

When to go

The city's altitude gives it a reliable climate: temperate during the rainy season from May to October; warm, with cool nights in March and April; and cool and dry with cool nights from November to April. See also the climate chart on page 11.

Tegucigalpa
& around

Built on the region's mineral wealth, Tegucigalpa, the capital of Honduras, is a relentless urban dynamo, neither beautiful nor compelling, but as a hub of business and transport, essential and unavoidable.

The chaotic Tegucigalpa – or Tegus as it is called by locals – is cramped and crowded, but still somehow retains a degree of charm in what remains of the colonial centre. If you can bear to stay away from the Caribbean for a few days, it has much more history and charisma than its rival San Pedro Sula, to the north.

Surrounded by sharp, high peaks on three sides, the city is built on the lower slopes of El Picacho. Its smattering of Spanish colonial plazas, churches and townhouses contrast with much newer structures – high-rise office blocks, condos and shopping malls – which are signs of the city's growing, if unevenly distributed, wealth and commercialism. The commercial centre is around Boulevard Morazán, an area known as 'zona viva', full of cafés, restaurants and shops. For contrast to the modern functional city, you can visit some of the centuries-old mining settlements set in forested valleys among the nearby mountains that are ideal for hiking.

Sights

Crossing the river in Tegucigalpa (altitude 1000 m, population 1.1 million) from Comayagüela by the colonial Mallol bridge, on the left is the old **Casa Presidencial** (1919), home to the National Archive. When this was a museum, visitors could see the president's office and the Salón Azul state room. Try asking – you may be lucky. (The new Palacio Presidencial is a modern building on Boulevard Juan Pablo II in Colonia Lomas del Mayab.)

Calle Bolívar leads to the Congress building and the former site of the University, founded in 1847. The site adjoining the church in Plaza La Merced is now the

Tegucigalpa

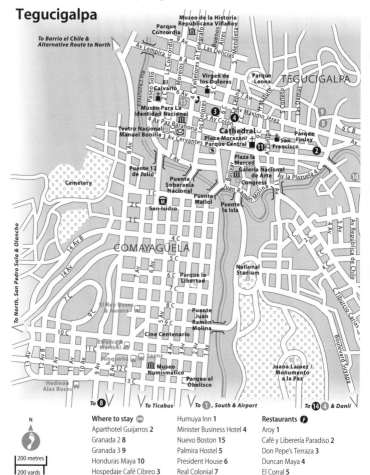

N	Where to stay	Humuya Inn 1	Restaurants
	Aparthotel Guijarros 2	Minister Business Hotel 4	Aroy 1
	Granada 2 8	Nuevo Boston 15	Café y Librería Paradiso 2
200 metres	Granada 3 9	Palmira Hostel 5	Don Pepe's Terraza 3
200 yards	Honduras Maya 10	President House 6	Duncan Maya 4
	Hospedaje Café Cibreo 3	Real Colonial 7	El Corral 5

Galería Nacional de Arte ⓘ *Tue-Fri 0900-1600, Sat 0900-1200, US$1.50*, a beautifully restored 17th-century building, housing a very fine collection of Honduran modern and colonial art, prehistoric rock carvings and some remarkable pre-Colombian ceramic pieces. There are useful descriptions of exhibits, and explanations of the mythology embodied in the prehistoric and pre-Colombian art.

Calle Bolívar leads to the main square, Plaza Morazán (commonly known as Parque Central). On the eastern side of the square is the **Palacio del Distrito Central**, and the domed and double-towered **cathedral**, built in the late 18th century but which have had a complete facelift. See the gilt colonial altarpiece, the fine examples of Spanish colonial art, the cloisters and, in Holy Week, the ceremony of the Descent from the Cross.

Avenida Miguel Paz Barahona, running through the north side of the square, is a key venue. To the east is the church of **San Francisco**, with its clangorous bells, and, on 3 Calle, called Avenida Cervantes, the old **Spanish Mint** (1770), now the national printing works.

From Plaza Morazán, heading west towards the river to Avenida Miguel Paz Barahona, opposite the post office is the **Museo Para La Identidad Nacional** ⓘ *T2238-7412, www.min.hn, Tue-Sat 0900-1700, Sun 1100-1700, US$3.30*, a museum that is unashamedly about Honduras for Hondurans. There is a good multimedia presentation (with an audioguide, in Spanish only), and a well-thought-out trip through Honduran history, from plate tectonics to the present day. Its star attraction is 'Virtual Copán' – a wide-screen CGI recreation of the Maya ruins, entrance US$1.65; there are also occasional temporary exhibitions. It offers just enough detail without getting heavy; every capital city in Central America should have a museum like this.

El Patio **6**
Gino's Pasta Café **7**
Hacienda Real **8**
La Cacerola **9**
Marjaba Café **10**
Merendero El Buen Gusto **11**

Rojo, Verde y Ajo **12**
Tony's Mar **14**

BACKGROUND
Tegucigalpa

Founded as a silver and gold mining camp in 1578, Tegucigalpa means silver hill in the original indigenous tongue; miners first discovered gold at the north end of the current Soberanía bridge. The present city is comprised of the two former towns of Comayagüela and Tegucigalpa which, although divided by the steeply banked Río Choluteca, became the capital in 1880 and are now united administratively as the Distrito Central.

Being off the main earthquake fault line, Tegucigalpa has not been subjected to disasters by fire or earthquake, unlike many of its Central American neighbours, so it has retained many traditional features. The stuccoed houses, with a single, heavily barred entrance leading to a central patio, are often attractively coloured. However, the old low skyline of the city has been punctuated by several modern tall buildings, and much of the old landscape changed with the arrival of Hurricane Mitch.

The rains of Hurricane Mitch in October 1998 had a devastating effect on the Distrito Central. But the damage caused by the Choluteca bursting its banks is hard to see these days, with the exception of the first avenue of Comayagüela, where abandoned homes and buildings remain empty. Bridges washed away by the floodwaters have now been replaced, power supplies are back and, in some respects, traffic is actually better now, since many routes were diverted from the heart of downtown. Today, Hurricane Mitch lives on as painful memory.

Heading east a block, then left (north) along 5 Calle (Calle Los Dolores), is the 18th-century church of **Iglesia de Nuestra Señora de los Dolores**. Two blocks north and three blocks west of the church is the beautiful Parque Concordia with good copies of Maya sculpture and temples. On a hilltop one block above Parque Concordia, on Calle Morelos 3A, is the **Museo de la Historia Republicana Villa Roy**, the former site of the Museo Nacional and, in 1936, home of the former president, Julio Lozano. Sadly, the building sustained severe structural damage from landslides in 2014 and at the time of research the museum was closed for the foreseeable future. It may or may not reopen; check with the tourist office for the latest news.

Back on Avenida Miguel Paz Barahona, and further west, are the **Teatro Nacional Manuel Bonilla**, with a rather grand interior (1915) inspired by the Athenée Theatre in Paris and, across the square, the beautiful old church of **El Calvario**. Built in elegant colonial style, El Calvario's roof is supported by 14 pillars.

In Colonia Palmira, to the southeast of the city, is Boulevard Morazán, with shopping and business complexes, embassies, banks, restaurants, *cafeterías* and bars. You can get a fine view of the city from the **Monumento a La Paz** ① *open till 1700*, on Juana Laínez hill, near the Estadio Nacional (National Stadium), but don't walk up alone.

The backdrop to Tegucigalpa is the summit of **El Picacho**, with the Cristo del Picacho statue looming up to the north (see Valle de Angeles, below), although this can be hard to see at times. From Plaza Morazán go up 7 Calle and the Calle de la Leona to **Parque La Leona**, a small handsome park with a railed walk overlooking the city and safer than Monumento a La Paz.

Higher still is the reservoir in El Picacho, also known as the **United Nations Park**, which can be reached by a special bus from the No 9 bus stop, behind Los Dolores church (in front of Farmacia Santa Bárbara, Sunday only, US$0.15); alternatively, take a bus to El Piligüin or Corralitos (daily at 0600) from the north side of Parque Herrera in front of the Teatro Nacional Manuel Bonilla.

Comayagüela

Crossing the bridge of 12 de Julio (quite near the Teatro Nacional Manuel Bonilla, see above) you can visit Comayagüela's market of San Isidro. In the Edificio del Banco Central, is the **Pinacoteca Arturo H Medrano** ⓘ *12 Calle entre 5 y 6 Av*, which houses approximately 500 works by five Honduran artists, and the **Museo Numismático** ⓘ *Mon-Fri 0900-1200, 1300-1600*, which has a collection of coins and banknotes.

Listings Tegucigalpa *map p22*

Tourist information

Instituto Hondureño de Turismo
Edif Europa, Av Ramón E Cruz and Calle República de México, 3rd floor, Col San Carlos, T2222-2124; also at Toncontín Airport, open 0830-1530.
Tourist offices provide lists of hotels and sell posters and postcards. Information on cultural events around the country from **Teatro Nacional Manuel Bonilla** is better than at regional tourist offices.

Where to stay

There is a 4% tax on hotel bills, plus 12% sales tax: check if it is included in the price.

$$$ Aparthotel Guijarros
Col Lomas del Guijarro, Calle Roma 3929, T2235-6851, www.guijarros.com.
Enjoying a good location in a safe residential neighbourhood, Aparthotel Guijarros offers a range of modern rooms, suites, and apartments, all fully kitted with 32 inch screens, microwave, mini-fridge, Wi-Fi, hair-dryers and more. Offerings in the restaurant include home-grown organic produce. A decent and reliable option with very accommodating staff.

$$$ Honduras Maya
Av República de Chile, Col Palmira, T2280-5000, www.hotelhonduras maya.hn.
Spacious rooms and apartments, dated decor, casino and pool, **Bar Mirador** with nightly happy hour 1700-1900, *cafeterías*, restaurant, very good buffet breakfast, conference hall and convention facilities for 1300, view over the city from upper rooms. Excellent travel agency in the basement. Expensive internet access.

$$$ Humuya Inn
Col Humuya 1150, 5 mins from airport, T2239-2206, www.humuyainn.com.

Helpful, homey and professionally run lodgings with lots of good reports. Accommodation includes rooms and service apartments, US owner. Quiet family atmosphere and nice views from the rooftop terrace. Recommended.

$$$ Minister Business Hotel
Col Florencia Norte, Blvd Suyapa 2340, T2280-6464, www.ministerbusiness.com.
This swish business hotel boasts stylish contemporary decor and a superb rooftop bar with 360-degree views of the city. Rooms are smallish but well-attired with plush fixtures and modern amenities, including cable TV, high-speed Wi-Fi and coffee machine. A very comfortable and presentable option. Recommended.

$$$ President House Hotel
Col Lomas del Guijarro, Av Enrique Tierno Galvan, T2231-0431, www.presidenthousehotel.com.
Well-situated in a quiet residential neighbourhood, this refurbished colonial-style townhouse was originally built for Honduran ex-president Ramón Ernesto Cruz. Perched on a hill, it offers airy terraces with a restaurant and coffeehouse. Accommodation is in comfortable rooms with a/c, cable TV, hot water, safe box and Wi-Fi. A good deal for single travellers ($).

$$$-$$ Real Colonial Hotel
Col Palmira, Calzada San Martín 458, T2220-7497, www.realcolonialhotel.hn.
The Real Colonial is a cosy, 6-storey hotel with attentive service, bright murals and a small outdoor patio where you can enjoy breakfast. Rooms are simple, comfortable and modern, featuring all the usual amenities including high-

speed Wi-Fi, a/c, and 32 inch screen. Nestled in an exclusive neighbourhood.

$$ Hospedaje Café Cibreo
Col Palmira, Calzada San Martín 452, T2220-5323, www.hospedajecafecibreo.cdvhotels.com.
Formerly Leslie's Place, this homely and well-established B&B has a restaurant-café serving Mediterranean-style cooking in an open-air courtyard. Rooms have high-speed Wi-Fi, hot water, cable TV and a/c. Close to bars and restaurants. Down-to-earth and pleasant.

$$ Nuevo Boston
Av Máximo Jerez 321, T2237-9411.
In a central location, this well-run, simple place has spotless rooms with good beds, and hot water. Rooms on the street side are noisy. Good value, no credit cards, free coffee, mineral water and cookies in lounge, stores luggage. Recommended.

$ Granada 2 and $ Granada 3
T238-4438 and T2237-0843, on the street leading uphill (to Barrio Casamate) from northeast corner of Parque Finlay.
Good beds, hot water and safe parking. It can be noisy from passing traffic so try to get a room at the back. Recommended.

$ Palmira Hostel
Av Juan Lindo, T2236-9143, www.palmirahostel.com.
A cheap, comfortable, reliable hostel located in a safe part of town opposite the French embassy and around the corner from the US embassy. They offer well-kept dorms and private rooms, clean and spartan. There is a small outdoor terrace and indoor communal areas, including a kitchen. Wi-Fi included.

Comayagüela

Comayagüela is convenient for buses to the north and west and there are many cheap *pensiones* and rooms. It is noisier and dirtier than Tegucigalpa and many places are unsuitable for travellers. If you are carrying luggage, take a taxi.

Restaurants

Most places close on Sun.

$$$ El Corral
4a Av, opposite Hotel Clarión, Col Alameda, T2232-5066.
Big, brash steakhouse, with excellent grilled meats and decent wine list. Lively at weekends, with live music, karaoke and dancing.

$$$ Gino's Pasta Café
Distrito Hotelero San Martín, Col Palmira, www.ginos-pastacafe.com.
Gino serves some of the best home-cooked Italian food in Honduras, fresh, simple, and flavourful, the way good Italian food should be. Soups, salads, pastas and pizza are among the authentic offerings at this cosy and popular eatery.

$$$ Hacienda Real
Plaza Colprosumah and Blvd Juan Pablo II, west side of Hotel Marriot, T2239-6860, www.hacienda-real.com.
One of the finest steakhouses in Honduras, set in a handsome colonial-style building and part of a high-end international franchise with branches in Guatemala and El Salvador. Prices are steep, but not by western standards. Popular for business lunches.

$$$ La Cumbre
Northeast of the city, El Hatillo Km 7.5, T2211-9000, www.lacumbrehn.com.

La Cumbre promises a memorable fine dining experience with its disarming hill-top setting and expansive views over the valley and city below. Prices for its pasta, steaks and seafood aren't cheap, but the cuisine and service are exceptional. Romantic and intimate, one of the best.

$$$ Rojo
Verde y Ajo, Av República de Argentina 1930, Col Palmira, T2232-5653, www.rojoverdeyajo.com.
A very stylish and well-executed restaurant with diverse international offerings such as beef medallions in cognac sauce and shrimp with champagne butter. Occasional live music, guest chefs and wine-tasting events. Warm and convivial. Recommended.

$$ Aroy
Blvd Morazán, T9481-9095, www.aroyhn.wix.com/aroy.
Aroy serves authentic Thai cuisine with a tempting menu of delectable delights such as summer rolls, stuffed cucumber, chicken satay, Thai coco soup, and green papaya salad. Wholesome home-cooking and a pleasant interior.

$$ Duncan Maya
Av Colón 618, opposite central Pizza Hut.
This popular locals' haunt is a lively place and it occasionally hosts live music. Food is filling and reasonably priced fare, including mostly national staples.

$$ Marjaba Café
Av República Dominicana 3641, T8880-7358, www.marjabacafe.com. Tue-Sun for lunch only.
Wholesome, tasty, affordable and

> **Tip...**
> There are good Chinese restaurants on Calle del Telégrafo in the centre; they offer huge servings at reasonable prices.

fully authentic Middle Eastern fare, and occasional belly dancers. For lunch, the buffet-style *menú del día* includes a meat dish, 5 sides and a drink. Friendly service and vegetarian options too.

$$ Tony's Mar
Col Florencia, Blvd Suyapa, T2232-5266, www.tonysmarrestaurante.com.
This reliable seafood joint has been serving up fish, prawns and ceviche for 25 years. Large servings, fresh, tasty, wholesome and reasonably priced. The current menu has lots of variety, including octopus and conch.

$$-$ El Patio
Easternmost end of Blvd Morazán, T2221-3842, www.elpatiohn.com.
Traditional food served in a large casual dining hall bedecked with old photos and fairy lights. Good service and atmosphere, and generous portions. A long-standing Tegus favourite. Recommended.

$ Don Pepe's Terraza
Av Colón 530, upstairs, T2222-1084.
Central, cheap, live music, but typical Honduran atmosphere. Heaty locals' joint with hearty grub. Recommended.

$ La Cacerola
Col Lomas del Mayab, Av República de Costa Rica 1692.
This chilled out little eatery specializes in *comida típica*, of which its hot soups are particularly renowned; the *sopa de caracol* (conch soup), a national favourite, is not to be missed. Sandwiches and wraps are also available. A light, cosy, friendly place, good for an inexpensive lunch.

$ Merendero El Buen Gusto
Calle Hipolito Matute, behind the cathedral.

An unpretentious downtown joint where you can rub shoulders with the locals and wolf down some hearty home-cooked grub. Convenient, but not fine dining.

Cafés and bakeries

Café y Librería Paradiso
Av Paz Barahona 1351.
Excellent coffee and snacks, good library, paintings and photos to enjoy, and newspapers and magazines on sale. A good meeting place with a bohemian atmosphere.

Salman's
Blvd Morazán, next to Centro Comercial Maya, www.pansalmans.com.
Several outlets. Good bread/pastries, including baguettes and doughnuts.

Bars and clubs

In front of the Universidad Nacional on Blvd Suyapa is La Peña, where every Fri at 2100 there is live music, singing and dancing, entrance US$1.40.
Blvd Morazán has plenty of choice in nightlife including **Taco Taco**, a good bar, sometimes with live mariachi music; next door **Tequila**, a popular drinking place only open at weekends. **Tobacco Road Tavern**, a popular gringo hang-out, in the downtown area on Calle Matute. **Iguana Rana Bar** is very popular with locals and visitors, similarly **La Puerta del Alcalá**, 3½ blocks down from Taca office on Blvd Morazán, Col Castaño Sur. Pleasant open setting.

Tierra Libre
Calle Casa de las Naciones Unidas 2118, 5 mins' walk from Plaza San Martín in Col Palmira, T3232-8923. Mon-Sat, 1700-2400.

Arty cinephile café/bar, with occasional screenings, small and friendly, with good cocktails and snacks.

Cinemas

Plazas 1 to 5 (in Centro Comercial Plaza Miraflores on Blv Miraflores). **Regis**, **Real**, **Opera**, and **Sagitario** (at Centro Comercial Centroamérica, Blv Miraflores), for good US films. **Multiplaza** (Col Lomas del Mayab), 6 screens. In the city centre, **Lido Palace**, **Variedades** and **Aries** (200 m up Av Gutemberg leading from Parque Finlay to Col Reforma).

Shopping

Bookshops

Editorial Guaymuras, *Av Miguel Cervantes 1055*.
Librería Paradiso, *see under Cafés and bakeries, above*. Books in Spanish.
Mercado San Isidro, *6 Av y 2 Calle, Comayagüela*. Second-hand bookstalls, cheap.
Metromedia, *Edif Casa Real, Av San Carlos, behind Centro Comercial Los Castaños, Blvd Morazán*. English books, new and second-hand, for sale or exchange.

Markets

Mercado de Artesanías, *3 Av, 15 Calle, next to Parque El Soldado*. Good value.
Mercado San Isidro, *6 Av at 1 Calle, Comayagüela*. Many fascinating things, but filthy; do not buy food here. Sat is busiest day.
     Good supermarkets: **La Colonia** (in Blvd Morazán); **Más y Menos** (in Av de la Paz). Also on Calle Salvador, 1 block south of Peatonal.

What to do

Explore Honduras Tour Service, *Col Zerón 21-23 Av, 10 Calle NO, San Pedro Sula, T2552-6242, www.explorehonduras. com*. Copán and Bay Islands tours.

Transport

Air

Toncontín Airport (TGU), www. interairports.hn, is 6.5 km south of the centre in a narrow valley creating difficult landing conditions: morning fog or bad weather can cause it to close. The airport opens at 0530. Check in at least 2 hrs before departure; there are snacks, souvenir shops, several duty-free stores and internet. Buses to airport from Comayagüela, on 4 Av between 6 and 7 Calle, or from Av Máximo Jerez in downtown Tegucigalpa; into town US$0.19, every 20 mins from left-hand side outside the airport; official airport taxis (recommended) to the centre cost US$12-15; street cabs cost around US$5-6.

Bus

Local Fares are US$0.08-0.12; stops are official but unmarked.

Long distance There is no central bus station and bus companies have offices throughout Comayagüela. To **San Pedro Sula** on Northern Hwy, 3¼-4 hrs depending on service. Several companies, including: **Sáenz**, Centro Comercial Perisur, Blv Unión Europea, T2233-4229, and **Hedman Alas**, 11 Av, 13-14 Calle, Comayagüela, T2237-7143, www.hedmanalas.com, US$18; both recommended; **El Rey**, 6 Av, 9 Calle, Comayagüela, T2237-6609; **Viajes Nacionales** (Viana), terminal on Blv de Las Fuerzas Armadas, T2235-8185. To

Tela and La Ceiba, Viana Clase Oro, and Etrusca, 8 Av, 12 y 13 Calle, T2222-6881. To Choluteca, Mi Esperanza, 6 Av, 23-24 Calle, Comayagüela, T2225-1502. To Trujillo, Cotraibal, 7 Av, 10-11 Calle, Comayagüela, T2237-1666. To La Esperanza, Empresa Joelito, 4 Calle, No 834, Comayagüela. To Comayagua, most going to San Pedro Sula and Transportes Catrachos, Col Torocagua, Blv del Norte, Comayagüela. To Valle de Angeles and Santa Lucía, from stop on Av La Paz (near filling station opposite hospital). To Juticalpa and Catacamas, Empresa Aurora, 8 Calle, 6-7 Av, Comayagüela, T2237-3647. For Danlí and El Paraíso, for the Nicaraguan border at Las Manos, see page 84, and box, page 158.

For travellers leaving Tegucigalpa, take the Tiloarque bus on Av Máximo Jerez, by Calle Palace, and get off in Comayagüela at Cine Centenario (Av 6) for nearby Empresa Aurora buses (for Olancho) and El Rey buses (for San Pedro Sula). 3 blocks northwest is Cine Lux, near which are Empresas Unidas and Maribel (8 Av, 11-12 Calle, T2237-3032) for Siguatepeque. Tiloarque bus continues to Mi Esperanza bus terminal (for Choluteca and Nicaraguan border). Take a 'Carrizal' or 'Santa Fe' bus ascending Belén (9 Calle) for Hedman Alas buses to San Pedro Sula and for Comayagua buses. The Norteño bus line to San Pedro Sula is alongside Mamachepa market, from where there are also buses for Nacaome and El Amatillo border with El Salvador.

International Ticabus, Centro Comercial Plaza Toncontin, Entrada Principal de Lomas de Toncontin, Calle Hacia El IPM, south of the airport, T2291-0022, www.ticabus.com, to Managua

(US$23, 8 hrs), San José (US$65), San Salvador (US$21), Guatemala City (US$21, 12 hrs) and Panama (US$173) daily. Note: fares listed above are one-way 'executive' class. Make sure you reserve several days ahead. Hedman Alas have a service to Guatemala City and Antigua that leaves Tegucigalpa for San Pedro Sula, 0545, 12 hrs, US$52. Alternatively to Nicaragua, take Mi Esperanza bus to San Marcos de Colón, then taxi or local bus to El Espino on border. To San Marcos, 4 daily from 0730, direct to border at 0400, US$2.50, 5 hrs (0730 is the latest one that will get you into Nicaragua the same day). Or Mi Esperanza bus to Río Guasaule border, several daily, 4 hrs, US$2. To San Salvador, Cruceros del Golfo, Barrio Guacerique, Blv Comunidad Económica Europea, Comayagüela, T2233-7415, US$18, at 0600 and 1300, 6 hrs travelling, 1 hr or more at border. Connections to Guatemala and Mexico; direct bus to border at El Amatillo, US$2.50, 3 hrs, several daily; alternatively from San Pedro Sula via Nueva Ocotepeque and El Poy. To San Salvador and Guatemala, with King Quality from Tegucigalpa (T2225-5415) from Cruceros del Golfo terminal, 0600 and 1300 and San Pedro Sula (T2553-4547) at 0630. Alternatively, to Guatemala go to San Pedro Sula and take Escobar, Impala or Congolón to Nueva Ocotepeque and the border at Agua Caliente, or via Copán (see page 60 and box, page 156).

Car

Car hire Avis, Edif Palmira and airport, T2232-0088. Budget, Blv Suyapa and airport, T2235-9531. Hertz, Centro Comercial Villa Real, Col Palmira, T2239-0772. Maya, Av República de Chile 202, Col Palmira, T2232-0992. Molinari, 1 Av,

2 Calle, Comayagüela and airport, T2237-5335. **Thrifty**, Col Prados Universitarios, T2235-6077. **Toyota**, T2235-6694.

Car repairs Metal Mecánica, 1 block south of Av de los Próceres, Col Lara. Volkswagen dealer near Parque Concordia, good.

Taxi
About US$4-6 per person, but you can often bargain down to around US$3 for short distances within the city. More after 2200, cheaper on designated routes, eg Miraflores to centre.

Around Tegucigalpa
ancient mining towns steeped in aromatic highland pine forests

Heading north out of Tegucigalpa on the Olancho road, you come to Talanga, with a post office and Hondutel near the market on the main road. From Talanga it is a short trip to the historic and beautiful settlements of Cedros and Minas de Oro. From the Parque Central an unpaved road leads south to the Tegucigalpa–Danlí road making a triangular route possible back to the capital.

Cedros
Cedros (altitude 1034 m), 77 km north of Tegucigalpa, is one of Honduras' earliest settlements, dating from Pedro de Alvarado's mining operations of 1536. It is an outstanding colonial mining town with cobbled streets, perched high on an eminence amid forests. The **festival of El Señor del Buen Fin** takes place in the first two weeks of January. Buses to Talanga, Cedros and nearby San Ignacio leave from Reynita de San Ignacio in Mercado Zonal Belén, Comayagüela, T224-0066, five daily.

Santa Lucía
About 14 km northeast of Tegucigalpa, on the way to Valle de Angeles, a right turn goes to the quaint old mining village of Santa Lucía (altitude 1400-1600 m) which is perched precariously on a steep, pine forested mountainside overlooking the valley with Tegucigalpa below. The town has a colonial church with a Christ statue given by King Felipe II of Spain in 1592. There is a charming legend of the Black Christ, which the authorities ordered to be taken down to Tegucigalpa when Santa Lucía lost its former importance as a mining centre. Every step it was carried away from Santa Lucía it became heavier. When it was impossible to carry it any further they turned round, and by the time they were back in Santa Lucía, it was as light as a feather.

The town is lively with parties on Saturday night, and there is a festival in the second and third weeks of January, celebrating the 15 January Día de Cristo de las Mercedes. There are souvenir shops in the town, including **Cerámicas Ucles** just past the lagoon, second street on left, and another ceramics shop at the entrance on your right. On the way into the town from the capital the road is lined with many nurseries, selling flowers and plants for which the region is famous. There are good walks up the mountain on various trails, with fine views of Tegucigalpa.

A good circuit is to descend east from the mountain towards **San Juan del Rancho** through lovely landscapes on a good dirt road, then connect with the paved road to **El Zamorano**. From there continue either to El Zamorano, or return to Tegucigalpa (see below for the opposite direction).

Valle de Angeles

About 30 minutes' drive from Tegucigalpa, Valle de Angeles (altitude 1310 m) is on a plain below **Monte San Juan**, with **Cerro El Picacho** (2270 m) and **Cerro La Tigra** nearby. It is a popular spot for trips from the city, with a cool climate year round, and is surrounded by pine forests. The town's shady little main plaza is decorated with brightly painted benches and bandstand, a pretty little twin-domed church and fringed by several restaurants with outdoor tables. The **tourist office** ⓘ *Sat, Sun 0900-1200, 1330-1800*, is helpful but has limited information. There are tracks going through the forests, old mines to explore, a picnic area and a swimming pool; it gets crowded on Sundays. At the top of Cerro El Picacho there is a stunning view of the city and a **zoo** ⓘ *daily, 0800-1500, US$0.20*, of mostly indigenous animals including jaguar, spider monkeys and other animals and birds.

Parque Nacional La Tigra

Open 0800-1600, US$10 entry. There are 2 visitor centres. To reach the Jutiapa centre, 24 km from the capital, take a bus from Parque Herrera opposite the Teatro Nacional and exit at Aldea El Chaparro, from where it is a 20-min walk. To reach the El Rosario visitor centre, take a bus from to San Juancito from the Gasolinera San Felipe, opposite the San Felipe Hospital, from where it is a 45-min walk to the entrance. Lodging and maps are available at both centres. There are hiking trails of varying difficulty and single hikers must have a guide, US$10-20 per trail. For more information, see Where to stay and Transport, below.

Only 11 km from Tegucigalpa, this cloudforest covers 238 sq km and is considered one of the richest habitats in the world with a great diversity of flora and fauna: bromeliads, orchids, arborescent ferns and over 200 species of bird. There are good climbs to the heights of Picacho and excellent hikes in the park. Crumbling remains of the old mine buildings are dotted around the hillsides, some abandoned, others inhabited. Local resident Miguel Angel Sierra (T964-8334) has some fascinating remnants, including an original gold mould and old photographs, all of which he is happy to show to visitors. The small **Pulpería-Cafetería El Rosario** sells snacks, coffee and groceries, which are useful if you're hiking in the park, and has lovely views from its tiny terrace and balcony.

A recommended hike is the **Sendero La Esperanza**, which leads to the road; turn right then take the **Sendero Bosque Nublado** on your left. The whole circuit takes about one hour 20 minutes. A few quetzal birds survive here, but you will need a good eye. In the rainy season (June, July, October and November) there is a spectacular 100-m waterfall (**Cascada de la Gloria**), which falls on a vast igneous rock. Do not leave paths when walking as there are steep drops. Also get advice about personal safety, as robberies have occurred.

At Km 24 on the road to Danlí, there are climbs to the highest peak through the Uyuca rainforest. Information is available from the Escuela Agrícola Panamericana in the breathtaking **Valle del Zamorano**, or from the **Amitigra office** ① *Col Palmira dos calles al sur (de la Nunciatura Apostólica), Av Santa Sede casa #210, Tegucigalpa, T2231-3641*. The school has rooms for visitors. Visits to the school are organized by some tour operators. On the northwest flank of Uyuca is the picturesque village of **Tatumbla**.

Suyapa

Southeast of Tegucigalpa, the village of Suyapa attracts pilgrims to its big church, home to a tiny wooden image of the Virgin, about 8 cm high, set into the altar. A fiesta is held 1-4 February, see page 12. Take a bus to the University or to Suyapa from 'La Isla', one block northwest of the city stadium.

Sabanagrande

Further south (40 km) is Sabanagrande, just off the main highway. This typical colonial town, complete with cobbled streets, is a good day trip from Tegucigalpa. There is an interesting colonial church (1809), Nuestra Señora del Rosario 'Apa Kun Ka' (the place of water for washing), with the fiesta of La Virgen de Candelaria from 1-11 February. At 1000 m, it has a mild climate, beautiful scenery with pleasant walks, including views to the Pacific and the Gulf of Fonseca. The town is famous for its *rosquillas* (a type of biscuit).

Ojojona

Ojojona (altitude 1400 m) is another quaint and completely unspoiled old village about 30 minutes (24 km) south of Tegucigalpa; turn right off the Southern Highway. The village pottery is interesting but make your selection carefully as some of it is reported to be of poor quality. **La Casona del Pueblo** offers the best handicrafts in town, including fine rustic ceramics. The local fiesta is 18-20 January. There are two well-preserved colonial churches in Ojojona, with fine paintings, plus two more in nearby **Santa Ana**, which is passed on the way from Tegucigalpa.

Listings Around Tegucigalpa

Where to stay

Santa Lucía

$$ Hotel Santa Lucía Resort
1.2 km before Santa Lucía, T2779-0540, www.hotelsantaluciaresort.com.
Set among pine trees dripping with moss (*rigil*). Spacious and comfy log cabins, with cable TV, lounge area, and balcony; pleasant grounds and ample parking space.

$$ La Posada de Doña Estefana
T2779-0441, meeb@yahoo.com.
Overlooking the church in the heart of the well-preserved colonial town, this place has pretty rooms with cable TV and great views from balcony. There is a lounge and a pool; breakfast is included.

$$ Texas Guesthouse
1.5 km from the entrance to town, located right off the main street, T9891-2374, www.texasguesthousehn.com.
The Texas Guesthouse offers 14 cosy, comfortable and presentable rooms with hot water, minibar, a/c, TV and Wi-Fi. There is secure parking, laundry service and exercise machines. Helpful, well-kept and down-to-earth. Recommended.

Valle de Angeles

$$ Hotel y Restaurante Posada del Angel
Northeast of centre, T2766-2233, hotelposada delangel@yahoo.com.
Swimming pool, indifferent service, moderate prices.

$$-$ Villas del Valle
500 m north of town, T766-2534, www.villasdelvalle.com.
Selection of rooms, cabins and suites. Honduran and European food in the restaurant.

Parque Nacional La Tigra
Basic guesthouse accommodation ($) is also an option in San Juancito if you're stuck.

$ Eco-Albergue El Rosario.
Accommodation for 30 which includes bathrooms and a cafeteria.

$ Eco-Albergue Jutiapa
6 triple rooms and a cabin for 3 people, each with bath. Camping is available.

Restaurants

Santa Lucía

$$$-$$ La Placita de Susy
Barrio Lodo Prieto, 1 km after the turning for the highway, www.laplacitadsusy.com.

This popular family restaurant has a lovely rural setting with green lawns, good views and homely wood-built architecture. Food is international with a particular emphasis on Argentine meat dishes, which are also their best offerings.

$$ Miluska.
A Czech restaurant serving Czech and Honduran food. Recommended.

Valle de Angeles

$$$-$$ Los 4 Vientos
Valle de Angeles Km 20, T9473-4711.
This secluded rural retreat has beautiful rambling grounds filled with trees and immaculately landscaped flower beds. They serve a diverse range of international fare, including burgers, pizzas, seafood, and vegetarian dishes. Relaxed alfresco dining, good for families.

$$ Epocas
Calle Mineral, opposite the Town Hall on the main plaza, T9636-1235.
A wonderful ramshackle place, full of antiques and bric-a-brac, from old French horns to vintage cash registers (some items for sale); mixed menu of steak, chicken and fish as well as *típicos*; cheerfully talkative parrots in the backyard.

$$ La Casa de las Abuelas
1 block north of Parque Central, T2766-2626.
Pleasant courtyard with wine bar, café, library, satellite TV, email, phone, information and art gallery.

$$ Las Tejas
Opposite the Centro Turístico La Florida.
A Dutch-owned restaurant, serving traditional mix of meat and *típico* dishes.

$ Restaurante Turístico de Valle de Angeles
T2766-2148.
On the top of the hill overlooking town, with rustic decor, cartwheel table tops and lovely views over the forested valley. Good meat and fish dishes but slow service.

Cafés

Café La Estancia
Calle Principal, frente al Salon Comunal.
A superb coffeehouse set in a very appealing colonial building with wooden platforms, open-air balconies and arresting antique flourishes. Lots of character.

Parque Nacional La Tigra

$ Grocery store
Next door to Hotelito San Juan, San Juancito.
Sells fuel, drinks and can prepare *comida corriente*; same owners as hotel, T2766-2237.

Festivals

Suyapa
1-4 Feb Fiesta, with a televised *alborada* with singers, music and fireworks, from 2000-2400 on the 2nd evening.

Sabanagrande
1-11 Feb Fiesta of La Virgen de Candelaria.

Ojojona
18-20 Jan Fiesta.

Transport

Santa Lucía
Bus To Santa Lucía from Mercado San Pablo, **Tegucigalpa**, Bus 101, every 45 mins, US$0.50, past the statue of Simón Bolívar by the Esso station, Av de los Próceres.

Valle de Angeles
Bus To **Valle de Angeles** every 45 mins, US$0.50, 1 hr, leaves from San Felipe, near the hospital. To **San Juan de Flores** 1000, 1230, 1530.

Parque Nacional La Tigra
Bus Buses to the **Jutiapa visitor centre** leave from Parque Herrera, Mon-Fri 0700, 0900, 1400, 1600, 1700; Sat-Sun 0800, 1000, 1200, 1300, 1500, 1 hr, US$1.10; exit at Aldea El Chaparro and walk for 20 mins. Return buses to Tegucigalpa depart every 1-2 hrs 0530-1500; check with the visitor centre for specific times. Buses to **El Rosario visitor centre** depart from the Gasolinera San Felipe, opposite the San Felipe Hospital, 1400, 1500 and 1700, 1 hr, US$1.10; exit at San Juancito and walk for 45 mins. Return buses at 0530, 0630 and 0800.

Ojojona
Bus Buses leave **Comayagüela** every 15-30 mins from Calle 4, Av 6, near San Isidro market, US$0.50, 1 hr. From same location, buses go west to **Lepaterique** ('place of the jaguar'), another colonial village, over 1-hr drive through rugged, forested terrain. Distant view of Pacific on fine days from heights above village.

Tegucigalpa
to Copán

Treasured for its exceptional artistry, the serene ruins of Copán are Honduras' big Maya attraction. Located close to the Guatemalan border, the city once marked the eastern extent of Mayan civilization, a network of competing city-states which reached as far west as Chiapas in Mexico. The journey to Copán from Tegucigalpa involves traversing some highly convoluted countryside. Rising and falling with sublime mountain vistas, the road connects a procession of indigenous and mining communities steeped in age-old legends, lore, tradition and crafts.

The town of Gracias is one of the country's most historical settlements, popular with adventurers for the nearby mountain of Celaque, the highest peak in Honduras. Further north, Santa Rosa de Copán is rich in colonial heritage, while Copán itself is situated near the colonial town of Copán Ruinas with its bonus of nearby hot springs and flocks of gregarious macaws.

highway pitstops and low-key family diversions

Highway CA5, also known as the Carretera del Norte (Northern Highway), leaves the capital at Comayagüela and enters the vast valley of Támara, with the village of the same name. A turning leads to the San Matías waterfall, in a delightful area for walking in cool forested mountains.

The road climbs to the forested heights of **Parque Aventuras** ⓘ *open at weekends*, at Km 33, good food, swimming pools, horses, bikes, then to **Zambrano** (altitude 1450 m) at Km 34 and, at Km 36, midway between Tegucigalpa and Comayagua, **Parque Aurora** ⓘ *T9990-3338, camping US$0.50 per person, admission US$0.70, food supplies nearby*. It has a small zoo, good swimming pools and a picnic area among pine-covered hills, a lake with rowing boats (hire US$1 per hour), a snack bar and lovely scenery. The birdwatching is good too.

Before descending to the Comayagua Valley, the Northern Highway reaches another forested mountainous escarpment. Stalls selling home-made honey and garish chunky pottery line the roadside. A track leads off to the right (ask for directions), with about 30 minutes' climb on foot to a tableland and the natural fortress of **Tenampua**, where the indigenous inhabitants put up their last resistance to the *conquistadores*, even after the death of Lempira. It has an interesting wall and entrance portal.

Listings Támara and Zambrano

Where to stay

Támara

$ Posada Don Willy
500 m southwest of the toll station near Balneario San Francisco.
With bath (electric shower), clean, quiet, fan, excellent value.

Zambrano

$$$ Caserío Valuz
1.5 km from the highway, 20 mins' walk on the road to Catarata Escondida, T9996-4294 (mob), www.caseriovaluz. wordpress.com.
This charming country inn has 15 rooms with bath, most with balconies, 1- to 3-night packages including meals, also rooms for backpackers, with use of kitchen, volunteer work in exchange for room and board possible, a great place to relax, hike, read and paint.

$$$-$ Casitas Primavera
Barrio La Primavera, 1.5 km west of main road, T2898-26625/ T2239-2328.
Cosy houses, lovely setting, sleeps 6 (arrangements can be made for 1-2 people, $).

On Highway CA5, approximately 34 km after Zambrano, westbound Highway CA7 branches off towards Marcala (altitude 1300 m), 77 km away in the Department of La Paz. The region's staggered hills and mountains enjoy comfortable temperatures during the day and cool temperatures at the night, making them a particularly good place to escape the lowlands during the sweltering months of March to May.

It's ideal hiking country with beautiful scenery and dramatic waterfalls in the surrounding area. Marcala is also a good base from which to visit Yarula, Santa Elena, Opatoro, San José and Guajiquiro. The region is one of the finest coffee-producing areas of Honduras and a visit to Comarca, at the entrance to town, gives an idea of how coffee is processed. Semana Santa is celebrated with a large procession through the main street and there is a fiesta in honour of San Miguel Arcángel in the last week of September.

Around Marcala

Near Marcala is **Balneario El Manzanal** ⓘ *3 km on the road to La Esperanza, open weekends only*, which has a restaurant, two swimming pools and a boating lake. For panoramic views high above Marcala, follow this hike (one hour): head north past **Hotel Medina**, turn right (east) after the hotel and follow the road up into hills. After 2 km the road branches. Take the left branch and immediately on the left is a football field. A small path leaves from this field on the west side taking you through a small area of pine trees then out onto a ridge for excellent views. The track continues down from the ridge back to town, passing an unusual cemetery on a hill.

There are caves nearby on **Musula** mountain, the Cueva de las Animas in Guamizales and Cueva de El Gigante and Cueva de El León near La Estanzuela with a high waterfall close by. Other waterfalls are El Chiflador, 67 m high, Las Golondrinas, La Chorrera and Santa Rosita. Transport goes to La Florida where there is good walking to the village of **Opatoro** and climbing **Cerro Guajiquiro**. Between Opatoro and Guajiquiro is the **Reserva las Trancas**, a heavily forested mountain where quetzales have been seen.

Yarula and **Santa Elena** are two tiny municipalities, the latter about 40 km from Marcala, with beautiful views (bus Marcala–Santa Elena 1230 returns 0500 next day, 2¾ hours, enquire at Gámez bus office opposite market; truck daily 0830 returns from Santa Elena at 1300). Sometimes meals are available at *comedores* in Yarula and Santa Elena. The dirt road from Marcala gradually deteriorates, the last 20 km being terrible, high clearance essential, 4WD recommended. In **La Cueva Pintada**, south of Santa Elena, there are pre-Columbian cave paintings (*pinturas rupestres*) of snakes, men and dogs; ask for a guide in Santa Elena. Ask also in this village about the Danza de los Negritos, performed at the annual **Fiesta de Santiago**, 24-25 March, in front of the church. A special performance may be organized, the dancers wearing their old wooden masks, if suitable payment is offered.

The village of **San José** (altitude 1700 m) is a Lenca community where the climate can be cool and windy even in the hottest months. The scenery is superb, there's good hill walking (see box, page 47, for two examples; there are many others) and also rivers for swimming. Frequent pickups from Marcala, and two daily minibuses at about 0815 and 0900; from San José to Marcala minibuses depart at 0615 and 0645, one hour, US$1.

Listings Marcala and around

Where to stay

$ Medina
On main road, T2898-1866.
The most comfortable, clean, modern with bath, *cafetería*, free purified water. Highly recommended.

$ Unnamed hotel
San José.
Run by Brit Nigel Potter ('Nayo'). Basic but comfortable and clean, with meals. He also takes groups to stay in Lenca villages, US$5 per person plus US$10 per person for accommodation in a village; ask for the house of Doña Gloria, Profe Vinda, Nayo or Ruth. At least one of these will be present to meet visitors.

Restaurants

$$ Riviera Linda
Opposite Hotel Medina.
Pleasant atmosphere and spacious restaurant. It's a little pricey but serves good food.

$ Café Express
Beside Esso.
Good breakfast and *comida corrida*. Recommended.

$ Darwin
Main street in centre.
Cheap breakfasts from 0700. Recommended.

$ El Mirador
On entering town by petrol station.
Nice views from veranda, good food. Recommended.

Around Marcala
$ Comedor
500 m before plaza on main road.
Good, clean and cheap.

What to do

For trips to visit Lenca villages see the unnamed hotel in San José, Where to stay, above.

Transport

Bus To **Tegucigalpa** 0500, 0915 and 1000 daily via La Paz, 4 hrs, US$2.40 (bus from Tegucigalpa at 0800 and 1400, **Empresa Lila**, 4-5 Av, 7 Calle, No 418 Comayagüela, opposite Hispano cinema); bus to **La Paz** only, 0700, 2 hrs, US$1; several minibuses a day, 1½ hrs, US$1.50. Bus also from Comayagua. Pickup truck to **San José** at around 1000 from market, ask for drivers, Don Santos, Torencio, or Gustavo. Bus to **La Esperanza** at about 0830, unreliable, check with driver, Don Pincho, at the supermarket next to where the bus is parked (same street as Hotel Medina), 1½-2 hrs, otherwise hitching possible, going rate US$1.20. Bus to **San Miguel**, El Salvador, Transportes Wendy Patricia, 0500, 1200, 7 hrs, US$3.50.

North of Marcala, Highway CA11A connects with La Esperanza (altitude 1485 m) 30 km away, an old colonial town in a pleasant valley. It has an attractive church in front of the park and there is a grotto carved out of the mountainside west of the town centre, a site of religious festivals. There is a market on Thursdays and Sundays when the Lenca from nearby villages sell wares and food, but no handicrafts. Nearby is the indigenous village of Yaramanguila.

The surroundings include forested hills with lakes and waterfalls, great for walking although they are very cold in December and January. One option is to hike to **Cerro de Ojos**, a hill to the northwest and visible from La Esperanza. It is forested with a clearing on top littered with many strange cylindrical holes; no one knows how they were formed. The turning to this hill is on the La Esperanza to San Juan road. Ask for directions.

Erandique

It is 45 km from La Esperanza to **San Juan del Caite** on Highway CA11A (a few *hospedajes*, **Lempira**, **Sánchez**, and the comfortable **Hacienda**, two restaurants nearby, helpful people and Peace Corps workers). From here a dirt road runs 26 km south to the small town of Erandique. Founded in 1560 and set high in pine-clad mountains not far from the border with El Salvador, it is a friendly town, and very beautiful. Lempira was born nearby, and was killed a few kilometres away. The third weekend in January is the local **Fiesta de San Sebastián**. The best time to visit is at the weekend and market days are Friday and Sunday. Each of the three *barrios* has a handsome colonial church.

There are lakes, rivers, waterfalls, springs and bathing ponds in the vicinity; ask around for directions. Nearby is **San Antonio** where fine opals (not cut gems, but stones encased in rock) are mined and may be purchased. The many hamlets in the surrounding mountains are reached by roads that have been either resurfaced or rebuilt and the landscapes are magnificent.

There are several roads radiating from Erandique, including one to **Mapulaca** and the border with El Salvador (no immigration or customs or bridge here, at the Río Lempa), a road to San Andrés and another to Piraera (all passable in a car).

Listings La Esperanza and around

Where to stay

La Esperanza
There are several simple but pleasant pensiones around town.

$$ Casa Arroyo
Northwest of town past Supermercado Melissa (see website for map), T2783-1721, www.casadelarroyohn.com.
Surrounded by nature and highland views, this tranquil B&B enjoys a

lovely hacienda setting in the hills. Accommodation includes clean, cosy and homely rooms and cabins with cable TV and hot water. Quiet and romantic, would suit couples or families.

$$-$ Posada Papa Chepe
Frente al Parque Lopez, T2783-0443, http://posadapapachepe.cdvhotels.com.
Conveniently located in the centre of town, Papa Chepe's is a solid colonial-style option with simple, good value rooms and a tranquil garden-courtyard overflowing with leafy plants. There's a restaurant on-site and all the usual amenities including cable TV and Wi-Fi.

Restaurants

La Esperanza

$$ Casa Vieja
Opposite Parque Lopez.
Set in a well-renovated colonial townhouse, Casa Vieja boasts a great atmosphere with its spacious dining hall and high wood-beam ceilings. They do very tasty burgers and other filling international fare. The best place in town, a good spot for a drink too. Recommended.

$$ Papa Chepe
Opposite Parque Lopez. Open for breakfast, lunch and dinner.
Papá Chepe serves wholesome home-cooked grub including national staples and solid international fare: chicken and rice, pancakes, grilled meats are among the offerings. Pleasant, clean, café-style interior.

$ Café El Ecológico
Corner of Parque Central.
Home-made cakes and pastries, fruit drinks, and delicious home-made jams.

Festivals

La Esperanza
3rd week in Jul Festival de la Papa.
8 Dec Fiesta de la Virgen de la Concepción.

Transport

La Esperanza
Bus
To **Tegucigalpa** several daily, 3½ hrs, US$5 (**Cobramil**, also to **San Pedro Sula**, and **Joelito**, 4 hrs, US$2.60). To **Siguatepeque** 0700, 0900, last at 1000, US$1.50, 1 hr; also to **Siguatepeque**, **Comayagua** at 0600; and to the **Salvadorean border**; bus stops by market. Hourly minibuses to **Yaramanguila**, 30 mins. Daily bus to **Marcala**, 2 hrs at 1230 (but check), US$0.80 (truck, US$1.20, 2¼ hrs). Minibus service at 1130, US$1.50. Daily minibus service to **San Juan**, departs between 1030-1200 from a parking space midway between the 2 bus stops, 2½ hrs, pickups also do this journey, very crowded; for **Erandique**, alight at Erandique turn-off, 1 km before San Juan and wait for truck to pass (*comedor* plus basic *hospedaje* at intersection). If going to Gracias, stay on the La Esperanza–San Juan bus until the end of the line where a pickup collects passengers 15 mins or so later, 1 hr San Juan–Gracias. Buses to **Lake Yojoa** (see page 67), 2 hrs, US$2.50.

Erandique
Bus
There are minibuses to Erandique from the bridge on the road to La Esperanza, 1100 daily, although most people go by truck from Gracias (there is sometimes a van service as far as San Juan) or La Esperanza (change trucks at San Juan

intersection, very dusty). Return minibus to Gracias at 0500 daily, which connects with the bus to La Esperanza in San Juan. Trucks leave Erandique 0700 daily, but sometimes earlier, and occasionally a 2nd one leaves around 0800 for Gracias, otherwise be prepared for a long wait for a pickup.

Gracias and around

colonial treasure set beneath mountain giants

★One of the oldest settlements in Honduras, dominated by Montañas de Celaque, Puca and Opulaca – the country's highest peaks – Gracias (altitude 765 m) is a charming, friendly town. Just 50 km from Santa Rosa, both the town and the surrounding countryside are worth a visit.

Tip...
A helpful tourist office in the Parque Central can store luggage and arrange transport to Parque Nacional Celaque.

Gracias was the centre from which Francisco de Montejo, thrice governor of Honduras, put down the great indigenous revolt of 1537-1538. Alonso de Cáceres, his lieutenant, besieged Lempira the indigenous leader in his impregnable mountain-top fortress at Cerquín, finally luring him out under a flag of truce, ambushed him and treacherously killed him. When the Audiencia de los Confines was formed in 1544, Gracias became the administrative centre of Central America.

There are three colonial churches, **San Sebastián**, **Las Mercedes** and **San Marcos** (a fourth, Santa Lucía, is southwest of Gracias), and a restored fort, with two fine Spanish cannon, on a hill five minutes' walk west of the centre. The fort, **El Castillo San Cristóbal**, has been well restored, and at the foot of the northern ramparts is the tomb of Juan Lindo, president of Honduras 1847-1852, who introduced free education through a system of state schools.

Balneario Aguas Termales
Daily 0600-2000, US$2.50, rental of towels, hammock, inner tube, restaurant/bar.

Some 6 km from Gracias along the road to Esperanza (side road signposted), are hot, mineral-rich, communal thermal pools in the forest for swimming and soaking. It takes an hour to walk there via a path, and 1½ hours by road. To find the path, walk 2 km beyond the bridge over Río Arcagual to a second bridge before which turn right by a white house. Climb the hill and take the first path on the left (no sign), cross the river and continue for about 15 minutes to the pools. The Balneario is a good place to have a barbecue and rest your weary limbs after hiking.

Parque Nacional Celaque
This protected park is home to **Monte Celaque**, which at 2849 m, is the highest point in Honduras. It takes at least a day to climb from Gracias to the summit but most people allow two days to enjoy the trip.

The Parque Nacional Celaque visitor centre (1400 m) is 8 km from Gracias, or two hours' walk. There are several intersections, so it's best to ask at each. Not much of the 8-km road from Gracias to the park is passable when wet, without a high-clearance or 4WD vehicle. Behind the visitor centre is a trail going down to the river where a crystal-clear pool and waterfall make for wonderful bathing.

The trail to the summit begins from behind the visitor centre. Along the trail the trees are marked with ribbons. It takes at least six hours to reach the summit from the visitor centre and it's four hours down. The first three hours of ascent are easy, to a campsite at 2000 m (**Campamento Don Tomás**) where there is small hut A better campsite if you can make it is **Campamento Naranjo**, with water, at about 2500 m – but you'll need a tent. Between these two sites, the climb is particularly steep and in cloudforest. Look out for spider monkeys. Above 2600 m quetzals have been seen. Many hikers don't bother with the summit as it is forested and enclosed. There is a trail westward from the summit to Belén Gualcho which is steep towards Belén. It takes a couple of days and a guide might be a good idea.

You can also enjoy a day walk to **Mirador La Cascada** ⓘ *entry fee US$3 plus US$3 per night camping in the mountain*, about three hours from the visitor centre, 1½ hours downhill going back. Transport can be arranged with the tourist office in the Plaza Central (US$10 per vehicle for up to four people).

For guides, contact **Dona Mercedes' Comedor** in Villa Verde (T2994-96681), **Don Luis Melgar**, or **Don Cándido** (T299715114), or one of their brothers; all recommended. Ask the guide the exact way or pay US$6 for the guide. There is a warden, Miguel, living nearby who can supply food and beer but it is safer to take supplies from Gracias. Contact **Cohdefor** or **CIPANAC** in Gracias before leaving for full information.

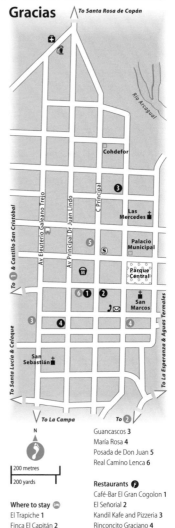

Gracias /\ To Santa Rosa de Copán

Río Arcagual

Cohdefor

Av Eleuterio Galeano Trejo

Av Principal Dr Juan Lindo

C Principal

& Castillo San Cristóbal

To ① & Castillo San Cristóbal

To Santa Lucía & Celaque

To La Campa

To ②

To La Esperanza & Aguas Termales

Las Mercedes

Palacio Municipal

Parque Central

San Marcos

San Sebastián

N

200 metres
200 yards

Guancascos **3**
María Rosa **4**
Posada de Don Juan **5**
Real Camino Lenca **6**

Where to stay
El Trapiche **1**
Finca El Capitán **2**

Restaurants
Café-Bar El Gran Cogolon **1**
El Señorial **2**
Kandil Kafe and Pizzeria **3**
Rinconcito Graciano **4**

Don't forget good hiking boots, warm clothing, insect repellent and, given the dense forest and possibility of heavy cloud, a compass is also recommended for safety. Also, beware of snakes.

Visiting the other peaks around Gracias is more complicated but interesting.

Listings Gracias *map p43*

Where to stay

$$$ Posada de Don Juan
Calle Principal opposite Banco de Occidente, T2656-1020, www. posadadedonjuanhotel.com.
An attractive colonial-style lodging with a pleasant garden, refreshing pool and 42 rooms. Good beds, great hot showers, nice big towels, cotton sheets, Wi-Fi and cable TV.

$$$-$$ Real Camino Lenca
Av Juan Lindo y Calle Jeremia Cisneros, T2656-1712, www.realcaminolencahotel. com.
Set in a converted colonial mansion, the centrally located Real Camino Lenca is one of the town's more upscale options. Rooms are spotless and well-attired, but the hotel's unique selling point is the breezy rooftop bar with a modern lounge ambience and panoramic views. There's a great restaurant too. Recommended.

$$ Guancascos
At the west end of Hondutel road, T2656-1219, www.guancascos.com.
A lovely little colonial guesthouse set on a former coffee farm on a hillside. Rooms are simple, clean and tranquil; also rents 2-room cabin at Villa Verde adjacent to Monte Celaque visitor centre. Strong green and sustainable ethos and lots of local community connections. Recommended.

$ Finca El Capitán
1 km from the centre of town, T2656-1659, www.hotelfincaelcapitan.galeon. com.
Simple *cabaña*-style lodgings set around a leafy garden, adobe-built and each with their own hammock, cable TV and hot water. There is a restaurant on site and a small pool for cooling off. A pleasant, good value option with natural surroundings, but you may need a moto-taxi to get into town.

$ Hotel El Trapiche
Next to the Terminal de buses Celaque Gracias, T3158-6102.
This motel-style option is set in pleasant verdant grounds and is a good option for drivers. Accommodation includes 14 rooms with cable TV, hot water and a/c.

$ Maria Rosa
Av Jose Maria Medina, 150 m south of the Central Park, Barrio El Rosario.
Another colonial option, this is a low-key and economical place. Rooms overlook a small courtyard with a dipping pool. Restaurant. Helpful, English-speaking staff. Unpretentious and reliable.

Parque Nacional Celaque

$ Visitor centre
There are 7 beds, shower and cooking facilities, drinks available, well maintained. There is another cabin nearby with 10 beds. Take a torch and sleeping bag.

Restaurants

For breakfast, try the *comedores* near the market or, better, the restaurant at Hotel Iris (good *comida corriente* too) or Guancascos.

$$$ Cafe-Bar El Gran Cogolon
Inside the Hotel Real Camino Lenca, Av Juan Lindo y Calle Jeremia Cisneros, www.realcaminolencahotel.com.
This elegant bar-restaurant enjoys commanding views of the town from its rooftop perch. They have a wine list and an array of cocktails. Pastas are their speciality. Lounge-style ambience, good for a drink.

$$$-$$ Kandil Kafe & Pizzeria
Av Jose Maria Medina 34, Barrio La Merced.
Set in a cosy colonial townhouse, this lovely little eatery offers an eclectic range of international food from nachos to chicken wings. Pizzas are what they do best, however. There's seating indoors and out with a pleasant garden-patio out back. Good atmosphere. Recommended.

$$ Guancascos
See Where to stay, above.
The popular Guanascos has pleasant views of the town from its terrace and it offers an array of local and international fare including spaghetti bolognese, black bean soup, Mexican tacos and Honduran breakfasts. Relaxing space. Recommended.

$$ Rinconcito Graciano
2½ blocks south of the Mercado Municipal, Av San Sebastián.
This well-established Graciano haunt serves a variety of local and international fare, including *nacatamales* with chicken or pork, sandwiches, soups and vegetarian dishes. Uses lots of local produce. Rustic and earthy ambience.

$ El Señorial
Main street.
Simple meals and snacks, once house of former president Dr Juan Lindo.

Parque Nacional Celaque

$ Comedor Doña Alejandrina
Just before the visitor centre.
Provides excellent breakfasts.

What to do

Tour operators
Guancascos Tourist Centre, *at the Guancascos Hotel, see Where to stay, above.* Arranges tours and expeditions to Monte Celaque Parque Nacional, local villages and other attractions.

Transport

Bus
A bus goes to **La Esperanza** at 0530 and 0730, or take bus to Erandique (they leave when full from La Planta) get off at San Juan from where frequent buses goes to La Esperanza (1 hr, US$2). There is a bus service to **Santa Rosa de Copán**, US$1.30, from 0530 to 1630, 5 times a day, 1½ hrs; beautiful journey through majestic scenery. Also to **San Pedro Sula** at 0500, 0800 and 0900, US$3, 4 hrs. Daily bus service to **Lepaera** 1400, 1½ hrs, US$1.50; daily bus to **San Manuel de Colohuete** at 1300. **Cotral** bus ticket office is 1 block north of Parque Central. **Torito** bus, a few metres from the main terminal, has buses to the Guatemalan border at **Agua Caliente**, one at 1000, change buses at Nueva Ocotepeque; see also box 156.

Santa Rosa (altitude 1160 m) is an important regional town with a colonial atmosphere of cobbled streets and some of the best architecture in Honduras. The town is set in some of the best scenery in Honduras and the fine weather makes it ideal for hiking, horses and mountain biking.

Originally known as Los Llanos, Santa Rosa was made a municipality in 1812 and became capital of the Department of Copán when it was split from Gracias (now Lempira). Santa Rosa owes its wealth to the fact that it's an agricultural and cattle-raising area. Maize and tobacco are grown here, and visitors can see traditional hand-rolling at the Flor de **Copán cigar factory** ⓘ *3 blocks east of the bus terminal, T2662 0185, Mon-Fri until 1700, closed 1130-1300, tours in Spanish at 1000 and 1400, US$2 per person; ask the guard at the gate.* The central plaza and church are perched on a hilltop. There is a quieter plaza, the **Parque Infantil** ⓘ *Calle Real Centenario y 6 Av SO*, a fenced playground and a pleasant place to relax. The main **market** ⓘ *1 Calle and 3 Av NE*, has good leather items. **Farmers' markets** are held daily in Barrio Santa Teresa (take 4 Calle SE past 5 Avenida SE) and at 4 Calle SE

Santa Rosa de Copán

To Carretara, San Pedro Sula & Gracias

To Carretara, Cucuyagua & Ocotepeque

Where to stay
Casa Real 1
Elvir 2
Hospedaje Calle Real 3
Posada de Juan B&B 4
San Jorge 5

Restaurants
El Café de las Velas 1
El Rodeo 2
Flamingos 3
Jireth Delicias
Alimentarias 4

Kaldi's Koffee 5
Las Haciendas 6
Lenca Maya 7
Weekends Pizza 8

ON THE ROAD

Walking from San Manuel Colohuete to Belén Gualcho

There is a well-defined, well-used and easy-to-follow mule trail linking these two villages, which makes a good one- or two-day hike. Maps are not essential as there are communities at many points along the way where advice can be sought.

As the local security situation is constantly changing, it is absolutely essential to check on the feasibility of this journey before setting out.

The path leading away from the village leaves from opposite the *pulpería* and *comedor* where the bus drops you, heading west and downhill into a valley. The path is used by 4WD vehicles and continues to San Sebastián. Just after the community of San José, after passing the last house, the path to Belén branches off. A smaller path leaves the 4WD track and climbs steeply up to your right and more northwest.

One hour Just after Peña Blanca, the path direction becomes unclear after it crosses an area of white chalky rocks. There are several other paths here. The main path heads north and steeply downhill at this point.

Two hours There is water all the year round in the Quebrada de Rogán.

Three hours All year round water in Río Gualmite, a short descent. After this there is a longish, steep ascent.

Four hours Just after this point the path branches on a large flat grassy area. Both paths lead to Belén Gualcho. The one to the left drops and crosses the river and then you are faced with a long, arduous and very steep ascent. We would recommend taking the path to the right, which exits to the far right of a grassy area by three small houses.

Five hours The path climbs as it skirts around the Cerro Capitán. Just after passing the steepest part, a small landslide forces the path into a descent almost to the river. From here, only 2 m above the river, you can walk steeply down off the path to the river bank where there is the most perfect campsite. Flat sandy soil in some shade on the edge of a coffee plantation and 2 m from the river.

Six hours From the camping site there is a long, continuous climb before dropping down sharply to cross the river. It is possible, but difficult, to cross the river at the point the path meets it. Take a small path off to the right just before the river, which leads to a suspension bridge. From the river it is a long continuous climb, not especially steep, to Belén Gualcho. It is between two small peaks that can be seen clearly after crossing the river. There are more houses after crossing the river and the odd *pulpería* where you can buy *refrescos* or food.

and 5 Avenida SE on Sunday 0500 to 1000. For further information, visit www. visitesantarosadecopan.com.

Around Santa Rosa de Copán

Taking time to explore some of the forested hills around Santa Rosa will lead you through spectacular scenery and give an insight into the life of agricultural Honduras.

There are buses from Santa Rosa west to the small town of **Dulce Nombre de Copán** (US$0.55). There are rooms available next to the Hondutel office. Hikers heading for Copán and the border can continue west through the mountains to stay at **San Agustín** (buses and pickups from Santa Rosa), take a hammock or sleeping bag, continuing next day through Mirasol to reach the Ruinas road at El Jaral, 11 km east of Copán ruins.

South of Santa Rosa, buses pass through **Cucuyagua**, with a scenic river, good swimming and camping on its banks, and **San Pedro de Copán**, an attractive village and an entry point into the Parque Nacional Celaque, see page 42.

A mule trail (see box, page 47) connects **Belén Gualcho**, a Lenca village in the mountains and a good base for exploring the surrounding area, with **San Manuel de Colohuete** (1500 m), which has a magnificent colonial church whose façade is sculpted with figures of saints. Buses go to San Manuel from Gracias at 1300, four hours, and there's usually a pickup returning in the evening. There are no hotels so you must ask villagers about places to stay. There is an equally fine colonial church 30 minutes by 4WD vehicle to the southwest at **San Sebastián Colosuca** (1550 m). The village has a mild climate (two *hospedajes*; or try Don Rubilio; food at Doña Clementina García or Doña Alicia Molina). The **Feria de San Sebastián** is on 20 January. An hour's walk away is the Cueva del Diablo and 6 km away is Cerro El Alta with a lagoon at the top. From San Sebastián, a mule trail goes via the heights of **Agua Fría** to reach the route near the border at **Tomalá**.

Listings Santa Rosa de Copán and around *map p46*

Where to stay

Santa Rosa de Copán

$$$ Elvir
Calle Real Centenario SO, 3 Av SO, T2662-0805, www.hotelelvir.com.
A stylish, comfortable lodging with 41 rooms and 2 suites. It's safe, clean and quiet, and all rooms have their own bath, TV, hot water and drinking water. Free internet is in the lobby and good but pricey meals are served in the cafetería or restaurant. There's also a gym and rooftop pool and bar.

$$ Casa Real
2 Calle entre 3 y 4 Av NE, next to the Instituto María Auxiliadora, Barrio El Carmen, T2662-0801, www.hotelcasarealsrc.com.
One of the larger hotels in town, a bit dated and definitely geared to nationals, but reasonable. Rooms have LCD TVs, Wi-Fi and hot water, and suites come with jacuzzi. There is also a restaurant, gym, pool and business centre on site.

$$ Posada de Juan B&B
Barrio El Carmen, half a block east of the Catholic university, T2662-0254, www.laposadadejuan.com.

This homely and pleasant B&B has cosy enclaves and a tranquil garden space where you can relax, read and have breakfast. There are just 5 rooms, each equipped with cable TV, hot water, a/c and Wi-Fi. Good value and very hospitable. Recommended.

$$-$ Hotel San Jorge
2 Av SO, entre Calle 1 y 2, T2662-0254, www.hotelsanjorgehn.com.
This attentive family-run hotel sometimes provides lodging for Canadian Habitat for Humanity groups. Rooms are large, clean, and unpretentious and all come with cable TV, Wi-Fi, hot water, fan or a/c. Simple, solid and economical.

$ Hospedaje Calle Real
Real Centenario y 6 Av NE.
A clean, quiet and friendly place, the best of the cheaper accommodation but sometimes there are water failures.

Around Santa Rosa de Copán
In Belén Gualcho hotels fill up quickly on Sat as traders arrive for the Sun market.

$ Hotelito El Carmen
Belén Gualcho, 2 blocks east down from the church in the plaza. Friendly, clean, good views.
Recommended.

$ Pensión
Corquín.
Good *pensión* with a charming garden. Recommended.

Restaurants

Santa Rosa de Copán
Carnivores are well-served here.

$$ El Rodeo
1 Av SE.

El Rodeo is a well-established restaurant and one of the better ones in Santa Rosa, although it's pricey. It specializes in succulent steak slabs and grilled beef. Good atmosphere, with plenty of dead animals on the walls. Things get jaunty at weekends with live ranchero music.

$$ Flamingos
1 Av SE, off main plaza, T2662-0654.
Popular and long-serving place that specializes in seafood. They also do reasonably priced and good pasta and chop suey; upstairs there's a lounge bar with painted flamingos on walls.

$$ Las Haciendas
1 Av Calle SE.
This colonial-style family restaurant dishes up generous portions of hearty grub. Steak and seafood, varied menu, filling *comida corriente*, and an attractive patio bar. Recommended.

$$ Restaurante Lenca Maya
Barrio Santa Teresa, 1 block south of Casa Bueso, T2662-1243.
Set in a cosy colonial townhouse complete with solid wood tables and a romantic outdoor patio (recommended), Restaurante Lenca Maya serves Honduran-style barbecued meat and soups. Hearty and comforting, a good spot for families, couples or friends.

$ Weekends Pizza
3 Av SO and 3C, T2662-4221. Wed-Sun 0900-2100.
Downhill on edge of town but worth the walk for good-value pizzas, pasta and unusual extras like cheese straws; bright and colourful with lime green and marigold yellow walls. Home-made bread, local honey and coffee for sale. Recommended.

Cafés

El Café de las Velas
Barrio El Carmen, half a block northeast of Hotel Elvir, www.elcafedelasvelas.com.
So-called for its staggering variety of candles, this elegant coffee shop grows its own Arabica beans. They also do superb smoothies and cooked breakfasts.

Jireth Delicias Alimentarias
3 Calle, 3 Av, Barrio Santa Teresa, www. jireth.com.
Jireth sells tasty artisanal breads, cakes, and hot coffee, as well as full plates of pasta.

Kaldi's Koffee Shop
South side of the cathedral, opposite Deporticentro Edwin.
Located next to the church, a cosy little coffee house serving delicious caffeinated fare and sweet treats.

Around Santa Rosa de Copán
In Belén Gualcho there are 2 *comedores* on south side of plaza and east side on corner with store.

$ Comedor Mery
Belén Gualcho.
1 block northwest of plaza. Good food in a welcoming family atmosphere.

Bars and clubs

Santa Rosa de Copán

Extasis
Shows videos Mon-Thu night.

Luna Jaguar
at 3 Av, between 1 Calle SE and Calle Real Centenario.
The hottest disco in town, but proper dress required.

Manzanitas
On the corner of 3 Av SE and Calle Real Centenario.
A good place if you fancy singing your heart out to a little karaoke.

Entertainment

Santa Rosa de Copán
Cinema
Plaza Saavedra, opposite Blanca Nieves. Films shown nightly at 1900.

Festivals

Santa Rosa de Copán
21-31 Aug Festival de Santa Rosa de Lima; the 'Tobacco Queen' is crowned at the end of the week.

Shopping

Santa Rosa de Copán
Supermercado Manzanitaz, *Calle Centenario.*

What to do

Santa Rosa de Copán
Tour operators
Lenca Land Trails, *at Hotel Elvir, T2662-1375.* Run by Max Elvir, who organizes cultural tours of the Lenca mountain villages in western Honduras, hiking, mountain biking, the lot; including a fascinating visit to a *purería* (cigar workshop), pilgrimage shrine and archaeological site at Quezailica, a village 38 km north of Santa Rosa. Excellent source of information about the region. Highly recommended.

Transport

Santa Rosa de Copán
Bus Buses depart from the city bus station on Carretera Internacional.

Local 'El Urbano' bus to centre from bus station (on Carretera Internacional, 2 km below town, opposite Hotel Mayaland), US$0.15,15 mins; taxi US$1.40.

Long distance If coming from the Guatemalan border at Nueva Ocotepeque, the bus will stop at the end of town near Av Centenario, 2 km below town, opposite **Hotel Mayaland**. To **Tegucigalpa**, **Toritos** leaves at 0400 from terminal Mon-Sat 0400 and 1000 Sun, US$6, 10 hrs; also **Empresa de Transportes la Sultana** (T2662-0940) has departures at 0500, 0700, and 0900. Alternatively, take an express bus to San Pedro Sula and an express bus on to Tegucigalpa (US$5, 6 hrs). To **Gracias**, **Transportes Lempira**, several 0630-1800, 1½ hrs, US$1.30. To **San Pedro Sula**, US$2.50, 4 hrs, every 45 mins 0400-1730, express service daily 2½ hrs, US$3.50 (**Empresa Torito**). Bus to **La Entrada**, 1 hr, US$1. To **Copán Ruinas**, 4 hrs on good road, US$2.90, several direct daily 1100, 1230 and 1400. Alternatively, take any bus to La Entrada, 1 hr, US$1, and transfer to a Copán Ruinas bus. South on paved road to **Nueva Ocotepeque**, 6 daily, US$1.80, 2 hrs. There you change buses for El Salvador and Guatemala (1 hr to border, US$1, bus leaves hourly until 1700).

Around Santa Rosa de Copán

Bus Numerous buses head south daily from Santa Rosa to **Corquín** (US$0.75, 2 hrs). **Belén Gualcho** to **Santa Rosa** daily at 0430 (Sun at 0930). To **Gracias** from main plaza at 0400, 0500 and 1330.

Nueva Ocotepeque

cloudforest hiking near the international borders

Heading south from Santa Rosa, Nueva Ocotepeque gives access to good hiking and leads to the borders with Guatemala and El Salvador. The old colonial church of La Vieja (or La Antigua) between Nueva Ocotepeque and the border is in the village of Antigua Ocotepeque, which was founded in the 1540s, but destroyed by a flood from Cerro El Pital in 1934.

El Pital, 30 km east of Nueva Ocotepeque, at 2730 m is the third highest point in Honduras with several square kilometres of cloudforest. The **Guisayote Biological Reserve** protects 35 sq km of cloudforest, about 50% virgin and is reached from the Western Highway, where there are trails and good hiking. Access is from El Portillo, the name of the pass on the main road north. El Portillo to El Sillón, the park's southern entrance, is three to five hours. There's a twice-daily bus from El Sillón to Ocotepeque. The park has not been developed for tourism.

The **Parque Nacional Montecristo** forms part of the Trifinio/La Fraternidad project, administered jointly by Honduras, Guatemala and El Salvador. The park is quite remote from the Honduran side, two to three days to the summit, but there are easy-to-follow trails. Access is best from Metapán in El Salvador. From the lookout point at the peak you can see about 90% of El Salvador and 20% of Honduras on a clear day. The natural resources office, for information, is opposite Texaco, two blocks from Hotel y Comedor Congolón at the south end of town. Raymond J Sabella of the US Peace Corps has written a very thorough description of the natural and historical attractions of the Department, including hikes, waterfalls and caves.

Listings Nueva Ocotepeque

Where to stay

$$ Maya Chortis
Barrio San José, 4 Calle, 3 Av NE, T2653-3377.
Good-value nice rooms with bath, double beds, hot water, fan, TV, minibar and phone. The quieter rooms are at back. There is also room service and a good restaurant. Breakfast included.

$$ Sandoval
Opposite Hondutel, T2653-3098.
Rooms and suites with private bath, hot water, cable TV, minibar, phone and room service; there's a good-value restaurant. Breakfast included.

$ Gran
About 250 m from town at the junction of the roads for El Salvador and Guatemala, just north of town, at Sinuapa.
Pleasant, clean place with bath and cold water, single beds only.

Restaurants

Comedor Nora ($), Parque Central, and **Merendera Ruth** ($), 2 Calle NE, just off Parque Central, both offer economical *comida corriente*, preferable to *comedores* around bus terminal.

$$ Sandoval and Don Chepe
At Maya Chortis.
The best options. Excellent food, small wine lists, good value. Recommended.

Transport

Bus Transportes Escobar daily service **Tegucigalpa** to Nueva Ocotepeque/ Agua Caliente, via La Entrada and Santa Rosa de Copán (12 Av entre 8 y 9 C, Barrio Concepción, Comayagüela, T2237-4897; **Hotel Sandoval**, T2653-3098, Nueva Ocotepeque). Buses to **San Pedro Sula** stop at La Entrada (US$1.70), 1st at 0030, for connections to Copán. There are splendid mountain views. From **San Pedro Sula** there are regular buses via Santa Rosa south (6 hrs, US$4.50); road is well paved.

★A charming town set in the hills just to the east of the border with Guatemala, Copán Ruinas (www.copanhonduras.org)– to give the town its full name – thrives and survives on visitors passing through to visit the nearby ruins (see page 63). Nevertheless, it is arguably the best-preserved and one of the most pleasant towns in Honduras. For those arriving from nearby Guatemala, it's a good place to stop for a few days before heading straight to San Pedro Sula (172 km) and the Bay Islands or Tegucigalpa (395 km). In addition to the enigmatic ruins of Copán, the town offers good hotels and restaurants, coffee plantation tours, hiking, caving, hot springs, horse riding, language schools and volunteer opportunities.

The **Museo de Arqueología** ① *on the town square, Mon-Sat 0800-1600, US$2*, has explanations in Spanish of the Maya empire and stelae. The exhibits are on the dusty side, but there is an interesting selection of artefacts, a burial site and a tomb that was unearthed during a road-building project. The completely

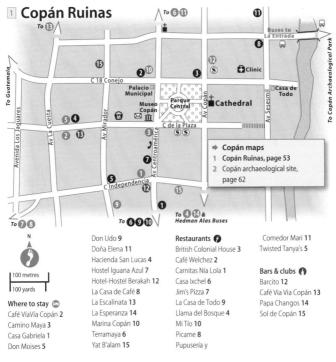

Copán Ruinas

Copán maps
1 Copán Ruinas, page 53
2 Copán archaeological site, page 62

Where to stay 🛏
Café VíaVía Copán 2
Camino Maya 3
Casa Gabriela 1
Don Moises 5
Don Udo 9
Doña Elena 11
Hacienda San Lucas 4
Hostel Iguana Azul 7
Hotel-Hostel Berakah 12
La Casa de Café 8
La Escalinata 13
La Esperanza 14
Marina Copán 10
Terramaya 6
Yat B'alam 15

Restaurants 🍴
British Colonial House 3
Café Welchez 2
Carnitas Nía Lola 1
Casa Ixchel 6
Jim's Pizza 7
La Casa de Todo 9
Llama del Bosque 4
Mi Tío 10
Picame 8
Pupusería y
Comedor Mari 11
Twisted Tanya's 5

Bars & clubs 🍸
Barcito 12
Café Via Via Copán 13
Papa Changos 14
Sol de Copán 15

restored Old Cuartel now houses the **Casa K'inich Interactive Children's Museum** ① *Up the hill from Hotel Marina Copán, www.asociacioncopan.org, US$1.10, Wed-Fri 1400-1700*, an interesting museum for everyone, not just for kids, and in a nice spot with great views of the town from towers in the perimeter wall. An excellent permanent **photography exhibition** ① *Mon-Fri, 0800-1600, free*, has opened at the Municipalidad on the main plaza. There are rare period photos and documentation from the first archaeological expedition to Copán at the turn of the 20th century, donated by Harvard University's Peabody Museum and archaeologists Barbara and Bill Fash.

Around Copán Ruinas

There are many caves around Copán to visit; some of which have unearthed Maya artefacts; ask locally. Also here, and in the neighbouring part of Guatemala, are a few remaining Chorti indigenous villages, such as La Pintada, surrounded by cornfields and forests, which is great countryside for hiking and horse-riding (see What to do, page 59). The villages are particularly interesting to visit on 1 November, Día de Los Muertos, when there are family and communal ceremonies for the dead. Nine kilometres east of Copán is **Santa Rita**, a small colonial town on the Copán River with cobblestones and red roofs.

Luna Jaguar Spa
20 km north from Copán, T2651-4746, www.lunajaguarspa.com, daily 0900-2100.

The mineral-rich hot springs at Luna Jaguar Spa are a great place to rest and unwind, especially if you've been trekking the hills. Reached by a road through villages and beautiful scenery, it's a 45-minute journey by vehicle from Copán; pickups sometimes go for about US$25, shared between passengers. The cheapest option is local transport from beside the soccer field (three buses daily, US$1.50), though it's a very rough unpaved road, only advisable by 4WD in wet season. It is best to use **Base Camp Adventures** for trips, US$15, plus entry to hot springs.

Imaginatively designed as a Maya spiritual centre, complete with a tunnel entry to a Xibalba 'underworld', Luna Jaguar offers a hedonistic treat, with 13 different hot pools, mud bath, hydrotherapy warm shower, DIY hot stone foot massage, nature trail and river bathing (US$10, plus extra for massage treatments), all set among the steamy lush forest with aloof Maya sculptures looking over the simmering bathers. There is a therapist on hand for advice; snacks and drinks are served at the poolside. There are changing facilities, toilets, drinks and snacks in the park. Cold water pools before entrance to spa, US$3.

Macaw Mountain
10 mins from the town centre, T2651-4245, www.macawmountain.org, open 0900-1700, US$10 (valid for 3 days).

Macaw Mountain is Honduras' largest bird park with 130+ parrots, toucans and macaws, all locally rescued or donated, including some injured and sick birds. There are also some birds of prey, including tiny pigmy owls, all lovingly cared for in clean, spacious enclosures; some tamer birds are in an open area. Activities include tours of the coffee *finca*, with expert bilingual naturalist guides; a riverside restaurant serving good, hearty food, including excellent coffee and freshly baked cakes; a visitor centre; and river swimming. Highly recommended.

La Entrada: Copán to San Pedro Sula

Approximately 60 km east of Copán Ruinas on Highway CA11, the hot, dusty town of La Entrada marks the junction with Highway CA4, also known as the Western Highway. The town offers bus connections with Santa Rosa (see page 46) to the south and San Pedro Sula 115 km away to the northeast, but due to the risk of highway robbery, it is recommended that you take a direct non-stop service from Copán.

El Puente ⓘ *daily 0800-1600, US$5*, is a national archaeological park reached by taking a turn-off, 4.5 km west from La Entrada on the Copán road, then turning right on a well-signposted, paved road 6 km to the visitor centre. It is near the confluence of the Chamelecón and Chinamito rivers and is thought to have been a regional centre between AD 600 and 900.

Listings Copán Ruinas *map p53*

Where to stay

$$$$ Hacienda San Lucas
Couth out of town, T2651-4495, www. haciendasanlucas.com.
This renovated hacienda home has lovely views of Copán river valley and is a great spot for calm and tranquillity. Accommodation and amenities include 8 rooms with hot water bath, Wi-Fi, restaurant and hiking trails. Secluded and romantic.

$$$ Camino Maya
Corner of main plaza, T2651-4646, www. caminomayahotel.com.
Another solid colonial-style option. Rooms are bright and airy; some have balconies, but those on the courtyard are quieter than those facing the street. Facilities include a good restaurant, cable TV, a/c and Wi-Fi. English spoken.

$$$ La Casa de Café
4½ blocks west of plaza, T2651-4620, www.casadecafecopan.com.

Renovated colonial home with beautifully designed garden and lovely views over the valley. Rates include breakfast, coffee all day, library and expert local information. Friendly and interesting hosts, English spoken. It's popular so it's best to reserve in advance. Protected parking. The Bamboo Patio massage pavilion offers 1-hr relaxation massage. Wi-Fi. Recommended.

$$$ Terramaya
2 blocks uphill from main plaza, T2651-4623, www.terramayacopan.com.
The town's first boutique-style hotel with 6 small but tasteful rooms, glorious countryside views from those upstairs, leafy little garden with massage area and outdoor shower; lounge areas and library. Breakfast included. Same owners as La Casa del Café (see above), very helpful and knowledgeable for local tours and activities.

$$$-$$ Casa Gabriela
Calle Independencia, 1 block south of the Parque Central, Barrio El Centro, T2651-4436, www.hotelcasagabriela.com.
A well-attired boutique option whose rooms combine airy simplicity, earthy tones and solid wood furniture to relaxing effect. Rooms have semi-orthopaedic beds, LCD TVs, cotton sheets, a/c and Wi-Fi. The colonial patio has leafy plants and a restaurant.

$$$-$$ La Esperanza
South of town on the banks of the Copán river, T2651-4676, www.haciendalaesperanza.org.
The delightfully secluded setting of La Esperanza, a colonial-style B&B just a short walk out of town, encompasses verdant landscaped grounds filled with green lawns, fountains, tropical trees and patios. Accommodation includes 4 fully appointed rooms with modern amenities and a touch of rustic chic. 100% of proceeds go to Paramedics for Children.

$$$-$$ Marina Copán
On the plaza occupying almost an entire block, T2651-4070, www.hotelmarinacopan.com.
A long-established colonial favourite with a pool, sauna, restaurant, bar, live marimba music at weekends; also caters for tour groups. Rooms and suites are tasteful and spacious with hand-crafted furniture and balconies overlooking the plaza. Friendly atmosphere. Recommended.

$$$-$$ Yat B'alam
Calle Independencia, Barrio El Centro, T2651-4388, www.yatbalam.com.
Offering an array of atmospheric boutique rooms, this handsome colonial townhouse retains its old school charm with cobblestone enclaves, terracotta tiles, wooden rocking chairs, wrought iron beds and other traditional touches. Modern amenities include Wi-Fi, a/c, fridge, cable TV and DVD player.

$$ Don Udo
Av Mirador, Barrio El Centro, T2651-4533, www.donudos.com.
This colonial-style, family-run B&B features a calming breakfast patio surrounded by abundant plants. Accommodation includes 14 rooms overlooking the central courtyard. There is transport, tours, Wi-Fi, massage, sauna, sun deck, laundry services and a fully stocked international bar with a daily happy hour.

$$ Doña Elena
Av Centroamérica, Barrio El Calvario, T2651-4029, www.casadonaelena.com.
Founded in 1998 by Doña Elena and her last son, Nery, this homely *hospedaje* prides itself on hospitality. They don't promise luxury, but rooms are comfortable and reasonably priced, all fully kitted with TVs, a/c, Wi-Fi, hot water and panoramic views of the gardens or mountains. Solid, helpful and reliable.

$$ La Escalinata
Av La Cuesta, Barrio Buena Vista, www.hotellaescalinata.com.
La Escalinata is a dependable guesthouse with 9 simple but well-equipped rooms: facilities include Wi-Fi, hot water and semi-orthopaedic beds. The inn's unique selling point is its view of the mountains and treetops, yours to enjoy if you snag a room with a private balcony.

$$-$ Don Moises
Calle de la Plaza, T2651-4543, www.hoteldonmoisescopan.com.

Don Moises offers simple budget rooms equipped with Wi-Fi, fan or a/c, hot water, and cable TV. There's also a shared kitchen, lockers, laundry and relaxing sun terrace with hammocks. Kind, helpful and hospitable; a good choice for thrifty wanderers.

$ Café Via Via Copán
T2651-4652, www.viaviacafe.com.
Great rooms, part of a worldwide Belgian network of cafés, breakfast US$2.75, special price for students with card and discounts for more than 1 night, hot water, good beds, bar and great vegetarian food.

$ Hostel Iguana Azul
Next to La Casa de Café and under same ownership, T2651-4620, www.iguanaazulcopan.com.
Good for backpackers, this clean, comfortable hostel with colonial decor offers dorm-style bunk beds in 2 rooms, with shared bath; also 3 more private double rooms. There is hot water, free purified water, lockers, laundry facilities, garden patio, common area, books, magazines, travel guides (including Footprint), maps, garden, fans and a safe box. English spoken.

$ Hotel-Hostel Berakah
1 block north of Parque Central, T9828-9827, www.hotelberakahcopan.hostel.com.
This pleasant and centrally located hotel-hostel has some of the cheapest dorm beds in town, which come complete with quality mattresses and useful amenities like Wi-Fi, a pool table, kitchen and hammocks. Intimate, friendly and affordable. There are a few private rooms too.

Apartments

Casa Jaguar Rental Home
Just 5 blocks from Parque Central, T2651-4620, www.casajaguarcopan.com.
Comfortable village residence with 2 double bedrooms with a/c, fully equipped for self-catering. Available for the night, week or month. Contact **La Casa de Café**, see above.

La Entrada
There are several other cheapies and no-frills guesthouses in town.

$$-$ San Carlos
T2661-2228, www.hotelelsancarlos.com.
Reliable and economical with very adequate rooms, all with a/c and cable TV. There's also a pool, bar and a restaurant. Excellent value.

Restaurants

$$$ Hacienda San Lucas
South out of town, T2651-4495, www. haciendasanlucas.com.
Using traditional recipes and old world cooking techniques, Hacienda San Lucas has developed an interesting style of Mayan fusion cuisine. Reservations are required for lunch (1200-1400) and dinner; drop-ins for groups of less than 4 welcome for breakfast. A great place for a special meal. Recommended.

$$$ Twisted Tanya's
Calle Independencia and Av La Cuesta, T2651-4182, www.twistedtanya.com. Mon-Sat 1500-2200.
Happy hour 1600-1800. Fine dining and quirky retro decor (ie mirror balls). The menu includes rich and creative international cuisine such as seasonal fish with a cream loroco flower bud sauce, tequila shrimp and slow-roasted

pork with sage and onion stuffing. Lovely open-air setting on the 2nd floor.

$$$-$$ British Colonial House
Av Copán y Calle 18 Conejo, Parque Central.

This popular British-run gastropub serves a diverse range of international fare in generous portions including Thai curries, chicken tikka masala, steaks and much more. For the homesick, there's 'pub grub' and comfort food straight from old Blighty, including shepherd's pie.

$$$-$$ Casa Ixchel
Approximately 25 mins out of town by car, shuttles offered for spa users, T2651-4515, www.spaixchel.com.

Casa Ixchel is a day spa and coffee finca. Its restaurant is set in a peaceful outdoor patio filled with potted palms and dazzling bougainvillea and their menu includes cooked breakfasts, light meals and international café fare, such as pancakes, burgers and pastas, all accompanied by seasonal fruit juices, medicinal tea and locally sourced coffee. A tranquil healing space.

$$$-$$ Mi Tío
Av Centroamericano, 1½ blocks south of the Parque Central, T9791-6572, www.mitiocopan.com.

This family-run Uruguayan restaurant serves hearty platters of beef, chicken and pork straight off the *parillada*, along with a few fish and vegetarian dishes, sandwiches and light snacks. Lots of flavour, recommended for carnivores.

$$ Café Vía Vía Copán
See Where to stay, above.

Vía Vía serves an eclectic range of international grub from hamburgers to lasagne to *comida típica*. Can be hit-and-miss but breakfasts are fairly reliable. A

pleasant space and a popular evening nightspot with the traveller crowd.

$$ Jim's Pizza
½ a block from Hotel Camino Maya.

Jim's Pizza claims to be the first and most authentic pizza joint in western Honduras with thin-crust pizzas prepared according to traditional family recipes. They also serve burgers, lasagne and subs and, at weekends, rotisserie chicken. A friendly, casual place, popular with tourists and expats.

$$ La Casa de Todo
1 block from Parque Central, www.casadetodo.com. Open 0700-2100.

In a pleasant garden setting, this restaurant has internet, a craft shop and book exchange. They often host NGOs and other community groups.

$$ Llama del Bosque
2 blocks west of plaza. Open for breakfast, lunch and dinner.

This attractive place offers large portions of reasonable food; try their *carnitas típicas*. Recommended.

$ Carnitas Nía Lola
2 blocks south of Parque Central, at the end of the road. Daily 0700-2200.

A busy bar with *comida típica* served in a relaxed atmosphere. Also has a book exchange.

$ Pupusería y Comedor Mari
Av Sesesmil.

The best cheap, typical food in town, with daily specials like seafood soup. Clean, decent service, and very popular with locals at lunchtime. Food is fresh, cheap and plentiful.

Cafés
Café Welchez
Next to Hotel Marina Copán, www.cafehonduras.com.

They serve their own gourmet coffee, good cakes and desserts, including coconut flan, but it's on the pricey side. There's a pleasant upstairs terrace.

Santa Rita
Unnamed outdoor restaurant, off the main road next to the Esso station. Speciality *tajadas*, huge portions, cheap. Recommended.

Bars and clubs

Barcito
1 block down from SW corner of main square.
Small, cosy, laid-back bar on an upstairs open terrace. Happy hour is 1700-1900. They also serve great and inexpensive gourmet snacks and tapas.

Café Via Via Copán
See Where to stay, above. Open every night till 2400.
European chill-out lounge vibe, comfortable and popular, food until 2100.

Papa Changos
Located a few blocks from downtown.
After hours spot, popular with young locals and traveller crowd. Gets going at midnight on Fri and Sat. The place to let loose and party till dawn.

Sol de Copán
Calle El Mirador, Barrio Buena Vista, look for the turret.
Managed by Tomas from Munich, the Sol de Copán is a bona fide German microbrewery with some excellent nectar on tap, undoubtedly the best German brews in Honduras. If all that authentic Bavarian beer leaves you peckish, order some bratwurst to soak it up. Recommended.

Shopping

Selling all sorts of local crafts are **La Casa de Todo** (down the street from **Banco de Occidente**), one of Copán's best crafts shop, with a popular café for light meals and snacks (see Restaurants, above); **Yax Kuk Mo** (the southwest corner of plaza), has biggest selection; **Mayan Connection** (opposite **Barcito**, see Bars and clubs, above), is a bit more expensive but offers better than average quality.
La Casa del Jade, *1 block uphill from Hotel Marina Copán (with another branch in lobby)*. Specializes in high-class designer jewellery.

What to do

Language schools
Academia de Español Guacamaya, T2651-4360, www.guacamaya.com. Classes US$160 a week, plus homestay US$60. Recommended.
Ixbalanque, T2651-4432, www. ixbalanque.com. This school offers one-to-one teaching plus board and lodging with a local family, US$300 for classes and a 7-day homestay.

Birdwatching and wildlife observation
Alexander Alvarado, *based in Copán Ruinas, T9751-1680, www.honduranbirds. com.* Alexander Alvarado also leads birdwatching and hiking tours around the country; he knows his stuff and speaks good English.
Bob Gallardo, *T2651-4133, www. birdsofhonduras.com.* A birding guide and naturalist, Bob Gallardo is an expert on Honduran flora and fauna. He leads birding trips, natural history tours, orchid and serpent tours around Copán and

other parts of Honduras, including La Mosquitia.

Canopy tours

Canopy Copán Ruinas, *2 km from downtown on the road to the hot springs, T9330-2024*. One of the best canopy tours in the country with 16 high-speed cables; the longest runs for a staggering 1 km. Stunning views of the countryside and rainforest. Contact the canopy directly or via a tour operator in town (around US$45 per person).

Coffee tours

Copán Coffee Tour, *Finca Santa Isabel, 40 mins' drive from Copán Ruinas, T2651-4202, www.cafehonduras.com.* Run by family producers of high-quality Welchez coffee for 3 generations. The 3- to 4-hr tour of grounds shows the whole production process in a lovely hillside setting, with expert multilingual guides; US$25-30. There is also a terrace restaurant overlooking river. Horse riding is available, through countryside rich with flora and fauna, including some 80 bird species and medicinal plants. The best tour of its kind in the area. Highly recommended.

Horse riding

You will probably be approached with offers of horse hire, which is a good way of getting to nearby attractions. Riding trips are available to Los Sapos and Las Sepulturas, US$15 for 3 hrs. Watch out for taxi and on the street recommendations as the quality and price can be poor.
Finca El Cisne, *T2651-4695, www.fincaelcisne.com.* Full-day tours to the coffee plantation high in the mountains including horse riding, lunch and transport, US$82 per person with overnight accommodation available for

an extra US$13. Also trips to hot springs on this working hacienda.

Tour operators

Base Camp Adventures, *T2651-4695, www.basecampcopan.wordpress.com.* Nature hikes US$10, treks, motocross tours US$40, horse riding US$15, expedition hikes US$20 and transport including shuttles to Guatemala City, Antigua US$20.
Copán Connections, *T2651-4182, www.copanconnections.com.* Tours, hotels, transport, specializing in Copán and Bay Islands. Run by Tanya of **Twisted Tanya** fame.
MC Tours, *Av Centroamérica, T2651 4154, www.mctours-honduras.com.* Local and countrywide tours.

Transport

Bus

Heading inland you normally have to go to San Pedro Sula before heading for the coast or south to the capital.

There is a 1st-class direct service to **San Pedro Sula** with connections to **Tegucigalpa** and **La Ceiba** with **Hedman Alas** (T2651-4037, www.hedmanalas.com), 3 a day, 3 hrs to San Pedro. US$16, at 1030 and 1430, with connections in San Pedro for Tegucigalpa and La Ceiba. Also 0515 daily connection to **Tela**, 8 hrs, US$22 and **San Pedro Sula Airport**, US$21. To **Guatemala City** (US$35) and **Antigua** (US$42) at 1420 and 1800. To **San Pedro Sula** Casasola Express for San Pedro Sula (T2651-4078) at 0400, 0500, 0600, 0700 and 1400. Both services are comfortable, efficient, good value and with reclining seats.

If heading for **Santa Rosa de Copán** or **Gracias** get a bus to the junction at

La Entrada and change there. Buses for **La Entrada** leave Copán Ruinas every 30 mins, 1 hr, US$1.80.

Plus+ Agency daily shuttle bus service (www.plustravelguate.com, T2651-4088), main office in Copán Ruinas, Comercial Handal, Calle Independencia, to many destinations around Honduras and to Guatemala City and Antigua (US$8). If travelling in a group, private express minibuses can be hired to **San Pedro Sula**, **Tela**, **La Ceiba**, and airport from **Hotel Patty** and **Yaragua Tours** – US$120 regardless of number of people. Numerous boys greet you on arrival to carry bags or offer directions for a small fee; while most are good kids, some will tell you hotels are closed when they aren't.

Tuk-tuk
As in much of Honduras, tuk-tuks have arrived, providing cheap, easy transport. Short trips around town cost US$0.50, **Macaw Mountain Bird Park** US$1.10, **ruins** US$0.80, **Hedman Alas** terminal US$1.10.

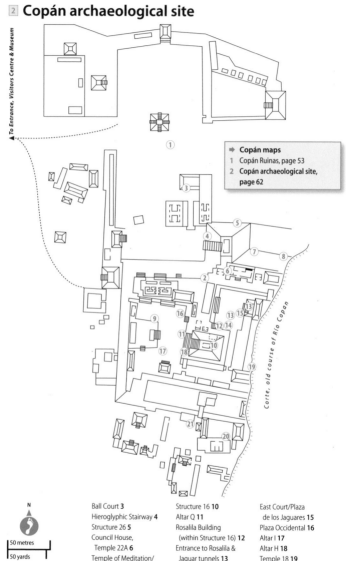

② Copán archaeological site

To Entrance, Visitors Centre & Museum

➡ **Copán maps**
1 Copán Ruinas, page 53
2 **Copán archaeological site, page 62**

Corte, old course of Río Copán

N

50 metres
50 yards

Main Plaza with Stelae **1**
Acropolis **2**

Ball Court **3**
Hieroglyphic Stairway **4**
Structure 26 **5**
Council House,
  Temple 22A **6**
Temple of Meditation/
  Temple 22 **7**
House of Knives **8**
Structure 13 **9**

Structure 16 **10**
Altar Q **11**
Rosalila Building
  (within Structure 16) **12**
Entrance to Rosalila &
  Jaguar tunnels **13**
Hunal Building
  (beneath Rosalila)
  & Tomb of Founder **14**

East Court/Plaza
  de los Jaguares **15**
Plaza Occidental **16**
Altar I **17**
Altar H **18**
Temple 18 **19**
Structure 32 **20**
Zona Residencial **21**

★The magnificent ruins of Copán are one of Central America's major Maya sites, certainly the most significant in Honduras, and they mark the southeastern limit of Maya dominance.

Site information Daily 0800-1600, US$15 entrance to ruins and Las Sepulturas, admission valid for one day. To explore the tunnels is a pricey and unnecessary, US$15. Bilingual guided tours available (US$25, two hours), recommended. The Copán Guide Association has a kiosk in the parking area where qualified bilingual guides can be hired at a fixed rate.

Tip...
Get to the ruins as early as possible, or stay late in the day so you have a chance to be there without hordes of people.

Just 1 km from the village, there is a path beside the road from Copán to the ruins which passes two stelae en route.

Photographs of the excavation work and a maquette of the site are located in a small exhibition room at the visitor centre. There is a cafetería by the entrance to the ruins, and also a handicrafts shop, in the Parque Arqueológico, next to the bookshop, with local and country maps, and a Spanish/English guidebook for the ruins, which is rather generalized. Useful books are: *Scribes, Warriors and Kings: City of Copán*, by William and Barbara Fash, and *History Carved in Stone, a guide to Copán*, by William Fash and Ricardo Argucía, published locally and available at the site. Luggage can be left for free.

Museo de Escultura Maya
US$7, ticket from the main ticket office not at the museum.

It is essential to visit the museum before the ruins. The impressive and huge two-storey Museum of Maya Sculpture and sculpture park houses the recently excavated carvings and has good explanations in Spanish and English. In the middle of the museum is an open-air courtyard with a full-size reproduction of the Rosalila temple, found intact buried under Temple 16 with its original paint and carvings (see below). A reproduction of the doorway to Temple 16 is on the upper floor. The museum houses the original stelae to prevent weather damage, while copies will be placed on site. More than 2000 other objects found at Copán are also in the museum. The exit leads to the ruins via the nature trail.

Archaeological site
The ruins were engulfed in jungle when John Lloyd Stephens and Frederick Catherwood examined them in 1839. Stephens, a lawyer, and Catherwood, an architect, were the first English-speaking travellers to explore the regions originally settled by the Maya. They are credited with recording the existence of many of the ruins in the Maya area. Some of the finest examples of sculpture from Copán are now in London and Boston.

In the 1930s, the Carnegie Institute cleared the ground and rebuilt the Hieroglyphic Stairway, and since then the ruins have been maintained by the government. Some of the most complex carvings are found on the 21 **stelae**, or 3-m columns of stones on which the passage of time was originally believed to have been recorded. Under many of the stelae was a vault; some have been excavated. The stelae are deeply incised and carved with faces, figures and animals. There are royal portraits with inscriptions recording deeds and the lineage of those portrayed as well as dates of birth, marriage and death. Ball courts were revealed during excavation, and one of them has been fully restored. The **Hieroglyphic Stairway** leads up a pyramid; its upper level supported a temple. Its other sides are still under excavation. The stairway is covered for protection, but a good view can be gained from the foot and there is access to the top via the adjacent plaza.

After Hurricane Mitch, the **Rosalila Temple**, in Temple 16, was opened to the public, as were other previously restricted excavations, in an effort to attract more visitors. The Rosalila and Jaguar tunnels below the site are now open to visitors at an additional cost (see above). Much fascinating excavation work is now in progress, stacks of labelled carved stones have been placed under shelters, and the site looks like it is becoming even more interesting as new buildings are revealed.

The most atmospheric buildings are those still half-buried under roots and soil. The last stela was set up in Copán between AD 800 and 820, after less than five centuries of civilized existence. The nearby river has been diverted to prevent it encroaching on the site when in flood.

Also near the ruins is a *sendero natural* (nature trail) through the jungle to the minor ball court; take mosquito repellent. The trail takes 30 minutes and has a few signposts explaining the plants, animals and spirituality of the forest to the Maya. After 1600 is the best time to see animals on the *sendero natural*, which is open until 1700. About 4 km from the main centre is the ceremonial site known as **Los Sapos** ⓘ *entry US$2* (The Toads), a pre-Classic site with early stone carvings. The toad was a Maya symbol of fertility. East of the main ruins near Los Sapos is a stone, **Estela 12**, which lines up with another, **Estela 10**, on the other side of the valley at sunrise and sunset on 12 April every year.

One kilometre beyond the main ruins, along the road to San Pedro Sula, or connected by a stone path from the main site, is an area called **Las Sepulturas** ⓘ *entrance is almost 2 km from the main site, entry to this site is included in the main Copán ticket*, a residential area where ceramics dating back to 1000 BC have been found. Exhibits from the site are on display in the Copán Museum. It is a delightful site, beautifully excavated and well maintained, peaceful and in lovely surroundings.

Tegucigalpa
to San Pedro Sula

Like the capital, San Pedro Sula is a rapidly developing and largely unappealing destination; a sweltering business and transport hub as much forged by North American commercial appetites as by the illicit cocaine trade. Most travellers pass through on their way to the Caribbean coast. For those seeking access to the languid shores of the Bay Islands, the Northern Highway from the capital to San Pedro remains the fastest option, but it is worth pausing en route to enjoy the fine colonial heritage of Comayagua, the entrancing mountain beauty spots of Lago Yojoa and Pulhapanzak waterfall, and the intriguing craft villages of Santa Bárbara department.

Comayagua and around
a historic colonial city and the former capital of Honduras

Founded on 7 December 1537 as Villa Santa María de Comayagua on the site of an indigenous village by Alonzo de Cáceres, Located Located on the rich Comayagua plain, 1½ hours' drive (93 km) north of the capital, Comayagua (altitude 550 m) has many old colonial buildings, reflecting the importance of Honduras' first capital after Independence in 1821. The centre has had an impressive makeover recently, and is worth a visit for the handsome colonial architecture in and around the main square, Plaza León Alvarado.

On 3 September 1543, it was designated the Seat of the Audiencia de los Confines by King Felipe II of Spain. President Marco Aurelio Soto transferred the capital to Tegucigalpa in 1880. Comayagua was declared a city in 1557, 20 years after its founding. Within a couple of centuries a rash of civic and religious buildings were constructed. The former university, the first in Central America, was founded in 1632 and closed in 1842 (it was located in the Casa Cural, Bishop's Palace, where the bishops have lived since 1558). Others include the churches of **La Merced** (1550-1588) and **La Caridad** (1730), **San Francisco** (1574) and **San Sebastián** (1575). **San Juan de Dios** (1590 but destroyed by earthquake in 1750), the church where the Inquisition sat, is now the site of the Hospital Santa Teresa. **El Carmen** was built in 1785.

The wealth of colonial heritage has attracted funds for renovation, which have produced a slow transformation in the town. The most interesting building is the **cathedral** ⓘ *daily 0700-1900,* in the Parque Central, inaugurated in 1711, with its plain square tower and façade decorated with sculpted figures of the saints, which contains some of the finest examples of colonial art in Honduras. Of the 16 original hand-carved and gilded altars, just four survive today. The clock in the tower was originally made over 800 years ago in Spain and is the oldest working clock in the Americas. It was given to Comayagua by Felipe II in 1582. At first it was in La Merced when that was the cathedral, but it was moved to the new cathedral in 1715. You can climb the tower to see the clock and the old bells, with tour guides on hand in the cathedral (Ever Villanueva, T2994-77551, is knowledgeable and friendly). A huge floor mosaic of the cathedral façade has been built on the square, best seen from the tower.

Half a block north of the cathedral is the **Ecclesiastical Museum** ⓘ *daily 0930-1200, 1400-1700, US$0.60.* One block south of the cathedral, the **Museo de Arqueología** ⓘ *at the corner of 6 Calle and 1 Av NO, Wed-Fri 0800-1600, Sat and Sun 0900-1200, 1300-1600, US$1.70,* housed in the former Palacio de Gobernación, is small scale but fascinating, with six rooms each devoted to a different period. Much of the collection came from digs in the El Cajón region, 47 km north of Comayagua, before the area was flooded for the hydroelectricity project. The **Casa Cultural** on a corner of the plaza, left of the cathedral, has permanent and temporary exhibitions of the city history and art.

There are two colonial plazas shaded by trees and shrubs. A stone portal and a portion of the façade of **Casa Real** (the viceroy's residence) still survive. Built in 1739-1741, it was damaged by an earthquake in 1750 and destroyed by tremors in 1856. The army still uses a quaint old fortress built when Comayagua was the capital. There is a lively market area.

Parque Nacional Montaña de Comayagua is only 13 km from Comayagua, reached from the villages of San José de la Mora (4WD necessary) or San Jerónimo and Río Negro (usually passable). Contact **Fundación Ecosimco** ⓘ *0 Calle y 1 Av NO in Comayagua, T772-4681,* for further information about the trails which lead through the cloudforest to waterfalls. The mountain (2407 m) has 6000 ha of cloudforest and is a major watershed for the area.

Siguatepeque

The Northern Highway crosses the Comayagua plain, part of the gap in the mountains which stretches from the Gulf of Fonseca to the Ulúa lowlands. Set in forested highlands 32 km northwest of Comayagua is the town of Siguatepeque (altitude 1150 m), which has a cool climate. It is the site of the Escuela Nacional de Ciencias Forestales (which is worth a visit) and, being exactly halfway between

Tegucigalpa and San Pedro Sula (128 km), is a collection point for the produce of the Intibucá, Comayagua and Lempira departments. The Cerro and Bosque de Calanterique, behind the Evangelical Hospital, is a 45-minute walk from the town centre. The Parque Central is pleasant, shaded by tall trees with the church of San Pablo on the north side on the east.

Southwest from Siguatepeque, the route to La Esperanza is a beautiful paved road through lovely forested mountainous country, via **Jesús de Otoro**, where there are two basic *hospedajes* and **Balneario San Juan de Quelala** ⓘ *US$0.30*, which has a *cafetería* and picnic sites. North from Siguatepeque, the highway goes over the forested escarpment of the continental divide, before descending towards Lago Yojoa. Just south of Taulabé on the highway are the illuminated **Caves of Taulabé** ⓘ *daily, US$0.40, guides available*, with both stalactites and bats. North of Taulabé, and 16 km south of the lake is the turn-off northwest of a paved road to Santa Bárbara.

★Lago Yojoa

For local information contact Enrique Campos or his son at Hotel Agua Azul (see Where to stay, below). For more information, contact Proyecto Humuya, behind Iglesia Betel, 21 de Agosto, Siguatepeque, T2773-2426.

Sitting pretty among the mountains is the impressive Lake Yojoa (altitude 635 m), which is 22.5 km long and 10 km wide. To the west rise the Montañas de Santa Bárbara which include the country's second highest peak and the **Parque Nacional de Santa Bárbara** (see page 69). To the east is the **Parque Nacional Montaña Cerro Azul-Meámbar**. Pumas, jaguars and other animals live in the forests, pine-clad slopes and the cloudforest forming part of the reservoir of the Lago Yojoa basin. The national parks also have many waterfalls. The 50-sq-km Azul-Meámbar park is 30 km north of Siguatepeque and its highest point is 2047 m.

To get to any of the entry points (Meámbar, the main one, Jardines, Bacadia, Monte Verde or San Isidro) a 4WD is necessary. A local ecological group, **Ecolago** ⓘ *Edif Midence Soto, Parque Central (Tegucigalpa), T2237 9659*, has marked out the area and can offer guided tours. **Ecolago** has guides who are expert in spotting regional birds; at least 373 species have been identified around the lake. At one time the lake was full of bass, but overfishing and pollution have decimated the stocks. Tilapia farming is now very important.

The Northern Highway follows the eastern margin to the lake's southern tip at **Pito Solo**, where sailing and motor boats can be hired. Frustratingly, there is no public access to the lakeshore, which is fenced off by farms and private properties. Lake excursions are also available at several of the waterfront hotels and restaurants (see Listings, below), which also offer the best views.

On the northern shore of Lago Yojoa is a complex of pre-Columbian settlements called **Los Naranjos** ⓘ *US$5*, which are believed to have had a population of several thousand. It is considered to be the country's third most important archaeological site spanning the period from 1000 BC to AD 1000, and includes two ball courts. The site is slowly being developed for tourism by the Institute of

Anthropology and History and has a visitor centre, small museum and coffee shop and a number of forest walking trails. Excavation work is currently in progress. The local office of the institute (T2557-8197) is at the **Hotel Brisas de Lago**. From the lake it is 37 km down to the hot Ulúa lowlands.

A paved road skirts the lake's northern shore for 12 km via Peña Blanca. A road heads southwest to **El Mochito**, Honduras' most important mining centre. A bus from 2 Avenida in San Pedro Sula goes to Las Vegas-El Mochito mine for walks along the west side of Lago Yojoa. Buses will generally stop anywhere along the east side of the lake. Another road heads north from the northern shore, through Río Lindo, to **Caracol** on the Northern Highway. This road gives access to the Pulhapanzak waterfall, with some unexcavated ceremonial mounds adjacent, and to Ojo de Agua, a pretty bathing spot near Caracol. **Peña Blanca** is, according to one reader, a "very ugly town" on the north side of the lake.

Pulhapanzak waterfall
T3319-7282, www.pulhahn.com, daily 0600-1800, US$2.80. The caretaker allows camping for US$0.85; cabins are also available ($$$).

The impressive 42-m-high waterfall at Pulhapanzak is on the Río Lindo. The waterfall is beautiful during, or just after the rainy season, and in sunshine there is a rainbow over the gorge. A path leads down to the foot of the falls, thick with spray, and is very slippery; you can swim in river just before the edge – if you dare! There is a picnic area, a small *cafetería* and a good *comedor* 15 minutes' walk away down in the village, but the site does get crowded at weekends and holidays. River tubing is a seasonal option and there is also a large zip-wire course inside the grounds, with 13 sections, including one breathtaking stretch over the falls (US$25).

Santa Bárbara and around
Santa Bárbara (altitude: 290 m), surrounded by high mountains, forested hills and rivers, lies in a hot lowland valley 32 km west of Lago Yojoa. One of the nicest main towns in Honduras, it has little of architectural or historical interest compared with Gracias, Ojojona or Yuscarán, but it is here that you will find Panama hats and other goods made from junco palm. The majority of the population is fair-skinned (some redheads).

In addition to being a pleasant place to stay, Santa Bárbara is also a good base for visiting villages throughout the Santa Bárbara Department. Nearby, the ruined colonial city of **Tencoa** has been rediscovered. A short local trek behind the town climbs the hills to the ruined site of **Castillo Bogran**, with fine views across the valley and the town. Heading south out of Santa Bárbara, the paved road joins the Northern Highway south of Lago Yojoa.

The Department of Santa Bárbara is called the Cuna de los Artesanos (cradle of artisans), with over 10,000 craftspeople involved in the manufacture of handicrafts. The main products come from the small junco palm; for example, fine hats and baskets. The main towns for junco items are **La Arada**, 25 minutes from Santa Bárbara on the road to San Nicolás, and then branching off south, and **Ceguaca**, on a side road off the road to Tegucigalpa. Flowers and dolls from corn husks are made in Nueva Celilac. Mezcal is used to make carpets, rugs and hammocks, which are easy to find in towns such as **Ilama**, on the road to San Pedro Sula, which has one of the best small colonial churches in Honduras (no accommodation). People here also make *petates* (rugs) and purses.

Between Santa Bárbara and Lago Yojoa is the **Parque Nacional de Santa Bárbara** which contains the country's second highest peak, Montaña de Santa Bárbara at 2744 m. The rock is principally limestone with many subterranean caves. There is little tourist development as yet, with just one trail, and you can track down a guide in Los Andes, a village above Peña Blanca and Las Vegas. The best time to visit is the dry season, January to June. For information contact **Asociación Ecológica Corazón Verde** ⓘ *Palacio Municipal, Santa Bárbara*. There is a **Cohdefor** office just below the market (look for the sign) but they are not helpful.

Listings Comayagua and around

Tourist information

Casa Cultural
Near the cathedral, Parque Central, T2772-2028. Tue-Thu 0900-1700, Fri and Sat 0900-2100, Sun 0900-1200.
Tourist information is available here, including city map for sale, US$1.20. City tours are available in an open-topped tram from outside the Casa Cultural, daily every 30 mins, US$1.50.

Where to stay

Comayagua

$$$ Santa María
Km 82 on the Tegucigalpa highway, T2772-7872, www.hotelsmc.com.
The best in town, although not in the centre. Rooms are comfortable, if generic. Amenities include spacious grounds with lawns and a large pool.

$$ Casa Grande
Barrio Abajo, ½ a block to the east of Cine Valladolid, T2772-0772.

This good-looking and well-restored 19th-century colonial-style *casa* has lots of attractive touches: solid antique furniture, clay tiles, wood beams, terracotta tones and a courtyard filled with tropical plants. It's an intimate and romantic place to stay with lots of character.

$$ Hotel Antigua Comayagua
6a Calle NO, T2772-0816, www. hotelantiguacomayagua.com.
The Antigua has a great central location just 50 m from the Parque Central. Its rooms are spacious and presentable and have hot water, a/c, mini-fridge, Wi-Fi and cable TV. The real draw, however, is the well-kept garden and sizeable pool.

$$ Posada de mi Viejo
Barrio San Sebastian, opposite Iglesia San Sebastian, T2771-9312, www. hotellaposadademiviejo.com.
Set around a central courtyard with a small pool, this reliable *posada* has 22 spacious, modern, down-to-earth rooms with hot water, Wi-Fi and cable TV. Safe and spotless. Breakfast included.

Siguatepeque

$$ Park Place
Parque Central, T2773-9212.
An unbeatable central location opposite the main plaza. Rooms are on the small side, but reasonable and recently renovated. There's a pool on the roof and views over the town. Comfortable and attentive. Good reports.

$$ Vuestra Casa
Blvd Morazán, Barrio Abajo, T2773-0885.
This comfortable B&B has a range of decent, modern rooms with all the usual amenities; the suites are particularly appealing and come with fireplaces. Safe, secure, friendly place with leafy grounds, pool and views of the mountains.

Lago Yojoa

$$$$ Gualiqueme
Cottage at edge of lake, for information contact Richard Joint at Honduyate, T2882-3129.
Has 4 bedrooms in main house, 2 in annexe. Daily, weekly, monthly rental, weekend packages include ferry and fishing boat.

$$ Brisas del Lago
Close to Peña Blanca at the northern end of the lake, T2608-7229, www. hotelbrisasdellago.com.
Large, 1960s concrete hotel now looking a bit dated and mildewed, but with spacious rooms with a/c, cable TV and balcony, good value family suites; great lake views from gardens and pool. Good restaurant but overpriced, launches for hire and horse riding.

$$-$ D&D Brewery and Guesthouse
T2994-9719, www.ddbrewery.com.
Probably the best place on the lake, complete with 3 spacious cabins, 11 private rooms, 2 mixed dorms and 4 campsites. There is a pool and a restaurant but the real draw is the craft beer on tap. Recommended.

$$-$ Los Remos
Pito Solo, at the south end of the lake, T2557-8054.
Has cabins and camping facilities. Clean, beautiful setting, good food, nice for breakfasts, no beach but swimming pool and boat trips. Parking US$3.

$ Boarding House Moderno
Barrio Arriba, T643-2203.
Quiet place offering rooms with a hot shower; those with a fan are better value than with a/c. Parking. Recommended.

$ Gran Hotel Colonial
1½ blocks from Parque Central, T2643-2665.
Friendly hotel with sparsely furnished rooms, some with a/c, cold water. There's a good view from the roof. Recommended.

$ Hotel Agua Azul
At north end of lake, about 3 km west from junction at Km 166, T2991-7244.
Set in beautiful gardens, basic clean cabins for 2 or more people, meals for non-residents, but the food and service in restaurant is poor. There's a swimming pool, fishing, horse riding and boating, launches, kayaks and pedalos for hire, around US$6 for 30 mins; mosquito coils. The manager speaks English and there's a good reduction in low season. Recommended (except when loud karaoke is in full swing).

Santa Bárbara and around

$ Ruth
Calle La Libertad, T2643-2632.
Rooms without windows, fan.

Restaurants

Comayagua

$$$-$$ El Torito
Colonia San Miguel, on the Tegucigalpa road, opposite Polaris.
This local steakhouse is one of Comayagua's better joints. They serve succulent and locally sourced beef cuts along with chicken, shrimp and fish dishes. Hearty, good value and authentically Hondureño.

$$ La Gota de Limon
5a Calle NO. Sun-Wed 1030-1900; Thu-Sat 1030-0200.
A hit with pretty young things, La Gota de Limón serves economical *comida típica* by day and spins Latin favourites by night; don your dancing shoes and rock up to the rooftop terrace.

San Pedro Sula and around

evolving business hub and notorious narco den

San Pedro Sula is the second largest and most industrialized city in the country and a centre for the banana, coffee, sugar and timber trades. It is a distribution hub for northern and western Honduras with good road links. Its business community is mainly of Arab origin, and it is considered one of the fastest-growing cities between Mexico and Panama. By Central American standards, San Pedro Sula is a well-planned, modern city, but it's not a city you'll be inclined to stay in for long.

San Pedro Sula (altitude 60-150 m, population 900,000) was founded in 1536 by Pedro de Alvarado in the lush and fertile valley of the Ulúa (Sula) River, beneath the forested slopes of the Merendón mountains. There are many banana plantations. In recent years, the city has gained international notoriety as one of the most violent places on earth. On average, there are three homicides per day in San Pedro Sula, a sprawling urban powerhouse ingloriously dubbed the 'murder capital of the world'. Like Ciudad Juárez in Mexico, its problems are at least partly a consequence of its strategic location on international drug trafficking routes.

The city is divided into four quadrants: Noreste (Northeast, NE), Noroeste (Northwest, NO), Sudeste (Southeast, SE) and Sudoeste (Southwest, SO), where most of the hotels are located, although newer hotels, shopping malls and restaurant chains are in the Noroeste.

Although pleasant in the cooler season from November to February, temperatures are very high for the rest of the year. It is, nevertheless, a relatively clean city and the traffic is not too bad. The higher and cooler suburb of Bella Vista, with its fine views over the city, provides relief from the intense heat of the centre.

Safety San Pedro Sula has a fearsome reputation, but it is also an important business centre that welcomes scores of international travellers annually. The vast majority of violent crime is gang-related; provided you follow big city rules and do not stray into outlying *barrios*, you are unlikely to encounter any problems. Stay alert at all times and avoid areas without a police presence (or armed security). San Pedro Sula is not a great city for pedestrians but do not use urban buses; instead use radio taxis to get around (ask your hotel to call one). Do not walk the streets at night.

Sights
The large neocolonial-style **cathedral** was completed in the 1950s. **Museo de Antropología e Historia** ① *3 Av, 4 Calle NO, Mon, Wed-Sat 0900-1600, Sun 0900-1500, US$0.75, first Sun of the month is free*, has displays of the cultures that once inhabited the Ulúa Valley up to Spanish colonization and, on the first floor, local history since colonization. There is a museum café in the adjacent garden with fine stelae and a good set lunch.

Parque Nacional Cusuco
Entrance is US$15, which includes a guided trip; you cannot go on your own. Contact the HRPF at 5 Av, 1 Calle NO, San Pedro Sula, T552-1014. Also contact Cohdefor, 10 Av, 5 Calle NO, Barrio Guamilito, San Pedro Sula, T553-4959, or Cambio CA, who run tours. Permission from HRPF is required to walk through the park to Tegucigalpita on the coast. There is a visitor centre but bring your own food. You cannot stay or camp in the park, but camping is possible outside. Access by dirt road from Cofradía (Cafetería Negro, 1 block northwest of plaza, good food), on the road to Santa Rosa de Copán, then to Buenos Aires: 2 hrs by car from San Pedro Sula, 4WD recommended.

Parque Nacional Cusuco, 20 km west of San Pedro Sula, offers some excellent hikes, trails and birdwatching in cloudforest. Now managed by the Fundación Ecológica Héctor Rodrigo Pastor Fasquelle (HRPF), the park was exploited for lumber until the 1950s. It was declared a protected area in 1959 when the Venezuelan ecologist, Geraldo Budowski, reported the pine trees there were the highest in Central America. Cutting was stopped and the lumber company abandoned the site.

Parque Nacional Cusuco is a splendid location and well worth the effort. The area includes tropical rainforest and cloudforest with all the associated flora and fauna. It includes **Cerro Jilinco**, 2242 m, and **Cerro San Ildefonso**, 2228 m. There are four trails, ranging from 30 minutes to two days. They use old logging roads traversing forested ridges with good views. HRPF produces a bird checklist that includes the quetzal.

Listings San Pedro Sula and around *map p73*

Where to stay

$$$$ Real Intercontinental San Pedro Sula
Blv del Sur at Centro Comercial Multiplaza, T2545-2500, www.ichotelsgroup.com.

A long-established favourite among business travellers. Reliable, secure and predictably comfortable. One of the best.

$$$ Casa del Arbol Galerias
Intersection of 7ma Calle, Colonia Jardines del Valle y 1ra Av de

la Colonia Villas del Sol, near the Galerias mall, T2566-4201, www.hotelcasadelarbol.com.
This environmentally aware hotel has solar panels and a tree growing through it. Clean, modern, minimalist rooms with crisp white sheets and all the usual comforts including cable TV, a/c and Wi-Fi. They have a second facility downtown. Continental breakfast included.

$$$ Casa El Mesón B&B
Bloque 10 Casa #8, Colonia Tara, T2551-3303, www.casaelmeson.com.

Super-friendly and hospitable, this cosy B&B is managed by Jimmy and Sandra Pinell, who have 20 years of experience working in hospitality as tour guides and restauranteurs. Homely accommodation with attentive service in tranquil surroundings.

$$$ Ejecutivo
2 Calle 10 Av SO, T2552-4289, www.hotel-ejecutivo.com.
A solid if uninspired business class option. They offer simple, reasonable, generic rooms with a/c, cable TV, hot

San Pedro Sula

Where to stay 🛏
Casa del Arbol Galerias **1**
Casa El Mesón B&B **2**
Dos Molinos B&B **3**
Ejecutivo **4**
Guaras Hostal **5**
Isabella Boutique **6**
La Madrugada Hostel **7**
La Posada B&B **8**
Real Intercontinental
San Pedro Sula **9**

Restaurants 🍴
Baranda **1**
Comidas Casas Viejas **2**
Entre Pisco y Nazca **3**
Garden Bistro **4**
Orange Deli and Burgers **5**
Pamplona **6**
Pat's Steakhouse **7**
Trattoria Bel Paese **8**

Bars & clubs 🍸
La Musa Gastropub **9**

water and Wi-Fi. Also have their own generator in case of grid problems.

$$$ Isabella Boutique Hotel
8 Calle NO, T2550-9191, www. hotelisabellaboutique.directotels.com.
Decked in swish contemporary decor, the Isabella Boutique is one of San Pedro Sula's more stylish options. They have 12 attractive rooms with cable TVs, coffee-makers, a/c and fridges. Facilities include a pool, business centre, airport pick-up and lounge-bar.

$$ La Posada B&B
Colonia Universidad, 21 Calle "A" 9 y 11 Av, Casa #172, T2566-3312, www.laposadahn.com.
Located within walking distance of the Galerias mall, the Posada B&B has simple, clean, comfortable rooms kitted with Wi-Fi, a/c and hot water. There is a small pool in the garden and some hammocks for chilling out. They also offer free bus station pickup and drop off (one trip per booking). Breakfast and local calls included. Good, quiet, reliable place.

$$-$ Dos Molinos B&B
Barrio Paz Barahona, 13 Calle 8 y 9 Av #34, T2550-5926, www.dosmolinos.hostel.com.
Dos Molinos is a favourite with Peace Corps volunteers whenever they're in town. A simple, safe, economical place with no-frills rooms and friendly, helpful service. They can pick you up from the bus terminal and provide information.

$$-$ La Madrugada Hostel
8 Calle 8 y 9 Av NO, T2540-1309, www.lamadrugadahostel.com.
A pleasant new place, clean and tidy, with a youthful vibe that will appeal to backpackers. Dorms are on the pricey side, but worth it for the good looks and comfort. Rooms have 42 inch TVs. The

adjoining bar-restaurant is a good place for a cool beer. Creatively rendered, with lots of potential.

$$-$ The Guaras Hostal
Colonia Andalucia, 13 Calle and 13 Av NE #6, T9650-4431, www.theguarashostal.com.
A very clean and secure hostel located in a gated community. Dorms ($) are cosy and well-kept. Rooms have a/c, cable TV and Wi-Fi, with ($$) or without private bath ($). Relaxed, homely place, family-run and hospitable. Bus terminal pick-up/drop-off included.

Restaurants

There are international restaurants in all the top hotels.

$$$ Baranda
20 Av, entre 1-2 calle NO, Colonia Moderna.
Drawing influence from Southeast Asia, Japan, India, France and Italy, Baranda serves intriguing international fusion cuisine, expertly prepared by Chef Ana Maria Selgado Pellman. Spicy Thai curries are among the recommended offerings.

$$$ Pamplona
On plaza, opposite Gran Hotel Sula.
Pleasant decor, good food, strong coffee and excellent service. Spanish-owned, as the name might suggest.

$$$ Pat's Steak house
5 Calle SO, Barrio Rio de Piedras, 1½ blocks uphill from Circunvalación Blvd.
Along with tempting Caribbean seafood, Pat's steakhouse serves the best beef cuts in town and has a good wine list too. One of the oldest restaurants in San Pedro Sula and still great. Consistent and reliable, an old favourite. Recommended.

$$$ Trattoria Bel Paese
5 Calle A, entre 13-14 Av, Barrio Los Andes.
Fettuccini with mushrooms and seafood ravioli are among the home-cooked treats cooked up Piero and his wife at this authentic Italian trattoria, claimed by many to be the best in town. A great place for friends and family. Don't miss the desserts!

$$$-$$ Garden Bistro
10 Calle 17 Av, next to the Hilton Princess Hotel.
Cosy and stylish, this smart little place has distinctly European airs, unsurprisingly given the English ownership. Their menu features an eclectic range of international favourites, British fish and chips, American turkey sandwiches, Spanish tapas, Italian pasta and Indian tikka masala included. Good reports.

$$$-$$ Orange Deli and Burgers
5 Calle, entre 18-19 Av, Barrio Rio de Piedras.
Delicious gourmet burgers cooked to taste; try the 'True Blue', which comes with blue cheese, or the 'Fidel Burger' with pulled pork. A friendly, fun, cosy place that serves good mojitos too.

$$ Entre Pisco y Nazca
3 Calle y 19 Avenida NO, Colonia Moderna, www.entrepiscoynazca.com.
Gourmet Peruvian good, including traditional ceviches and contemporary interpretations of old classics; order a selection and share. Don't miss the pisco sour.

$$-$ Comidas Casas Viejas
10 Calle, 10 Av, Barrio Los Andes, T2516-1472. Daily 0600-2200.
Hearty *comida típica* served indoors or outside on the terrace. Offerings include chicken soup, leg of pork and grilled meat, all served with tasty handmade tortillas. Authentic, casual and affordable.

Bars and clubs

A thriving nightlife exists beyond the casinos.

La Musa Gastropub
5 Calle, entre 17-18 Av, Barrio Río de Piedras.
A very hip and handsome place that serves tempting tapas and delicious cocktails, including mouth-watering margaritas, mojitos, piña coladas, lemon frappe daikiris and sangrias. Good for a meal, a drink, or both.

Entertainment

Cinemas
There are 8 cinemas, all showing Hollywood movies; look in local press for details.

Theatre
Centro Cultural Sampedrano. Stages productions.
Proyecto Teatral Futuro, is a semi-professional company presenting contemporary theatre of Latin American countries and translations of European playwrights, as well as ballet, children's theatre, and workshops. Offices and studio-theatre at 4 Calle 3-4 Av NO, Edif INMOSA, 3rd floor, T2552-3074.

Festivals

End Jun **Feria Juniana**, the city's main festival.

Shopping

Handicrafts

Large artisan market, **Mercado Guamilito Artesanía** (*6 Calle 7-8 Av NO, daily 0800-1700*), typical Honduran handicrafts, cigars and 'gifiti' – local moonshine, at good prices (bargain), with a few imported goods from Guatemala and Ecuador; also good for fruit and vegetables, and *baleada comedores*. **Danilo's Pura Piel** (*factory and shop 18 Av B/9 Calle SO*). **Honduras Souvenirs** (*Calle Peatonal No 7*), mahogany woodcraft. The **IMAPRO Handicraft School** in El Progreso has a retail outlet at 1 Calle 4-5 Av SE, well worth visiting, fixed prices, good value, good mahogany carvings. The **Museum Gift Shop**, at the Museo de Antropología e Historia has lots of cheap *artesanía* gifts open during museum visiting hours.

What to do

Tour operators
Maya Temple, *www.mayatempletours.com*. Also offers travel services.

Transport

Air San Pedro Sula is a more important international gateway than Tegucigalpa. Its airport, **Ramón Villeda Morales (SAP)** is 15 km from the city centre along a good 4-lane highway; for safety, use an authorised yellow airport taxi to get into town, US$20. Taxis to the airport costs US$12, but bargain hard. There are free airport shuttle from the big hotels. Buses and *colectivos* do not go to the airport terminal itself; you have to walk the final 1 km from the La Lima road. At the airport is a duty free shop, Global One phones, banks and a restaurant on the 2nd floor. Flights to **Tegucigalpa** (35 mins), **La Ceiba**, **Utila** and to **Roatán**. See page 153 for international flights.

Bus **Local** Local buses cost US$0.10, smaller minibuses cost US$0.20.

Long distance The Gran Central Metropolitana is clean, safe and a short US$3 taxi from the centre of San Pedro Sula. **Heading south**, buses pass **Lago Yojoa** for **Tegucigalpa**, very regular service provided by several companies, 4½ hrs, 250 km by paved road. Main bus services with comfortable coaches in the town centre are **Hedman Alas**, T2516-2273, 0830, 1330 and 1730, US$18; **Transportes Sáenz**, T2553-4969, US$7; **El Rey**, T2553-4264, or **Express**, T2557-8355; **Transportes Norteños**, T2552-2145, last bus at 1900; **Viana**, T2556-9261.

Heading west from San Pedro the road leads to **Puerto Cortés**, a pleasant 45-min journey down the lush river valley. With **Empresa Impala**, T2553-3111, from 0430 until 2200, US$1, or **Citul**, and also on to **Omoa** from 0600.

Heading east buses go to **La Lima**, **El Progreso**, **Tela** and **La Ceiba** (Tupsa and **Catisa**, very regular to El Progreso, hourly to La Ceiba from 0600 and 1800, 3 hrs, US$3), some with a change in El Progreso, others direct. Also 1st class to La Ceiba with **Viana** at 1030 and 1730, and with **Hedman Alas** at0600, 1030,1520 and1820. US$16 To **Trujillo**, 3 per day, 6 hrs, US$5, comfortable.

Heading southwest buses go to **Santa Rosa de Copán** through the Department of Ocotepeque, with superb mountain scenery, to the **Guatemalan border**. Congolón, and **Empresa Toritos y Copanecos**, serve **Nueva Ocotepeque** (US$8) and **Agua Caliente** on the Guatemalan border with 7 buses a day; **Congolón**, T2553-1174. For more information on Guatemala–Honduras border crossings, see box, page 156.

To **Santa Rosa de Copán**, with connections at La Entrada for **Copán Ruinas**, with **Empresa Toritos y Copanecos**, T2563-4930, leaving every 20 mins, 0345-1715, 3 hrs, US$3.70. Take a bus to the junction of La Entrada and change for connection to Copán Ruinas if you're not going direct. 1st-class bus to **Copán Ruinas** with **Hedman Alas**, T2516-2273, daily at 1030 and 1500, 3 hrs, US$16 with a/c, movie and bathrooms. Also direct service with **Casasola-Cheny Express** at 0800, 1300 and 1400.

International Services available from **Ticabus** covering the whole of Central America from Mexico to Panama.

Car Car rentals Avis, 1 Calle, 6 Av NE, T2553-0888; **Blitz**, Hotel Sula and airport (T2552-2405 or 668-3171); **Budget**, 1 Calle 7 Av NO, T2552-2295, airport T2668-3179; **Maya Eco Tours**, 3 Av NO, 7-8 Calle, and airport (T2552-2670 or 2668-3168); **Molinari**, Hotel Sula and airport (T2553-2639 or 2668-6178); **Toyota**, 3 Av 5 y 6 Calle NO, T2557-2666 or airport T2668-3174.

Car repairs Invanal, 13 Calle, 5 y 6 Av NE, T2552-7083. Excellent service from Víctor Mora.

Parque Nacional Cusuco

Bus San Pedro Sula–Cofradía, 1 hr, US$0.15, from 5 Av, 11 Calle SO (buses drop you at turn-off 1 km from town); pickup Cofradía-Buenos Aires 1½ hrs, US$1.75, best on Mon at 1400 (wait at small shop on outskirts of town on Buenos Aires road); the park is 12 km from Buenos Aires.

Tegucigalpa
to the Pacific

From the capital to the Golfo de Fonseca the route twists through mountain valleys down to the volcanic islands and Honduras' Pacific ports of San Lorenzo and Amapala. Near the coast the Pan-American Highway leads west to El Salvador and east though the hot plains of Choluteca to the quiet but popular beaches of Cedeña and Ratón and ultimately to Nicaragua. An alternative route to Nicaragua heads east, through the agricultural town of Danlí, to the border at Las Manos. Short detours from the highway lead to picturesque colonial villages and old mining centres in the hills.

The road to the Pacific
steamy Pacific ports and lesser-visited beaches

Tegucigalpa to Goascarán

From the capital a paved road runs south through fine scenery. Beyond Sabanagrande (see page 33) is **Pespire**, a picturesque colonial village with the beautiful church of San Francisco, which has triple domes. Pespire produces small, delicious mangoes. At **Jícaro Galán** (92 km) the road joins the Pan-American Highway, which heads west through **Nacaome**, where there is a colonial church, to the border with El Salvador at **Goascarán**; see also box, page 157. At Jícaro Galán, Ticabus and other international buses from San Salvador, Tegucigalpa and Managua meet and exchange passengers.

San Lorenzo

The Pan-American Highway continues south from Jícaro Galán, to the Pacific coast (46 km) at San Lorenzo, a dirty town on the shores of the Gulf of Fonseca. The climate on the Pacific litoral is very hot.

Amapala

A 31-km road leaves the Pan-American Highway 2 km west of San Lorenzo, signed to Coyolito. It passes through scrub and mangrove swamps before crossing a causeway to a hilly island, around which it winds to the jetty at **Coyolito** (no *hospedajes* but a *comedor* and *refrescarías*).

The Pacific port of Amapala, on Isla del Tigre, has been replaced by Puerto de Henecán in San Lorenzo, and is reached by a road which leaves the Pan-American Highway at the eastern edge of San Lorenzo. The **Isla del Tigre** is yet another place reputed to be the site of hidden pirate treasure. In the 16th century it was visited by a number of pirates, including Sir Francis Drake. Amapala was capital of Honduras for a brief period in 1876 when Marco Aurelio Soto was president. Today, in addition to a naval base, Amapala is a charming, decaying backwater. The 783-m extinct Amapala volcano has a road to the summit where there is a US army unit and a DEA contingent. You can walk round the island in half a day. There is a ferry service from Coyolito, but fishermen will take you to San Lorenzo for a small fee, not by motor launch, and the trip takes half a day. The deep-sea fishing in the gulf is good; it's possible to charter boats to La Unión in El Salvador.

Listings Tegucigalpa to the Pacific

Where to stay

Tegucigalpa to Goascarán
There are very basic hotels with restaurants at the border in Goascarán.

$$ Oasis Colonial
Jícaro Galán, T2881-2220.
Nice rooms, good restaurant and pool and an unnamed basic guesthouse.

San Lorenzo

$$ Miramar
Barrio Plaza Marina, T2781-2039.
Has 26 rooms, 4 with a/c, good restaurant, overpriced. As it's located in a rough dockside area it's best not to walk there.

$ Perla del Pacífico
On main street, T2781-3025.
In a central location, this friendly, charming place offers comfortable rooms with a fan and bath. Recommended.

Amapala
Ask for **Doña Marianita**, who rents the 1st floor of her house.

$$ Hotel Villas Playa Negra
Aldea Playa Negra, T2898-8534.
In an isolated lovely setting, this hotel has 7 rooms with a/c and 7 with fan, as well as a pool, beach and a restaurant.

$ Al Mar
Above Playa Grande.
With a lovely view of the mountains and sunset, Al Mar offers rooms with fans.

Restaurants

San Lorenzo

$$ Restaurant-Bar Henecán
Parque Central.
A/c, good food and service, not cheap but worth it.

Amapala

$ Mercado Municipal
Several clean *comedores*.

$ Restaurant-Bar Miramar
By the harbour.
Overlooking the sea, this is a pleasant
restaurant with very friendly staff,
good meals, including hamburgers
and *boquitas*, and you can hang your
hammock.

Transport

San Lorenzo
Bus Frequent *busitos* from **Tegucigalpa**
to San Lorenzo (US$1) and **Choluteca**
(US$1.50).

Amapala
Boat Motorized *lanchas* run between
Coyolito and Amapala, US$0.35 per
person when launch is full (about 10
passengers), about US$4 to hire a launch
(but you will probably have to pay for
the return trip as well). 1st boat leaves
Amapala at 0700 to connect with 1st
Coyolito–San Lorenzo bus at 0800; next
bus from Coyolito at 0900.

Choluteca and around

a trade hub with a colonial core

Choluteca is expanding rapidly on the back of the local industries of coffee, cotton
and cattle which flourish despite the hot climate. Founded in 1535, the town was
one of the earliest settlements in Honduras, and still has a colonial centre.

The church of **La Merced** (1643) is being renovated and is due to be reconsecrated.
The **Casa de la Cultura** and **Biblioteca Municipal** are in the colonial house of José
Cecilio del Valle on the corner of the Parque Central. A fine steel suspension bridge
crosses the broad river at the entrance into Choluteca from the north (it was built
in 1937). The social centre of **San José Obrero** ① *3 Calle SO*, is where handicrafts, in
particular carved wood and chairs, can be bought. The **Mercado Municipal** ① *7
Av SO, 3 Calle SO*, is on outskirts of town.

   Cedeño beach, on the eastern side of the Gulf of Fonseca 40 km from Choluteca,
is a lovely though primitive spot, with clean sand stretching for miles and often
thundering surf. Avoid public holidays, weekend crowds and take a good insect
repellent. There are spectacular views and sunsets over the Gulf of Fonseca south
to Nicaragua and west to El Salvador, and of the volcanic islands in the bay. There's
an hourly bus from Choluteca (US$0.60, 1½ hours). A turn-off leads from the
Choluteca–Cedeño road to Ratón beach, which is more pleasant than Cedeño.
There's a bus from Choluteca at 1130, returning next morning.

Listings Choluteca and around

Where to stay

$$ Camino Real
Road to Guasaule, T2882-0610.

Long-established place with a pool,
and good steaks in restaurant.
Recommended.

$$ La Fuente
Cra Panamericana, past bridge,
T2782-0253.
Reasonable highway pitstop with bath, swimming pool, Wi-Fi in the rooms, a/c and meals.

$ Hibueras
Av Bojórquez, Barrio El Centro,
T2882-0512.
With bath and fan, clean, purified water, *comedor* attached, good value.

$ Pacífico
Near Mi Esperanza terminal, outside the city.
Quiet place with clean, cool rooms, with fan and cable TV. Hammocks, safe parking, fresh drinking water, and breakfast US$1.50.

$ Pierre
Av Valle y Calle Williams, T2882-0676.
Central place offering rooms with bath (ants in the taps), a/c or fan and TV. There's free protected parking and the *cafetería* serves good breakfasts. Credit cards accepted. Recommended.

$ Santa Rosa
3 Calle NO, in the centre, just west of market, T2882-0355.
Some rooms with bath, pleasant patio, laundry facilities, clean, friendly. Recommended.

Restaurants

$$ Alondra
Parque Central. Open Fri-Sun only.
Old colonial house.

$ Comedor Central
Parque Central.
Comida corriente daily specials, *licuados*, sandwiches, good for breakfast. Local specialities are the drinks *posole* and *horchata de morro*.

$ El Burrito
Blv Choluteca between 4 and 5 Av N.
With good-value meals and fast service.

$ El Conquistador
On Pan-American, opposite **La Fuente**.
Steaks etc, outdoor seating but you have to eat inside, good but slow service. Will change money for customers. Recommended.

Festivals

8 Dec The feast day of the **Virgen de la Concepción**, a week of festivities, followed by the **Festival del Sur**, 'Ferisur'.

Transport

Bus To **El Espino** (Nicaraguan border) from Choluteca, US$1.15, 1 hr, 1st at 0700, last at 1400; see also box, page 158. Also frequent minibuses to **El Amatillo** (El Salvador border) via San Lorenzo, US$1, from bus stop at bridge; see also box, page 157. Buses to Choluteca from Tegucigalpa with **Mi Esperanza**, **Bonanza** and **El Dandy**; **Bonanza** continues to San Marcos and departs Tegucigalpa hourly from 0530, 4 hrs to Choluteca, US$1.90. The municipal bus terminal is about 10 blocks from the municipal market, about 8 blocks from cathedral/Parque Central; **Mi Esperanza** has its own terminal 1 block from municipal terminal.

former mining towns and tobacco plantations

A good paved road runs east from Tegucigalpa through the hills to Danlí, 92 km away in the Department of El Paraíso. There are no signs when leaving Tegucigalpa, so ask for directions. Some 40 km along, in the Zambrano Valley (see page 37), is the Escuela Agrícola Panamericana, which is run for all students of the Americas with US help: it has a fine collection of tropical flowers (book visits in advance at the office in Tegucigalpa).

Yuscarán

At Km 47.5, a paved road branches south to Yuscarán (altitude 1070 m), set in rolling pineland country preserved by the **Reserva Biológica de Yuscarán**, which protects much of the land around Montserrat mountain. The climate here is semi-tropical. Yuscarán was an important mining centre in colonial days and is a picturesque village, with cobbled streets and houses on a steep hillside. Ask to see the museum near the town plaza; you have to ask around to find the person who has the key, antiques and photographs are displayed in a restored mansion which belonged to a mining family. There is a **Casa de Cultura** ① *in the former Casa Fortín, open Mon-Sat*. The Yuscarán **distilleries** ① *one in the centre, the other on the outskirts, tours possible*, are considered by many to produce the best *aguardiente* in Honduras. The Montserrat mountain that looms over Yuscarán is riddled with mines. The old **Guavias mine** is close to Yuscarán, some 4 km along the road to Agua Fría. About 10 km further along, a narrow, winding road climbs steeply through pine woods to the summit of **Pico Montserrat** (1891 m).

Danlí

Danlí (altitude 760 m), 102 km from Tegucigalpa, is noted for sugar and coffee production, a large meat-packing company (Orinsa), and is a centre of the tobacco industry. There are four cigar factories. The **Honduras-América SA factory** ① *right-hand side of Cine Aladino, Mon-Fri 0800-1200 and 1300-1700, Sat 0800-1200*, produces export-quality cigars at good prices. At **Placencia Tabacos**, on the road to Tegucigalpa, you can watch cigar-making. Prices are better than at Santa Rosa. From Danlí to the north are **Cerro San Cristóbal** and the beautiful **Lago San Julián**.

El Paraíso

A paved road goes south 18 km to El Paraíso, and beyond to the Nicaraguan border at Las Manos/Ocotal; see box, page 158. El Paraíso is a pretty town in an area producing coffee, bananas and rice.

Where to stay

Yuscarán

$ Hotel
T2892-7213.
Owned by Dutch man Freek de Haan
and his Honduran wife and daughter,
private or dormitory rooms, with
beautiful views of Nicaraguan mountains
in the distance.

$ Hotel Carol
Set in an annex to the owner's fine
colonial house, this small, safe hotel
with a family atmosphere has 6 modern,
good-value rooms with bath and
hot water.

Danlí

$$-$ Gran Hotel Granada
T2883-2499.
Bar, cable TV, accepts Visa. Restaurant
and swimming pool, locals pay
half price.

$ La Esperanza
*Gabriela Mistral, next to Esso station,
T2883-2106.*
Friendly place offering rooms with bath,
hot water, fan (more expensive with a/c),
TV and drinking water. Parking.

El Paraíso

$ 5a Av Hotel y Restaurant
5 Av y 10 Calle, T2893-4298.
Rooms with bath and hot water. The
restaurant specializes in Mexican-
American food. Parking.

Restaurants

Yuscarán

$ Cafetería Colonial
Opposite **Banco de Occidente.**
Serves excellent *desayuno típico* and
comida corriente.

Danlí

$ Comedor Claudio.
Serves tasty *comida corriente* and you
can pick up some good information
from the locals.

Festivals

Danlí
3rd week Aug **Fiesta del Maíz** lasts
all week, with cultural and sporting
events, all-night street party on the Sat;
it gets very crowded with people from
Tegucigalpa.

Transport

Yuscarán
Bus Frequent buses to **Zamorano** and
Tegucigalpa; from the capital buses
leave from Mercado Jacaleapa. For
information, ask anyone in the Parque
Central in Yuscarán.

Danlí
Bus From **Tegucigalpa**, US$2, from Blv
Miraflores near Mercado Jacaleapa (from
left-hand side of market as you face it),
Col Kennedy, Tegucigalpa, hourly, 2 hrs,
arrive 1½ hrs before you want to leave,
long queues for tickets (take 'Kennedy'
bus from C La Isla near the football
stadium in central Tegucigalpa, or taxi,

US$1.20, to Mercado Jacaleapa). **Express** bus from Col Kennedy, 0830, 1230 and 1700, US$2. One road goes east from Danlí to **Santa María** (several buses daily), over a mountain range with great views.

El Paraíso

Bus Minibuses from **Danlí** terminal to El Paraíso, frequent (0600 to 1740), US$0.40, 30 mins, don't believe taxi drivers who say there are no minibuses. **Emtra Oriente**, Av 6, Calle 6-7, runs 4 times a day from **Tegucigalpa** to El Paraíso, 2½ hrs, US$1.50. Buses from El Paraíso to **Las Manos**, about every 1½ hrs, US$0.35, 30 mins, or taxi US$4, 15 mins.

Bay Islands

A string of beautiful islands of white sandy beaches, coconut palms and gentle sea breezes, off the northern coast of Honduras, the Bay Islands (Islas de la Bahía) are the country's most popular tourist attraction.

The rich and extensive underwater environment is one of the main attractions; reefs surround the islands, often within swimming distance of the shore. The warm, clear Caribbean waters provide excellent diving, which is some of the cheapest in the Caribbean. Equally enjoyable are the magnificent beaches, tropical sunsets and the relaxed atmosphere which positively encourages you to take to your hammock, lie back and relax.

The culture is far less Latino than on the mainland. English is spoken by many and there are still Black Carib – Garífuna – descendants of those deported from St Vincent in 1797.

The islands

offshore hideaways and world-class diving

★Located some 32 km north of La Ceiba, the three main islands are Utila, Guanaja and, the largest and most developed, Roatán. At the eastern end of Roatán are three smaller islands: Morat, Santa Elena, and Barbareta, with many islets and cayes to explore.

Underwater, caves and caverns are a common feature, with a wide variety of sponges and the best collection of pillar coral in the Caribbean. There are many protected areas including the marine parks of Turtle Harbour on Utila, and Sandy Bay/West End on Roatán, which has permanent mooring buoys at the popular dive sites to avoid damage from anchors. Several other areas have been proposed as marine reserves by the Asociación Hondureña de Ecología: the Santuario Marino de Utila, Parque Nacional Marino Barbareta and Parque Nacional Marino Guanaja. The Bay Islands have their own conservation association (see under Roatán, page 96).

Basic etiquette for snorkelling and diving applies. Snorkellers and divers should not stand on or even touch the coral reefs; any contact, even the turbulence from a fin, will kill the delicate organisms.

The traditional industry is fishing, mostly shellfish, with fleets based at French Harbour; but the supporting boat-building is a dying industry. Tourism is now a major source of income, particularly because of the scuba-diving attractions.

English-speaking blacks constitute the majority of the population, particularly on Roatán. Utila has a population that is about half black and half white, the latter of British descent mainly from the settlers from Grand Cayman who arrived in 1830. Columbus anchored here in 1502, during his fourth voyage. In the 18th century the islands were the base for English, French and Dutch buccaneers. They were in British hands for over a century, but were finally ceded to Honduras in 1859. Latin Hondurans have been moving to the islands from the mainland in recent years

> **Tip...**
> Beware of the strong sun (the locals bathe in T-shirts), sandflies and other insects.

Utila

the cheapest and least developed of the islands

With a a laid-back ambience, Utila (area 41 sq km) is only 32 km from La Ceiba and is low lying, with just two hills, Pumpkin and the smaller Stewarts, either side of the town known as East Harbour.

The first inhabitants were the Paya and there is scant archaeological evidence of their culture. Later the island was used by pirates; Henry Morgan is reputed to have hidden booty in the caves. The population now is descended from Black Caribs and white Cayman Islanders with a recent influx from mainland Honduras.

Utila

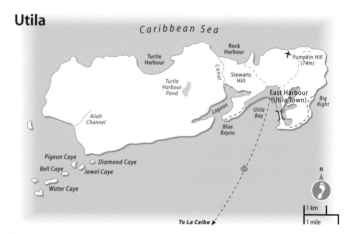

Utila's dive sites

There are currently around 50 dive sites around Utila, where permanent moorings have been established to minimize damage to the coral reef. Although the reef is colourful and varied, there are not a lot of fish, and lobster have almost disappeared. The dive sites are close to shore at about 20 m depth but they are all boat dives. Diving off the north coast is more spectacular, with drop-offs, canyons and caves. Fish are more numerous, helped by the establishment of the Turtle Harbour Marine Reserve and Wildlife Refuge.

Independence Day (15 September) festivities, including boxing and climbing greased poles, are worth staying for.

Around Utila

There are no big resorts on the island, although a couple of small, lodge-style, upmarket places have opened; otherwise the accommodation is rather basic. Sunbathing and swimming is not particularly good; people come for the diving. **Jack Neal Beach** has white sand with good snorkelling and swimming. **Chepee's White Hole** at the end of Blue Bayou peninsula has a beach for swimming. Snorkelling is also good offshore by the Blue Bayou restaurant, a 20-minute walk from town, but you will be charged US$1 for use of the facilities. There are hammocks and a jetty, which is great for fishing at sunset, and the only place to get away from the terrible sandflies. **Bandu Beach** is another option on the northern end of the island. Sun chairs, drinks and clean toilets are provided. Buy a drink or pay a US$2 charge. There is also sandfly relief at **Big Bight**, **Redcliff** and **Rocky Point**.

You can hike to **Pumpkin Hill** (about 4 km down the lane by HSBC, bikes recommended) where there are some freshwater caves with a beach nearby (watch out for sharp coral). It is also possible to walk on a trail from the airfield to Big Bight and the iron shore on the east coast, about 2 km, exploring tidal pools; there a good views and a great beach but it is rocky so wear sandals.

You can visit the **Iguana Station** ⓘ *Mon-Fri 0900-1200 and 1330-1700, T2425-3946, www.utila-iguana.de, US$3*, a short walk up hill from the fire station; follow the signs. Paying volunteer options are possible. They also offer great trips through the mangroves to explore the more hidden parts of the island for around US$12 per person, with a two-person minimum.

Utila's cayes

A 20-minute motorboat ride from East Harbour are the cayes, a chain of small islands populated by fisherfolk off the southwest coast of Utila, which are known as the Cayitos de Utila. **Jewel Caye** and **Pigeon Caye** are connected by a bridge and are inhabited by a fishing community, which reportedly settled there to get away from the sandflies on Utila. Basic accommodation and food is available. **Diamond Caye** is privately owned and the snorkelling offshore here is excellent. **Water Caye** is a coconut island with 'white hole' sandy areas and with wonderful bathing in the afternoons. It is the only place where you can camp, sling a hammock or, in an emergency, sleep in or under the house of the caretaker; take food and fresh water, or rent the caretaker's canoe and get supplies from Jewel Caye.

Listings Utila *map p86*

Tourist information

See the island's official website, www. aboututila.com, for details of hotels, restaurants and diving.

Where to stay

$$$$ Utila Lodge
On Utila Bay, west of the main dock, T1-855-846-3483 (US), www.utilalodge.com.
Set on a large pier over the water, this wood-built diving lodge offers spacious, calming, comfortable rooms with cable TV, Wi-Fi, porch, sun-deck, hammock, and ocean views. Amenities include restaurant-bar and a hyperbaric chamber which serves the local community. Various scuba packages are available. The divers' mecca.

$$$$ Utopia Village
Southwest coast, resort will arrange transport, T512-333-1684 (US), www.utopiautila.com.
Utopia Village is, for those who can afford it, the swanky resort option, complete with infinity pool, gym, library lounge, massage room, dive shop, beach bar and *palapas*. Secluded on a hard-to-reach part of the island, it has an exclusive feel, but it is still relatively small, intimate and low-key. Rooms are modern and impeccably attired.

$$$$-$$$ Laguna Beach Resort
On the point opposite Blue Bayou, T2668-68452, www.utila.com.
A comfortable lodge, with bungalows each with their own jetty. The 8-day package includes meals and diving for US$970, non-diver US$840. Fishing is offered, and they can accommodate a maximum of 40.

$$$ Jade Seahorse
T2425-3270, www.jadeseahorse.com.
5 great cabins, artistic, unusual and very funky, restaurant, bar, fantastic artistic gardens. Recommended.

$$$-$$ Lazy Daze on the Bay
The Point, T2425-3170, www.myutilahotel.com.
This small hotel on the waterfront is set in a converted family compound. It has down-to-earth and well-equipped rooms complete with a/c, fan, cable TV, Wi-Fi, coffee-maker, toaster, microwave, fridge and hot water. Their apartments, however, are much larger and better value. There is also a boat house.

$$$-$$ Mango Inn
La Punta, T2425-3326, www.mango-inn.com.
Spotless rooms with bath, cheaper without, and fan. Helpful staff, and there's a pool and a roof terrace. Reduction for students with **Utila Dive Centre**. **Mango Café** and **La Dolce Vita Pizzeria** for brick-oven pizzas on the premises. Recommended.

$$$-$$ The Lighthouse
Eastern Harbour, T2425-3164, www.utilalighthouse.com.

Perched over the water, the Lighthouse is a Caribbean colonial-style 2-storey hotel with wraparound balconies and panoramic views of the water and harbour. Rooms are simple but comfortable and have their own hammocks and the sound of relaxing rhythms of the waves. Good central location and lots of recommendations.

$$$-$$ Trudy's
5 mins from airport, T2425-3103.
Rooms with a/c and hot water. Also **Trudy's Suites**, with colour TV, fridge and microwave. **Underwater Vision** dive shop on site. Recommended.

$$-$ Pirate's Bay Inn
On Utila Bay, T2425-3818, www.piratesbayinn.com.
This dynamic dive lodge caters to mid-range and budget travellers with 5 a/c private rooms and 3 shared dorms, all equipped with hot water and Wi-Fi. There's also a shared balcony overlooking the bay complete with hammocks. Best rates for divers with Captain Morgan's Dive Centre.

$ Cooper's Inn
Main Street, towards the Point, T2425-3184.
This helpful, hospitable, family-run guesthouse features unpretentious rooms with a/c, private bathroom and kitchenette. Cheap, clean, tidy and chilled.

$ Rubi's Inn
Main Street, towards the Point, T2425-3240.
Rubi's is a spotless and economical 2-storey guesthouse with tranquil, wood-built rooms equipped with fridges and hot water. There is a shared kitchen. Locally owned, central, convenient, and a good choice for budget travellers.

Utila's cayes
All hotels are small family-run affairs ($).

$ Hotel Kayla
www.utilacaysdiving.com.
Free accommodation at Jewell Cay with PADI courses. Jewell Cay and Pigeon Cay are linked by a bridge.
You can rent out **Little Cay** and **Sandy Cay** completely, details available from cayosutila@hotmail.com.

Restaurants

Menus are often ruled by the supply boat: on Tue and Fri restaurants have everything, by the weekend some drinks run out. For more recommendations, see www.utilaguide.com.

$$$ Jade Seahorse
Fri-Wed 1100-2200.
A variety of home-made seafood dishes and *licuados*, with the coolest decor in town. It includes the very popular **Treetanic** bar; see Bars and clubs, below.

$$$-$$ Mango Inn Bar and Grill
Rocky Hill Rd, near the crossroads and the Banco Atlantida, www. mangoinnbarandgrill.com.
Breakfast burritos, buttermilk pancakes, French toast and yogurt with granola are among the morning options; choose from burgers, burritos, beer-battered shrimp, sandwiches, salads and pizzas (recommended) for lunch or dinner. Lovely setting and atmosphere.

$$ Babalu Bar and Grill
Main St, Barrio La Punta.
Babalu is the oldest dock bar in Utila, hosts to popular open mic nights and live music on Monday. They serve mostly tapas and Italian, including almond and olive pesto on homemade focaccia,

baked pasta with sweet pepper sauce and *salame di cioccolato*.

$$ Driftwood Café
Texan barbecue-style place with good burgers and grilled seafood. Wood-built with a deck and an open-air setting above the water. Fun place, popular with expats and often buzzing.

$$ El Picante
Up towards Mango Inn.
Upscale Mexican restaurant in a good location. Good nachos and tasty margaritas. A fine view from the balcony.

$$ Foo King Wok
Main St, opposite Tranquila Bar. Mon, Wed and Fri 1800-2200.
The name may be tongue-in-cheek, but the changing menu of authentic Asian cuisine is definitely a winner. Offerings include flavourful delights such as steamed dumplings, Thai curries, Vietnamese spring rolls and Szechuan fare.

$$ Jungle Café
At the end of Iguana Station road, www.utilaguru.com.
The Jungle Café's changing set menu and daily specials usually include a variety of seafood, meat and vegetarian options, all prepared with love (some roasted dishes can up to 48 hrs to get ready!). Possibilities include paprika lamb goulash, Thai coconut calamari rings and filet mignon.

$$ La Piccola.
Upscale yet relaxed atmosphere offering lunch and dinner; one of the best places in town. Dishes include pasta, garlic bread, fish and pizza; great service.

$$-$ Che Pancho
Main St, under the cinema, 5 mins east of the centre.
Che Pancho is a casual little eatery with outdoor tables. They serve light meals, snacks and café fare, including Spanish omelette, sandwiches, crepes, fried eggs, catch of the day and French fries. Good drinks – try the mango *licuado*, papaya smoothie or iced coffee.

$ Big Mamas.
Lovely little place serving authentic home-cooked grub and café fare, including *comida típica*, shrimp burger, wraps. The prettiest restaurant on Utila. Friendly and relaxed.

$ RJ's BBQ and Grill House
Open Wed, Fri, Sun 1730-2200.
Great Caribbean-style barbecue dishes, including steaks and fresh seafood. Very popular, busy, buzzing, and fills up fast. Recommended.

$ Skidrow Bar and Restaurant
In front of Ecomarine Dive shop.
Great burritos, popular with expats. Mon night is pub quiz night.

Cafés

Rio Coco Café
Main St, between Utila Dive Center and Free Dive Utila, www.riococobeans.com.
Rich, tasty, sustainably sourced coffee from the headwaters of the Río Coco. Great cakes and sweet treats too. Fun place, Wi-Fi included.

Utila Tea Cup
Cola del Mico road, inside the museum.
Refreshing herbal infusions to wash down sweet and savoury treats, including quiche, apple French toast and pineapple coconut pie.

Utila's cayes
There are a few restaurants, a Sat night disco and little else.

Bars and clubs

Bar in the Bush
100 m beyond the Mango Inn, Wed 1800-2330, Fri (Ladies' Night) and Sun 1800-0300.
Bar in the Bush is the place to go, very popular, lots of dancing and always packed.

Coco Loco
On the jetty at the harbour front near Tranquila Bar.
Very popular with young divers, together these 2 places are the anchors and reigning kings of late-night Utila nightlife.

La Pirata Bar
At the dock.
High up, breezy, with great views.

Treetanic Bar
Inside Jade Seahorse; see Restaurants, above. Open 1700-2400.
High up in the trees; a hot spot on the island.

Entertainment

Cinema
Reef Cinema, *opposite Bay Islands Originals shop.* Shows films at 1930 every night, at US$3 per person. Popcorn, hotdogs, a/c, comfortable seats, big screen. Also inside the cinema is **Funkytown Books and Music**, an excellent bookshop to trade, sell and rent. Stock up here before you travel anywhere else. Also trades MP3s.
Utila Centre for Marine Ecology, *opposite Trudy's, www.utilaecology.org.* Offers free presentations on Tropical Marine Ecology, the 1st and 3rd Mon of each month, 1830-1930.

Festivals

Aug **Sun Jam** on Water Caye at a weekend at the beginning of Aug, www.sunjamutila.com. Look out for details locally. They charge a US$2.50 entrance fee to the island; bring your own tent/hammock, food and water.

Shopping

Arts and crafts
Bay Islands Original Shop. *Mon-Fri 0900-1200 and 1300-1800, Sat and Sun 0900-1200.* Sells T-shirts, sarongs, coffee, hats, etc.
Gunter Kordovsky. A painter and sculptor with a gallery at his house, with a good map of Utila, paintings, cards and wood carving.
Utila Lodge Gift Shop. Also worth trying.

What to do

The **Utila Snorkel Center**, for all those who do not want to dive, organizes trips. Inside Mango Tree Business building. See also box, page 92.

Dive operators
Altons Dive Center, *T2425-3704, www.diveinutila.com.* Offers NAUI and PADI certification, weekly fish talk, popular, owned by the mayor of Utila. Recommended,
Bay Islands College of Diving, *on main street close to Hondutel tower, T425-3291, www.dive-utila.com.* 5-star PADI facility, experienced and well qualified staff, good boats ranging from 50 ft, for large parties to skiff for smaller ones, environmentally sound. Only dive shop on the island with in-house pool and hot tub. The trauma centre and

Diving

Dive with care for yourself and the reef at all times; www.roatanet.com has plenty of information about Utila and its dive sites.

Utila is a very popular dive training centre. Learning to dive is cheaper here than anywhere else in the Caribbean, especially if you include the low living expenses. It is best to do a course of some sort; students come first in line for places on boats and recreational divers have to fit in. In recent years, Utila has developed a reputation for poor safety and there have been some accidents requiring emergency treatment in the recompression chamber on Roatán. Serious attempts have been made to change this by the diving community of Utila. The three or four accidents that happen annually are a result of cowboy divers and drug or alcohol abuse.

Instructors Choose an instructor who you get on with, and one who has small classes and cares about safety; follow the rules on alcohol/drug abuse and pay attention to the dive tables. There is a rapid turnover of instructors; many stay only a season to earn money to continue their travels, and some have a lax attitude towards diving regulations and diving tables. Check that equipment looks in good condition and well maintained. Boats vary; you may find it difficult to climb into a dory if there are waves. While a dive shop has a responsibility to set standards of safety, you also have a responsibility to know about diving times. If you don't, or are a beginner, ask.

Price There is broad price agreement across dive shops in Utila. Out of the revenues the **Utila Dive Supporters' Association** can budget for spending,

recompression chamber, shared by all dive shops, is located here. 5-star facility.
Captain Morgan's, *T2425-3349, www. divingutila.com*. Has been recommended for small classes, good equipment, friendly staff. The only dive shop that offers accommodation on nearby Pigeon Key. Popular with travelling couples.
Deep Blue Divers, *T2425-3211, www. deepblueutila.com*. One of the newer operators on the island. The friendly owners are getting good feedback through word of mouth.
Gunter's Ecomarine Dive Shop, *T2425-3350, http://ecomarinegunters. blogspot. co.uk*. Dive school with 4 divers per group maximum, 7 languages spoken. Most laid-back dive shop and the only

dive school that does not hassle divers arriving at the ferry dock.
Underwater Vision Dive Center, *Trudy's, T2425-3103, www. utilascubadiving.com*. With accommodation. Very nice location at the Bay.
Utila Dive Centre, *Mango Inn, PADI CDC, T2425-3326, www.utiladivecentre. com*. Well-maintained equipment, daily trips to north coast in fast dory, recommended. All boats covered and custom-built, surface interval on cayes.
Utila Watersports, *T2425-3264, run by Troy Bodden*. 4 students per class. Troy also hires out snorkelling gear, photographic and video equipment and takes boat trips. Good reports.

facilities and eventually conservation. Whatever you may think of the idea, one benefit, is greater safety and better organized protection of the reef. Whether this works remains to be seen, but the price of saving a few dollars could end up costing lives. Dive insurance at US$3 per day for fun divers, US$9 for students (Advanced, or Open Water), US$30 for divemasters is compulsory and is available from the BICA office. It covers air ambulance to Roatán and the recompression chamber. Treat any cuts from the coral seriously, they do not heal easily.

PADI courses A PADI Open Water course costs from around US$260 (including certificate) with 4 dives, an Advanced course costs US$260 with 5 dives, slightly less if you do the Open Water course with the dive shop first. You can work your way up through the courses with rescue diver (US$260) and dive master (US$800). The Open Water usually comes with two free fun dives. Credit cards, if accepted, are 6% extra. Not permitted by credit cards but as all companies on the island do it you can't go elsewhere. Competition is fierce with over 15 dive shops looking for business, so you can pick and choose. Once qualified, fun dives are US$50 for two tanks. Dive shops offer free basic accommodation with packages. Most schools offer instruction in English or German; French and Spanish are usually available somewhere, while tuition handbooks are provided in numerous languages including Japanese. A variety of courses is available up to instructor level. If planning to do a diving course, it is helpful but not essential to take passport-sized photographs with you for the PADI card. Many dive shops have affiliated hotels or hostels where they may offer discounts or all-inclusive packages if you decide to take a course.

Whale Shark & Oceanic Research Centre (WSORC), *T2425-3760, www. wsorc.com.* A professional scientific organization committed to education and preserving Utila's oceans, offers speciality courses including whale shark research, naturalist courses, research diver, fish ID, Coral ID. Free presentation 1930 Sun nights about whale sharks.

Transport

Air Utila receives flights from **Tegucigalpa**, **La Ceiba** and **Roatán**. Domestic airlines serving the Bay Islands include Aerocaribe, Aerolineas Sosa, CM Airlines, Isleña/Sansa Regional, Island Air and Lanhsa. International airlines include American Airlines, United, Delta, Sunwing and Taca (for more information, see page 104).

Boat Services to/from Utila with the Utila Princess, T2408-5163, www. utilaprincess.com, **La Ceiba–Utila** 0930 and 1600; **Utila–La Ceiba**, 0620 and 1400, US$25. Daily sailings Utila–**Roatán**, on Captain Vern's catamaran *Nina Elisabeth II*, T3346-2600 (mob), or ask at **Gunter's Dive Shop** on Utila and **Coconut Divers**, Half Moon Bay, Roatán. US$55 one way, no fixed schedule. Dock fee required when leaving Utila (US$1)

Cycling Bike hire about US$5 per day. Try **Delco Bike**.

Despite its size and development, Roatán (area 127 sq km) has managed to retain its idyllic charm and quiet beaches are often just a short walk away. There is a paved road running from West End through to French Harbour, almost to Oak Ridge, continuing unpaved to Punta Gorda and Wilkes Point, as well as other unmade roads.

Coxen Hole

The capital and administrative centre of the department, Coxen Hole, or **Roatán City**, is on the southwest shore. Planes land and boats dock here and you can get transport to other parts of the island. It is a colourfully scruffy little town with not much of tourist interest but some souvenir shops are opening.

Besides being the seat of the local government, it has immigration, customs and the law courts. There is a post office, supermarket, handicraft shops, restaurants, banks, travel agents, a bookshop and various other stores. Buses leave from outside the supermarket. All public transport starts or ends here. If taxis are shared, they are *colectivos* and charge the same as buses. A huge, swanky cruise-liner dock has opened outside the western end of town, with the Town Center shopping mall, offering pricey cafés, gift shops, duty-free stores, and – probably unique on the island – free and spotless public toilets.

Sandy Bay

A short journey from Coxen Hole, en route to West End, is Sandy Bay, one of the quieter towns on the island. The **Carambola Botanical Gardens** ⓘ *opposite Anthony's Key Resort, www.carambolagardens.com, daily 0800-1700, US$10, guided tours (US$5) or self-guided nature trails*, created in 1985, contain many flowering plants, ferns and varieties of trees which can be explored on a network of trails; it is well worth a visit. The **Roatán Museum** ⓘ *T2445-3003, US$4*, has displays

Roatán

covering the history of the island, with plenty of information about the pirates who called Roatán home, and a collection of artefacts.

West End

Five minutes by road beyond Sandy Bay, the popular community of West End, at the western tip of the island, is the most popular place to stay. It's a narrow beach on a palm-fringed bay with a distinctly laid-back atmosphere. The **Sandy Bay/West End Marine Park** protects marine life in the area and large numbers of fish have flourished along the coast creating spectacular snorkelling. There are numerous good foreign and local restaurants with lots of pizza/pasta places, as well as hotels, *cabañas* and rooms to rent for all budgets. It is a stiff walk from Coxen Hole over the hills (three hours) to West End, or take the bus on the paved road (US$1; 20 minutes). See www.roatanmarinepark.com for more details.

West Bay

A beautiful clean beach with excellent snorkelling on the reef, particularly at the west end, where the reef is only 10-20 m offshore and the water is shallow right up to where the wall drops off 50-75 m out and scuba-diving begins. Biting sandflies – *jejenes* – can be a pest here at dusk, but since the hotel staff started raking the beach every day, which exposes their eggs to the sun and kills them, they are no longer such a nuisance. Developers have discovered the delights of West Bay and the atmosphere is changing fast. Apartments, hotels, bars and restaurants are springing up, though mostly low-rise, and hidden behind the palm trees, so it's still pretty quiet here during the week.

East of Coxen Hole

French Harbour, on the south coast, with its shrimping and lobster fleet, is the main fishing port of Roatán. There is no beach and there are two seafood-packing plants. The road passes Coleman's (Midway) Bakery, where you can buy freshly baked products. The bay is protected by the reef and small cayes, which provide safe anchorage. Roatan Dive and Yacht Club and Romeos Marina (at Brick Bay) offer services for visiting yachts. Several charter yachts are based here. There are a few cheap, clean places to stay, as well as expensive hotels and dive resorts. Eldon's Supermarket is open daily and has a range of imported US food.

Across the island

The main road goes across the mountain ridge along the island with side roads to Jonesville, Punta Gorda and Oak Ridge. You can take a bus on this route to see the island's hilly interior, with beautiful views from coast to coast. Alternatively, hire a small 4WD, which is almost as cheap if shared between four people and allows you to explore the dirt roads and empty bays along the island's northern tip. **Jonesville** is known for its mangrove canal, which is best reached by hiring a taxi boat in Oak Ridge. **Oak Ridge**, situated on a caye (US$1 crossing in a dory from the bus stop), is built around a deep inlet on the south coast. It is a sleepy little fishing port, with rows of dwellings on stilts built on the water's edge (a bus from Coxen Hole to Oak

Ridge takes about one and a half hours, depending on passengers, US$1.70). Much of the town has been rebuilt after widespread destruction by Hurricane Mitch in 1998, but the new buildings have retained the same traditional stilt design and pastel colours. Boatmen offer tours around the bay and through mangroves to caves allegedly used by pirates; US$20 for 45 minutes, but it's worth bargaining.

Listings Roatán *map p94*

Tourist information

Local information maps are available from Librería Casi Todo, West End. The Voice Book is a useful online directory of island services and businesses, as well as local news and reviews; a monthly magazine edition is available in most hotels: www.bayislandsvoice.com.

Bay Islands Conservation Association (BICA)
Casa Brady, 1st floor, Sandy Bay, 200 m off road to Anthony's Key Resort, T2445-3117, www.bicaroatan.com.
Irma Brady, director of BICA, which manages the Sandy Bay/West End Marine National Park and Port Royal National Park in the eastern tip of island, has lots of information about the reef and its conservation work; volunteers are welcome.

Where to stay

Coxen Hole
There are a few basic options if stuck, but nothing great. Try:

$$ Cay View
Calle Principal, T2445-1202.
A/c, bath, TV, phone, laundry, restaurant, bar, dingy rooms, one with seaview, no breakfast, overpriced, but just about adequate if you're desperate.

Sandy Bay

$$$$-$$$ Anthony Key Resort
Off Sandy Bay on Anthony Key, T800-227-3483 (from USA), www.anthonyskey.com.
Secluded and intimate, the far-flung island hideaway of Anthony Key offers very comfortable bungalows with hard wood floors, elevated decking, hammocks, and spectacular ocean views. Various dive packages are available.

$$$ Hobbies Hideaway
T9929-4720,
www.hobbies-hideaway.com.
With a tranquil and secluded location, Hobbies Hideaway has clean, comfortable, ocean-view apartments with fully equipped kitchens, a/c, and orthopaedic beds. Lots of activities on offer from fishing to island tours. Helpful and hospitable hosts.

$$$ Tranquilesas EcoLodge and Dive Center
Cra Principal, T9958-4719, www.tranquilseas.com.
Set among lush landscaped tropical gardens, this PADI dive resort has a range of luxury wood-built *cabañas* some with ocean views. Also a restaurant overlooking the water and free use of kayaks. Packages available. Rustic chic.

$$$-$ Roatan Backpackers' Hostel
T9714-0413,
www.roatanbackpackers.com.

One of the island's better economical options, this low-key hostel offers simple dorms with wooden bunks, each with their own fan. Communal facilities include Wi-Fi, book exchange, kitchen, shaded porch and pool. *Casitas* and apartments are also available ($$$).

West End

$$$$ The Beach House
At the entrance to West End, T515-4266, www.thebeachhouseroatan.com.
Constructed in typical Caribbean colonial style, this wood-built hotel overlooks the waves with a breezy veranda and a bar on the upper deck. It offers a range of rooms, all very tastefully attired with classy modern furnishings, some with beachside views. Suites boast a full kitchen. Continental breakfast included.

$$$ Half Moon Bay Cabins
Half Moon Bay, T445-4242.
Bungalows and cabins with bath, and a restaurant with excellent seafood.

$$$ Mariposa Lodge
T8983-7259, www.mariposa-lodge.com.
An intimate little lodging nestled among gardens about 100 m from the beach. Accommodation includes rooms and apartments with a/c and use of an upper deck with hammocks. Dive and stay packages available. Good hosts and attentive service.

$$$ Splash Inn Dive Resort
T9626-7919, www.roatansplashinn.com.
Set in leafy grounds by the beach, Splash Inn Dive has simple, cool, whitewashed rooms with a/c, cable TV and Wi-Fi. Amenities include a dive shop and international restaurant. The generator ensures there are no power outages. Personable service and lots of good reports.

$$$ The Lily Pond House Hotel
T3265-0220, www.lilypondroatan.com.
The Lily Pond claims to be the most luxurious boutique accommodation in Roatan's West End. Set on 3 levels, its rooms are comfortable and stylish, with tasteful hardwood furniture and flooring, cable TV, private entrances, a/c and 4-poster beds. Their restaurant serves good seafood in a garden setting.

$$ Posada Arco Iris
Half Moon Bay, T2445-4264, www.roatanposada.com.
Apartments with kitchen, hot water, fan and large balcony, with friendly owners. There's a restaurant specializing in grilled meats. Highly recommended.

$$ Roatan Bed and Breakfast apartments
T8990 3887, www.roatan-bed-and-breakfast.com.
Roatán Bed and Breakfast iss a lovely property in a secluded location on a hill a short distance from the tourist hub of West End. Its 3 rooms are tranquil, wood-built and environmentally friendly, and each has Wi-Fi, cable TV, fan and ocean views. There are also 2 self-catering apartments with full kitchen and garden access. Recommended.

$$ Sea Breeze
North of West End, T2445-4026, www.seabreezeroatan.com.
Nice rooms, hot water, baths, a/c optional, suites and studios available with kitchens. Windsurfers and kayaks for rent.

$$ Seagrape Plantation Resort
Half Moon Bay, T2445-4428, www.seagraperoatan.com.

In a good location on a rocky promontory, this resort offers cabins and rooms with private bath and hot water. There's a friendly, family atmosphere, no beach, but snorkelling possible, a full-service restaurant and bar. Fun dives for US$35 with equipment. Inclusive packages available; Visa accepted.

$$-$ Chillies
Half Moon Bay, T2445-4003, www. nativesonsroatan.com/chillies.htm.
Double rooms and dorm, clean, fully equipped kitchen, lounge, big balcony, camping and hammocks available. Excellent value for money.

$ Buena Onda
Next to the gas station, Cra Principal, T9770-0158, www.hbuenaonda.com.
Buena Onda is the dream project of a long-term traveller who understands what makes a good backpacker hostel tick. It is a youthful, sociable place with 3 dorms and a private room, weekly barbecue and cinema, roof terrace, kitchen, hot showers, DVD player and hammocks.

West Bay

$$$$ Island Pearl
On the beach, T2445-5005, www.roatanpearl.com.
Double-storey well-decorated apartments with hand-painted furniture, a/c, hot water and a tiled kitchen.

$$$$ Las Sirenas
Midway along the beach, T2445-5009, www.hmresorts.com.
Rooms, suites and enormous apartments, with a/c, cable TV and kitchen; small swimming pool. Full board and shared amenities with adjacent HM

resorts: Henry Morgan, Mayan Princess and Paradise Beach. Quiet, clean and well run. Recommended.

$$$$ Xbalanque Resort
Tamarind Dr, T9719-5282, www. xbalanque-roatan.com.
With impeccable contemporary design, Xbalanque is a stylish luxury resort overlooking the ocean. It offers beautiful suites and beachfront villas, a suave rooftop bar, infinity pool, lounge and gym. Set it in 3 ha of grounds, there are also many tranquil walking trails. Recommended, if you can afford it.

$$$ West Bay B&B
T2445-5080, www. westbaybedandbreakfast.com.
Managed by Glen from San Diego, the hospitable West Bay B&B offers a range of clean, comfortable, well-appointed rooms equipped with fridge, a/c, DVD player and satellite TV. General amenities include backup generator, internet café, DVD collection, laundry, snorkel gear, book exchange and home-cooked food. Discounts for stays of over 5 nights. Just 2 mins from the beach and good value for the area.

$$$-$$ Bananarama
Centre of West Bay beach, T2992-9679.
Good-value rooms with bath, hot water and fan. PADI dive courses available; breakfast included. Recommended.

$$$-$$ Las Rocas
Next to Bite on the Beach, T2445-1841, www.lasrocasresort.com.
Duplex *cabañas*, very close together, hot water, balcony, smaller cabins sleep 3, larger ones sleep 6. Free boat transport to West End and back, and there's a dive shop and a restaurant.

East of Coxen Hole

$$$$ Reef House Resort
Oak Ridge, T2435-1482,
www.reefhouseresort.com.
Meals and various packages, including
diving. Wooden cabins with sea-view
balconies, and a seaside bar a private
natural pool. Dock facilities, and good
snorkelling from the shore.

$$$$-$$$ Mango Creek
Port Royal, boat access, T8916-8704,
www.mangocreeklodge.com.
Spacious, calming, wood-built and fully
equipped with an open-air deck and
hammock where you can chill out to the
sounds of the ocean, accommodation
at Mango Creek consists of 6 wonderful
over-the-water *cabañas*. There are
cheaper, less exotic rooms in the main
lodge too. Packages are available.

$$$-$ Marble Hill Farms
Less than 1 km past Oak Ridge, T3335-
5409, www.marblehillfarms.com.
Marble Hill Farms offers a wide range
of accommodation including well-
furnished sea view rooms complete with
sofa, DVD, a/c and kitchenette; island-
style 'adventurer casitas' with private
bedrooms, kitchenettes and enclosed
decking; 'explorer treehouses', which
consist of yurt-style thatch roof cabins
on elevated decking; and backpacker
dorms ($).

Evening meals cost US$4-10. There is
a good seafood restaurant on Osgood
Caye a few mins by free water taxi from
the wharf.

Coxen Hole

$$ Le Bistro
10 mins' walk along seafront between
Coxen Hole and West Bay, T9527-3136.
Perched on a rocky outcrop on the
beach. Thai and Vietnamese cuisine,
with spicy seafood and curries. Beautiful
spot with deck overlooking the sea.
French owner François also takes
snorkelling trips.

$ Madah's Kitchen
Main St. Open for breakfast and lunch.
Founded by Deenie Edania Webster,
better known as Madah (Mother), this
authentic locals' joint serves wholesome
home-cooked Caribbean fare, including
fresh seafood and barbecue chicken.

$ Tacos al Pastor
Main St, west of the dock.
Cheap and easy eats close to the dock.
As the name suggests, fully authentic
Mexican fare. Friendly and casual.

Sandy Bay

$$$-$$ Blue Bahia Beach Grill
Inside the Blue Bahia Resort,
www.beachgrillroatan.com.
Dependable international fare in a
resort setting. Weekly specials include:
bottomless mimosas on Sun; all-you-
can-eat pasta on Mon; steak night on
Tue; barbecue on Wed; 2-for-1 on rum
on Thu; all-you-can-eat lionfish on Fri;
burgers on Sat. Great location by the
waves and views of the sunset.

$$$-$$ Blue Parrot
Sandy Bay Rd.
This low-key Jamaican eatery serves jerk pork and chicken. A fun and friendly place with typical Caribbean hospitality. Popular with the expats, a lively scene.

West End

$$$ Half Moon Bay Restaurant
Half Moon Bay.
Lovely location sitting on the terrace overlooking sea, with excellent food. But it's more expensive than most and service can be very slow.

$$$ Tong
Restaurant in a good location serving Asian and Middle East specialities, with a salad buffet. It's expensive but worth it.

$$$-$$ Roatan Oasis
Carretera Principal, at the entrance to the village, www.roatanoasis.com. Mon-Fri 1700-2300.
The popular Roatan Oasis cooks up a diverse range of international cuisine: American, Asian fusion, Mediterranean, Italian, Moroccan, Thai and vegetarian, to name a few. Past offerings include Jack Daniels chicken wings, Korean barbecue ribs, and duck and blue cheese salad. Live music and menu changes every Mon. Recommended.

$$ Café Escondido
West End Rd, www.cafeescondido.com.
A relaxed and sociable place, open-air and overlooking the water. They serve cooked breakfasts, café snacks and international fare, with a special emphasis on Chinese, including rice bowls and noodles. Beverages include ice coffees, smoothies, cocktails, local and imported beers. A popular watering hole.

$$ Cindy's Place
Next to Sunset Inn.
Local family breakfast, lunches and dinner in garden, serving fish caught the same morning, as well as also lobster and king crab. Recommended.

$$ Monkey Island Beach Café
West End Rd, near the entrance to West End.
This Tex Mex and seafood restaurant has found an innovative solution to the region's invasive lion fish problem – turn them into fish tacos! Other good grub includes pig roast and barbecued chicken in a beer can. A fun place with live music during the week.

$$ Por Que No
Between Eagle Ray and Fosters.
A friendly German-owned café serving good coffee and reasonable breakfasts. Evening menu includes 'Wiener Art' schnitzel and Jagerschnitzel. For dessert, try the crepe in rum-orange sauce.

$$-$ C Level Café and Bar
Next to Reef Glider's Dive Center.
A casual little open-air bar-restaurant, friendly and popular with divers. They serve café fare, including cooked breakfasts and subs, but most people come for the evening pizza (Mon-Fri, slices only on Wed). A good place to sip beer. 'Build your own Bloody Mary' may suit those seeking hair of the dog.

$ Anthony's Chicken and more
West End Rd, in front of Beach House.
A low-key locals' joint. Their home-cooked fare includes roast chicken, fried fish, jerk chicken, chicken burrito and grilled pork. Tasty and great value. A good lunch spot.

$ Creole Rotisserie Chicken
West End Rd.
As the name might suggest, wholesome home-cooked rotisserie chicken served with rice and beans. If you get there for lunch, there's usually some cinnamon rolls on offer too. A classic locals' joint managed by Dola.

West Bay

$$$ Bite on the Beach
On the point over West Bay.
Excellent place offering Wed-Sun brunch, served on a huge deck in a gorgeous position; fresh food and great fruit punch. Nightly feeding of moray eels, which swim – or wriggle – up to the edge of the dock. A fun place, very friendly, and very much what Roatán is about. Recommended.

$$$ Nice 'N Spicy
Behind the mall in the side road to the beach.
A cosy little restaurant serving reliable Asian grub. Choose from noodles with beef, pork, chicken, shrimp or vegetables served with a variety of Chinese, Malaysian and Thai sauces, among others. Traditionalists may enjoy the Indian or Thai curry.

$$$ Vintage Pearl Restaurant and Wine Cellar
Cra Principal, www.roatanpearl.com.
Gourmet offerings at the Vintage Pearl include succulent steak and fresh seafood. There's also a selection of fine wine. Intimate and extravagant, the place for gourmands and lovers. Fixed price 3-course meals available.

$$$-$$ Beachers
West Bay Beach.
This open-air restaurant by the waves serves typical Caribbean seafood, including coconut shrimp and catch-of-the-day with your choice of French fries or rice. There's international fare too (when in stock) including BLTs and burgers. Good service and impeccable views. Occasional live music.

$$ Pizzarama
Inside Bananarama dive resort, www.bananarama.com.
The stone-baked pizzas at this fun beachside restaurant can't be faulted for their tasty toppings and Italian-style crusts. Go on a Mon night and get 2 for 1 on large ones.

East of Coxen Hole

There is a *taquería* close to HSBC on the main road in French Harbour serving good tacos, burritos and hamburgers.

$$$ Gios
French Harbour.
Top-quality seafood, with king crab a speciality.

$$$ Roatan Dive and Yacht Club
French Harbour.
Daily specials, pizza, salads, sandwiches, usually very good.

$$ BJ's Backyard Restaurant
Oak Ridge, at the harbour.
Island cooking, with fishburgers and smoked foods, all at reasonable prices. There is a pizzeria and, next door, a supermarket.

$$ Romeo's
French Harbour.
Romeo, who is Honduran-Italian, serves good seafood, and continental cuisine.

Entertainment

Most clubs come alive about midnight, play reggae, salsa, *punta* and some rock.

Coxen Hole

Harbour View. *Open Thu-Sun nights late.* Hot, atmospheric and very local. There are usually no problems with visitors, but avoid getting involved in disputes. US$0.50 entrance.

West End

Bahía Azul. Fri is party night, with DJs and dancing.

C-bar. In a fantastic location on the beachfront near Seagrape Plantation.

Foster's. The late night hotspot, with dance music Thu night as well as band nights.

Lone's Bar, *Mermaid Beach*. Nightly barbecue, with reggae music.

Sundowners Bar. Popular bar with a happy hour from 1700-1900 and a Sun quiz followed by a barbecue.

East of Coxen Hole

Al's, *Barrio Las Fuertes, before French Harbour. Closed Sat night.* Salsa and plenty of *punta*.

Shopping

Supermarkets

It's best to buy supplies in Coxen Hole; **Coconut Tree** at West End is expensive. **Woods** is cheaper. **Eldon** in French Harbour is also expensive. **Ezekiel**, West End, opposite church, sells fruit and veg. **Mall Megaplaza**, French Harbour. New shopping mall by roadside east of town, with fast-food outlets.

What to do

Boat trips

Kayak rentals and tours from **Seablades**, contact Alex at **Casi Todo**, 3- to 7-day kayak tours, US$150-250. Full and ½-day rental US$20 and US$12 (with instruction), kayaks available at **Tyll's**. From Rick's American Café, **Casablanca** charters on yacht *Defiance III*, sunset cruises, party trips, full-day snorkelling, also can be arranged through **Casi Todo**. At West Bay beach is a glass-bottomed boat, **Caribbean Reef Explorer**, US$20 per 1½ hrs, unfortunately includes fish feeding, which upsets the reef's ecological balance. Glass-bottomed boat and 3-person submarine tours from the dock at Half Moon Bay, US$25 per person.

Diving

If you don't want to dive, the snorkelling is normally excellent. The creation of the Sandy Bay/West End Marine Park along 4 km of coast from Lawson Rock around the southwest tip to Key Hole has encouraged the return of large numbers of fish in that area and there are several interesting dive sites. Lobsters are still rare, but large grouper are now common and curious about divers. If the sea is rough off **West End** try diving around **French Harbour** (or vice versa) where the cayes provide some protection. There are more mangroves on this side, which attract the fish. **Flowers Bay** on the south side has some spectacular wall dives, but not many fish, and it is calm during the 'Northers' which blow in Dec-Feb. Few people dive the east end except the live-aboards (**Bay Islands Aggressor**, **The Aggressor Fleet**, **Romeo Tower**, French Harbour, T2445-1518) and people on camping trips to

Pigeon Cay, so it is relatively unspoilt. Because fishing is allowed to the east, tropical fish are scarce and the reef is damaged in places. In addition to a few stormy days from Dec to Feb, you can also expect stinging hydroids in the top few feet of water around Mar and Apr which bother people who are sensitive to stings. Vinegar is the local remedy.

Courses As on Utila, the dive operators concentrate on instruction but prices vary (the municipal government sets minimum prices). You can normally find a course starting within 1 or 2 days. There is more on offer than in Utila; not everyone teaches only PADI courses. Prices for courses and diving vary with the season. In low season good deals abound. Open Water US$320, advanced US$280, fun dives US$40 (2-9 dives are US$35 each, 10+ US$30 each). Despite the huge number of dive students, Roatán has a good safety record but it still pays to shop around and find an instructor you feel confident with at a dive shop which is well organized with well-maintained equipment. As in other 'adventure' sports, the cheapest is not always the best. Dive insurance is US$2 per day, and is sometimes included in the course price. If you do not have dive insurance and need their services, the hyperbaric chamber charges a minimum of US$800.

Dive operators
Anthony's Key Resort, *Sandy Bay, T2445-3049, www.anthonyskey.com.* Mostly hotel package diving, also swim and dive with dolphins.
Bananarama, *West Bay, in centre of beach, next to Cabaña Roatana, T2445-5005.* Small, friendly dive shop,

run by young German family, boat and shore diving.
Native Son's Water Sports, *next to Mermaid cabins, West End, T2445-4003.* Run by Alvin, local instructor, PADI and PDSI courses and fun dives.
Ocean Connections at **Sunset Inn**, *West End, T3327-0935, www.ocean-connections. com.* Run by Carol and Phil Stevens with emphasis on safety and fun, good equipment, multilingual instructors, PADI courses, BSAC, the only shop with nitrox instruction, fast boats, also rooms and restaurant, dive/accommodation packages available. Recommended. Also at West Bay, entrance through Paradise Beach Resort – though not attached to the resort – one of the few independent operators, T2445-5017. Very friendly and highly recommended.
Scuba Romance, *Dixon Cove.* Shop and equipment, large diesel boat and compressor, diving the south wall and the reef at Mary's Place, overnight trips to Barbareta, 6 dives, US$80, sleeping on the boat, work with Palm Cove Resort, cabin-style accommodation, home cooking.
Sueño del Mar Divers, *T2445-4343.* Good, inexpensive, American-style operation, which tends to dive the sites closest to home.
Tyll's Dive, *West End, T9698-0416, www. tyllsdive.com.* Multilingual instructors, PADI, SSI courses. Accommodation also available.
West End Divers, *West End, T2445-4289, www.westendivers.com.* Italian owned, competent bilingual instructors, PADI Dive Centre.

Fishing
Trips can be arranged through Eddie, contact at **Cindy's** next to Ocean Divers, West End, small dory, local expert, good

results, US$30 per hr, but prices can vary. Alternatively, go fishing in style from French Harbour, **Hot Rods** (T445-1862) sports fisher, US$500 per day charter. Contact **Casi Todo** (T2445-1347), for fishing tours, ½- and full day. Fishing trips also available on **Flame** (contact Darson or Bernadette, T445-1616), US$20 per hr.

Submarine trips
Karl Stanley offers a probably unique opportunity with deep-sea submarine trips down to 2000 ft. At US$600 per person, a little on the pricey side, but then it's not an everyday option. **Stanley Submarines**, www.stanleysubmarines.com.

Tour operators
The airport travel agency has information on hotels, and will make bookings, with no commission. **Bay Islands Tour and Travel Center**, in Coxen Hole (Suite 208, Cooper Building, T2445-1585) and French Harbour. **Casi Todo 1** in West End or **Casi Todo 2** in Coxen Hole can arrange tours, locally and on the mainland, including fishing, kayaking, island tours, trips to Barbareta and Copán. Local and international air tickets also sold here as well as new and second-hand books, Mon-Sat, 0900-1630. **Columbia Tours** (Barrio El Centro, T2445-1160), good prices for international travel, very helpful. **Carlos Hinds**, T2445-1446, has a van for trips, reasonable and dependable.

At **Belvedere's Lodge** on the headland at Half Moon Bay, Dennis runs snorkelling trips to secluded bays beyond Antony's Key in a glass-bottomed yacht. He also takes charters and sunset cruises all along the coast.

Horse riding available from **Keifitos** or **Jimmy's** in West End. Alex does day trips to Punta Gorda and 2- to 3-day trips in his sailboat *Adventure Girl*, which is moored at **Ocean Divers** dock, contact here or at **Tyll's**. **Far Tortugas** charters, trimaran *Genesis*, does sailing trips with snorkelling and reef drag (snorkellers towed behind slow-moving boat), US$45 per day, US$25 per ½ day, contact **Casi Todo** (West End, T2445-1347). **Coconut Tree** have a rainforest tour to Pico Bonito, US$112 (guide, transport, lunch and snorkelling).

Zip-wire
High-wire canopy tour circuits are the latest craze on Roatán, with half a dozen sites strung around the island, including **Pirates of the Caribbean** (T2455-7576), **Mayan Jungle Canopy** (www. boddentours.com), and **South Shore Canopy Tour** (on West Bay Rd, T9967-1381, www.southshorezipline.com).

Transport

Air The airport is 20 mins' walk from Coxen Hole, or you can catch a taxi from outside the airport for US$1.50. There is a hotel reservation desk in the airport, T2445-1930. Change in Coxen Hole for taxis to West End. US$1 per person for *colectivos* to West End, US$2 to Oak Ridge. If you take a taxi from the airport they charge US$10 per taxi; if you pick one up on the main road you may be able to bargain down to US$5. Domestic airlines serving the Bay Islands include **Aerocaribe**, www.aerocaribehn.com; **Aerolineas Sosa**, www.aerolineasosahn. com, CM Airlines, **www.cmairlines**.com; **Isleña/Sansa Regional**, www.flyislena. com, and **Lanhsa**, www.lanhsa.com. Always buy your ticket in advance (none on sale at airport), as reservations are not always honoured.

Boat Services to/from Roatán with Roatán Ferry, T2445-1795 (La Ceiba), www.roatanferry.com, **La Ceiba–Roatán**, 0930 and 1630, **Roatán–La Ceiba**, 0700 and 1400, US$31 regular class, US$36 1st class. No sailings in bad weather. At times the crossing can be rough, seasickness pills available at ticket counter, and steward gives out sick bags; smart modern ship, with café, and 2 decks, comfortable seating. Irregular boats from **Puerto Cortés** and **Utila**. Cruise ships visit from time to time, mostly visiting **Tabayana Resort** on West Bay.

Bus From Coxen Hole to Sandy Bay is a 2-hr walk, or a US$1.70 bus ride, every 30 mins 0600-1700 from market, a couple of blocks in from Calle Principal. **Ticabus** buses go to French Harbour, Oak Ridge and Punta Gorda, daily every 45 mins from 0600-1630, US$1.75; from parking lot opposite Centro Médico Euceda east end of Calle Principal.

Car Car rental Captain Van, West End, vans, also mopeds and bicycles, good information about the islands; **Roatan Rentals**, West End, range of vehicles, pickups and vans for rent; **Sandy Bay Rent-A-Car**, US$42 per day all inclusive, jeep rental, T2445-1710, agency also in West End outside Sunset Inn; **Toyota**, opposite airport, have pickups, US$46, 4WD, US$65, Starlets US$35 per day, also 12-seater bus, US$56 per day, T2445-1166.

Cycling and mopeds Captain Van's Rentals, West End; also from **Ole Rentavan**, T445-1819.

Taxi If you take a private taxi, *privado*, negotiate the price in advance. The official rate from the airport to Sandy Bay/West End is US$15 per taxi regardless of the number of passengers; from ferry dock to West End is US$20. Luis (waiter at **Bite on the Beach** restaurant West End), runs taxi tours, very informative and knowledgeable, T9892-9846. Water taxis from West End to West Bay, every few minutes depending on passengers, US$3, from jetty next to **Foster's Bar**.

Isla Guanaja

a forest reserve and national marine park

Columbus called Guanaja (area 56 sq km) the Island of Pines, but Hurricane Mitch swept most of them away. Since then, a great replanting effort has been completed and, until the pines have regrown, flowering and fruiting plants thrive on the island. Good (but sweaty) clambering on the island gives splendid views of the jungle and the sea and there are several attractive waterfalls, which can be visited on the hills rising to the summit of 415 m.

The first English settler was Robert Haylock, who arrived in 1856 with a land title to part of the island, the two cayes that now form the main settlement of Bonacca and some of the Mosquito coast. He was followed in 1866 by John Kirkconnell who purchased Hog Caye, where the Haylocks raised pigs away from the sandflies. These two families became sailors, boat builders and landowners, and formed the basis of the present population.

Much of Guanaja town, locally known as **Bonacca** and covering a small caye off the coast, is built on stilts above sea water, with boardwalks and concrete pathways, hence its nickname: the 'Venice of Honduras'. There are three small villages, **Mangrove Bight**, **Savannah Bight** and **North East Bight**, on the main island. Much of the accommodation is all-inclusive resorts, but you can visit independently as well. Sandflies and mosquitoes cannot be escaped on the island, and none of the beaches offer respite (coconut oil, baby oil or any oily suntan lotion will help to ward off sandflies).The cayes are better, including Guanaja town. South West Caye is especially recommended.

Listings Isla Guanaja

Where to stay

$ Harry Carter
T2455-4303, ask for fan.
Rooms are clean.

$ Miss Melba
Just before Hotel Alexander sign on left, house with flowers.
Run by a friendly old lady with lots of island information, 3 rooms in boarding house, with shared bathroom and cold water. Great porch and gardens.

Restaurants

$$ Harbour Light
Through Mountain View nightclub.
Good food, reasonably priced for the island.

What to do

Diving and sailing
The most famous dive site off Guanaja is the wreck of the *Jado Trader*, sunk in 1987 in about 30 m on a flat bottom surrounded by some large coral pinnacles which rise to about 15 m. Big black groupers and moray eels live here, as does a large shy jewfish and many other fish and crustaceans.

End of The World, *next to Bayman Bay Club, T2402-3016.* Diving instruction, beachfront bar, restaurant, cabins, kayaks, canoes, hobie cats, white-sand beach, fishing. Highly recommended resort.
Jado Divers, *beside Melba's, T2453-4326.* US$26 for 2 dives, run by Matthew from US. Preston Borden will take snorkellers out for US$25 per boat load (4-6 people), larger parties accommodated with larger boat, or for customized excursions, very flexible.

Transport

Air The airport is on Guanaja but you have to get a water taxi from there to wherever you are staying; there are no roads or cars; **Sosa** and **Isleña** (T2453-4208) fly daily from **La Ceiba**, 30 mins. Other non-scheduled flights available.

Boat The *Suyapa* sails between Guanaja, **La Ceiba** and **Puerto Cortés**. The *Miss Sheila* also does this run and on to **George Town** (**Grand Cayman**). *Cable Doly Zapata*, Guanaja, for monthly sailing dates to Grand Cayman (US$75 1 way). Irregular sailings from Guanaja to **Trujillo**, 5 hrs.

North
coast

Along the Caribbean lowlands are a mix of banana-exporting ports, historic towns and Garífuna villages. As the historic base for the United Fruit Company, the region claims kudos as the symbolic birthplace of the world's first banana republic. Throughout the early 20th century, the influx of plantation labourers from Jamaica and other English-speaking colonies infused the coast with a distinctive African-Caribbean culture that takes great pride in its unique forms of music, dance and cooking.

Steeped in steamy rainforests, brackish swamps and tangled mangroves, the coast has abundant exotic flora and fauna too. All its natural and cultural vibrancy contrasts with decaying United Fruit infrastructure – railways, ports, rusting machinery – partially or wholly reclaimed by the jungle. In between the main towns of interest – Omoa, Puerto Cortés, Tela, La Ceiba and Trujillo – you will find isolated beaches and resorts, and national parks like Pico Bonito, which are perfect for hiking and whitewater rafting. Close to the shore and accessible from La Ceiba, are the small, palm-fringed Hog Islands, more attractively known as Cayos Cochinos (see page 117). Back on the mainland, the route west takes in the 'Jungle Trail' to Guatemala.

Running parallel to the coast, a route from El Progreso leads to rarely visited national parks, pristine cloudforest and an alternative route to La Ceiba.

Puerto Cortés

Stuck out on the northwestern coast of the country and backed by the large bay of Laguna de Alvarado, Puerto Cortés is hot, tempered by sea breezes and close to many beautiful palm-fringed beaches. However, most people find little in Puerto Cortés to detain them and instead head straight to the infinitely more attractive village of Omoa.

The economic success of the place is due to its location and the fact that most Honduran trade passes through the port, which is just 58 km from San Pedro Sula by road and rail, and 333 km from Tegucigalpa. It has a small oil refinery, a free zone and, being two days' voyage from New Orleans, is one of the most important ports in Central America.

The Parque Central contains many fine trees but focuses on a huge Indian poplar, planted as a sapling in 1941, in the centre that provides an extensive canopy.

★Omoa

Omoa, 18 km from Puerto Cortés, is set in the beautiful Bahía de Omoa where the mountains, lusciously carpeted in jungle, tumble towards the sea. You can watch fine purple sunsets from the quiet laid-back bars on the beach and, if you're lucky, see dolphins in the bay. It has an 18th-century castle, **Fortaleza de San Fernando**, now renovated and worth a visit. It was built by the Spaniards in 1759 to protect the coast and shipments of silver, gold and cacao from British pirates. There is a **visitor centre** and a small, interesting **museum** ⓘ *Mon-Sun 0900-1600, US$1.40, tickets on sale at gate, guides available.*

During the week Omoa is a quiet, friendly fishing village, but at weekends it gets a little busier with Hondurans from San Pedro and the place becomes littered, followed by a grand clean-up on the Monday morning. Near Omoa are two waterfalls (**Los Chorros**), with lovely walks to each, and good hiking in attractive scenery both along the coast and inland.

It's a fair walk from the main road. Get a tuk-tuk for US$0.50 to the beach. Note: there are no ATMs in Omoa.

Listings Puerto Cortés and Omoa

Where to stay

Puerto Cortés

Avoid 4 Calle between 1 and 2 Av and the area on 1 Av opposite the dockyards; it is unpleasant by day and dangerous at night.

$$$ Costa Azul
Playa El Faro, T2665-5215,
www.hotelcostazul.net.
One of the town's better places, with restaurant, disco-bar, billiards, table tennis, pool, horse riding, volley ball. Good value.

$$ Villa del Sol
Barrio El Porvenir, in front of the municipal beach, T2665-4939, www.villadelsolhn.com.

In an interesting location by the beach, Villa del Sol has very reasonable guestrooms, which are spacious but simple. Each is fully equipped with a/c, hot water, private balcony, cable TV and phone. There's a restaurant and helpful staff. Safe and secure. Recommended.

$ Formosa
3 Av 2 Calle E.

Good-value, clean rooms with fan, bath (some without), no towel, but with soap and toilet paper. Friendly Chinese owner.

Omoa

$$ Sueño de Mar
T2658-9047, www.suenosdemar.com.

Chilled out hotel at the quiet end of the beach with a handful of rooms of differing sizes, run by Canadian couple Karen and Mark. A great spot, offering Canadian breakfasts, laundry and Wi-Fi. Recommended.

$ Roli's Place
T2658-9082, http://yaxpactours.com.

Located 80 m from beach, this great place has clean rooms with private bath and hot water, and good information of the region. It offers bikes and kayaks for guests' use, games, a shady garden and a campground. Roli will change TCs, quetzals, euros and dollars. As it's quiet after 2200 it's not a party place.

Restaurants

Puerto Cortés

$$$-$$ Restaurante La Ola
Inside Hotel Villa del Sol, Barrio El Porvenir, opposite the municipal

beaches, T2665-4939, www.villadelsolhn.com.

La Ola serves typical Honduran fare from *steak típico* to a host of fresh seafood such as prawns, conch, king crab (when in season) and fish fillet. Solid and reliable.

$$ Pekín
2 Av, 6-7 Calle.

Excellent Chinese, with a/c and good service. It's a bit pricey but recommended. **Supermercado Pekín** is next door.

Omoa

$$-$ Family Restaurant
Mila 2, 7 km before Omoa on the highway to Guatemala.

Perched on the seafront, this modest eatery serves wholesome home-cooked fare and is often crowded with loyal patrons. Fresh and economical. Try the seafood soup.

$ Fisherman's Hut
200 m to right of pier.

Clean, good food, seafood, recommended. Don't expect early Sun breakfasts after the partying the night before.

Festivals

Puerto Cortés
Aug **Noche Veneciana** on 3rd Sat.

Shopping

Puerto Cortés
There is a souvenir shop, **Marthita's**, in the customs administration building (opposite Hondutel). The market in the town centre is worth a visit, 3 Calle between 2 and 3 Av. **Supertienda Paico** is on the Parque.

Transport

Puerto Cortés

Boat To Guatemala Information from **Ocean Travel** at 3 Av, 2 blocks west of plaza. See also box, page 156.

To Belize Boats connecting to Belize leave from beside the bridge over the lagoon (Barra La Laguna), at the Muelle de Mariscos, next to El Delfín restaurant (also known as the 'Pescaderia'). The **D-Express, www.belizeferry.com,** leaves Puerto Cortés on Mon at 1100, for **Mango Creek** and on to **Placencia**, 4 hrs arriving around 1340, US$65. The *Pride of Belize* also departs Mon at 1100 and calls at Dangriga and Belize City. Check-in closes 15 mins prior to departure, though it is best to get on the passenger list as early as possible.

Remember to get your exit stamp from the Immigration office, located next to the D-Express ticket office at the Muelle de Mariscos. If arriving from Belize and heading on straight away you don't need to go into town to catch a bus. Get on to the bridge, cross over the other side and keep walking 200 m to the main road. Buses going past are going to San Pedro Sula and beyond.

Bus Virtually all buses now arrive and leave from 4 Av 2-4 Calle. Bus service at least hourly to **San Pedro Sula**, US$2.30, 45 mins, **Citul** (4 Av between 3 and 4 Calle) and **Impala** (4 Av y 3 Calle, T2255-0606). **Expresos del Caribe**, **Expresos de Citul** and **Expresos del Atlantic** all have minibuses to **San Pedro Sula**. Bus to **Omoa** and **Tegucigalpita** from 4 Av, old school bus, loud music, very full; guard your belongings. **Citral Costeños** go to the Guatemalan border, 4-5 Av, 3Calle E. Regular buses leave for **Omoa** (US$0.70) at 0730 to get to **Corinto** at the Guatemalan border. See also box, page 156.

Omoa

Boat Boats leave for **Lívingston**, Guatemala, on Tue and Fri around 1000. Ask around to confirm. Ask at **Fisherman's Hut** for Sr Juan Ramón Menjivar.

Bus Frequent buses to the Guatemalan border at 1000, 1400 and 1700. See box, page 156 for border crossing information.

East of San Pedro Sula
a former United Fruit outpost enveloped in remote beaches and humid wetlands

Tela

Tela used to be an important banana port before the pier was partly destroyed by fire. Easily reached from San Pedro Sula with a bus service via El Progreso, it is pleasantly laid out with a sandy but dirty beach.

Tela Viejo to the east is the original city joined by a bridge to Tela Nuevo, the residential area built for the executives of the American banana and farming company **Chiquita**. There is a pleasant walk along the beach east to Ensenada, or west to San Juan. More information is available at www.telahonduras.com.
Note Make sure you take a cab after midnight; US$1.50 per person at night.

ON THE ROAD

Environmental challenge

The **Fundación Para la Protección de Lancetilla, Punta Sal y Texiguat (Prolansate)** is a non-governmental, non-profit organization based in Tela. Originally set up by Peace Corps volunteers, it is now operated by local personnel and is involved in environmental programmes to protect and educate in conjunction with community development and ecotourism. It manages four protected areas: Parque Nacional 'Jeannette Kawas' (Punta Sal), Jardín Botánico Lancetilla, Refugio de Vida Silvestre Texiguat and Refugio de Vida Silvestre Punta Izopo. The Prolansate visitor centre, Calle 9 Avenida 2-3 NE, Tela, T2448-2042, www.prolansate.org, organizes trips to Punta Sal, Punta Izopo and Lancetilla, with guides, and provides information about other national parks, wildlife refuges and bird sanctuaries.

Around Tela

Local buses and trucks from the corner just east of the market go east to the Garífuna village of **Triunfo de la Cruz**, which is set in a beautiful bay. Site of the first Spanish settlement on the mainland, a sea battle between Cristóbal de Olid and Francisco de Las Casas (two of Cortés' lieutenants) was fought here in 1524.

Beyond Triunfo de la Cruz is an interesting coastal area that includes the cape, **Parque Nacional Punta Izopo** (1½-hour walk along the beach, take water; 12 km from Tela) and the mouth of the Río León. This, and its immediate hinterland, is a good place to see parrots, toucans, turtles, alligators and monkeys as well as the first landing point of the Spanish conqueror Cristóbal de Olid. For information, contact **Prolansate** (see box, above). To get right into the forest and enjoy the wildlife, it is best to take an organized tour (see What to do, page 114). A trip to Punta Izopo involves kayaking through mangrove swamps up the Río Plátano, Indiana Jones style.

Parque Nacional Punta Sal 'Jeannette Kawas'

US$2, daily 0800-1500. It is recommended that you contact Prolansate for more information, www.prolansate.org.

Encompassing 80,000 ha of sublime palm-fringed shoreline, the Parque Nacional Punta Sal 'Jeannette Kawas' is one of the most important parks in Honduras. It has two parts: the peninsula and the lagoon. During the dry season some 350 species of bird live within the lagoon, surrounded by forest, mangroves and wetlands.

Once inhabited only by Garífuna, the area has suffered from the immigration of cattle farmers who have cleared the forest, causing erosion, and from a palm oil extraction plant on the Río San Alejo, which has dumped waste in the river and contaminated the lagoons. Conservation and environmental protection programmes are now underway. To get there you will need a motor boat, or take a bus (three a day) to Tornabé and hitch a ride 12 km, or take the crab truck at 1300 for US$0.40 (back at 1700), on to Miami, a small, all-thatched fishing village (two hours' walk along beach from Tornabé), beer on ice available, and walk the remaining 10 km along the beach. There are also pickups from Punta Sal to Miami, contact Prolansate for information.

Lancetilla Jardín Botánico

T2448-1740, www.jblancetilla.esnacifor.hn. It's not well signposted; a guide is recommended, ask at the Cohdefor office. Guide services daily 0800-1530, US$8. Good maps are available in English or Spanish US$0.30. Simple cabin accommodation is available ($). To get here, take a taxi from Tela, US$4, but there are few in the park for the return journey in the afternoon, so organize collection in advance.

Located 5 km inland, the Lancetilla Jardín Botánico was founded in 1926 by the United Fruit Company as a plant research station. Today, it is the second largest botanical garden in the world. It has more than 1000 varieties of plant and over 200 bird species have been identified in its grounds. It has fruit trees from every continent, the most extensive collection of Asiatic fruit trees in the western hemisphere, an orchid garden, and plantations of mahogany and teak alongside a 1200-ha virgin tropical rainforest. But be warned, there are many mosquitoes.

Listings East of San Pedro Sula

Where to stay

Tela

During Easter week, the town is packed; room rates double and advance booking is essential.

$$$ Capitán Beach
Calle 9, T 3233-8182, www.hotelcapitanbeach.com.
Located 6 blocks from the main plaza and right across from the beach, this is a relatively recent edition to Tela's hotel scene. They have 10 clean, comfortable rooms with cable TV, Wi-Fi and a/c, all overlooking a tempting pool, and a well-stocked restaurant-bar upstairs with views of the ocean. Good choice.

$$$ Gran Central
Just south of the centre of town, T448-1099, www.hotelgran central.com.
This French-owned, beautifully restored historic banana-port-era hotel has

1 suite, kitchen, hot water, cable TV, a/c, security and a safe box in each room. Local excursions available. Highly recommended.

$$$ Posada Las Iguanas
Barrio Buena Vista, near Escuela Luis Landa, T2448-4625, www.posadaslasiguanas.biz.
Set inside a former United Fruit Company property, Posada Las Iguanas is a stylish boutique option with lots of character and comfort. Accommodation includes a range of handsome villas, suites and rooms, all kitted out with the usual amenities. Grounds are verdant and tranquil and there's also a sauna and pool to keep you entertained. Recommended.

$$$-$$ Hotel Marsol
Calle del Comercio, Av Nicaragua, T2448-1782, www.hotelmarsoltela.com.

Located 200 m from the beach, Hotel Marsol is chiefly recommended for its attached dive centre. Even if you're not planning any underwater forays, it's a very reasonable lodging with 23 smart rooms and breakfast included.

$$$-$$ Maya Vista
Top of hill, steep flight of steps starting opposite Preluna, T2448-1497, www.mayavista.com.
Canadian-owned, this place has fantastic views and a restaurant serving delicious French-Canadian cuisine. Rooms have bath, hot water and a/c. French and English spoken. Very highly recommended.

$$ Coco Cabaña
Playa Barrio El Tigre, Triunfo de la Cruz, T3335-4599, www.hotelcaraibe.com.
These 'eco-cabins' were thoughtfully constructed using waste plastic bottles. Each unit has Wi-Fi, a kitchenette and a private terrace with hammocks. No frills, unpretentious and on the rustic side, as all beach lodgings should be.

$$ Ejecutivos Aparthotel
Av 4, Contiguo a Hondutel, T2448-1076, www.ejecutivosah.com.
Marketed to nationals, this down-to-earth downtown lodging offers a range of comfortable and reliable rooms and apartments. Simple, solid place with the usual amenities, including cable TV, Wi-Fi, hot water and some a/c.

$ Sara
11 Calle, 6 Av, behind the restaurant Tiburón Playa, T2448-1477.
Basic in a rickety old building, with bath, or without, poor sanitation. Cheapest in town, popular with backpackers, friendly, noisy especially at weekends from all-night discos.

Around Tela
There are cheap houses and *cabañas* for rent in Triunfo de la Cruz. There is a small hotel in Río Tinto, near Parque Nacional Punta Sal; accommodation is available in private houses.

$$$-$$ Caribbean Coral Inn
Triunfo de la Cruz, T9957-8605, www.caribbeancoralinns.com.
Simple, homely rooms and bungalows with hammock, terrace, Wi-Fi and garden or sea views.

$$$-$$ The Last Resort
Tornabé, T2984-3964.
Has 8 bungalows for rent, some a/c, some fan, hot water, with breakfast. There are several cabins for different sized groups.

Restaurants

Tela
The best eating is in the hotel restaurants.

$$$ Casa Azul
Barrio El Centro. Open till 2300.
Run by Mark from Texas, subs, dinner specials, book exchange. Helpful.

$$ César Mariscos
Open from 0700.
Attractive location on the beach, serves good seafood and has a very good breakfast menu.

$$ Luces del Norte
Of Doña Mercedes, 11 Calle, 2 Av NE, towards beach from Parque Central, next to Hotel Puerto Rico.
Very popular place serving delicious seafood and good typical breakfasts. Also has good information and a book exchange.

$$ Maya Vista
In hotel (see Where to stay, above).
Run by Québécois Pierre, serving fine
cuisine; one of the best in Tela. Highly
recommended.

$$-$ Bungalow
Calle Cabañas, Barrio El Centro.
Kitsch and ramshackle, Bungalow is
a typical Caribbean eatery serving
typical Caribbean grub, such as fried
chicken and whole fish. Creaky wooden
floorboards and chequered table cloths.
The owner Norman is larger than life.

$ Bella Italia
www.pizzeriabellaitalia.weebly.com.
Italian-owned restaurant serving pizza,
on the walkway by the beach.

Festivals

Tela
Jun Fiesta de San Antonio.

What to do

Tela
Garífuna Tours, *southwest corner
of Parque Central*, T2448-2904, *www.
garifunatours.com*. Knowledgeable
and helpful with mountain bike hire,
US$5 per day. Day trips to Punta Sal
(US$31, meals extra), Los Micos lagoon
(US$31) and Punta Izopo (US$24). La
Ceiba–Cayos Cochinos (US$39), La
Ceiba–Cuero Salado (US$68), Pico Bonito
(US$33). Also trips further afield to La
Ceiba, Mosquitia (4 days, US$499) and a
shuttle service between San Pedro Sula
and La Ceiba, US$18 per person. Also La
Ceiba–Copán, US$45. Good value. Highly
recommended.

Language schools
Mango Café Spanish School, T2448-
0338, www.mangocafe.net. Mon-Fri 4
hrs' tuition a day, US$115, with a local
tour on Sat.

Transport

Tela
Bike Hire from **Garífuna Tours**, 9 Calle y
Parque Central (see What to do, above),
and from **Hotel Mango**.

Bus **Catisa** or **Tupsa** lines from San Pedro
Sula to **El Progreso** (US$0.50) where
you must change to go on to **Tela** (3 hrs
in total) and **La Ceiba** (last bus at 2030
with **Transportes Cristina**). On **Catisa**
bus ask to be let off at the petrol station
on the main road, then take a taxi to the
beach, US$0.50. Also 1st-class service with
Hedman Alas at 1010, 1415 and 1810.

Bus from Tela to **El Progreso** every
25 mins; last bus at 1830, US$1.50. To **La
Ceiba**, every 30 mins, from 0410 until
1800, 2 hrs, US$2. Direct to **Tegucigalpa**,
Traliasa, 1 a day from Hotel Los Arcos,
US$4.50, same bus to **La Ceiba** (this
service avoids San Pedro Sula; 6 a day
with **Transportes Cristinas** (US$9.20).
To **Copán**, leave by 0700 via El Progreso
and San Pedro Sula; to arrive same day.
To **San Pedro Sula**, 1130 and 1715 with
Diana Express (US$2.50), or 8 a day with
Transportes Tela Express, last bus at
1700 (US$3). To **Trujillo** through Savá,
Tocoa and Corocito.

Shuttle **Garífuna Tours**, see page
114, offers a shuttle service direct to **San
Pedro**, US$18 and **Copán Ruinas**, US$45.

Around Tela
Bus To **Triunfo de la Cruz**, US$0.40
(about 5 km, if no return bus, walk to
main road where buses pass).

La Ceiba, the capital of Atlántida Department and the third largest city in Honduras, stands on the narrow coastal plain between the Caribbean and the rugged Nombre de Dios mountain range crowned by the spectacular Pico Bonito (2435 m), see page 117. The climate is hot, but tempered by sea winds. Maritime trade has now passed to Puerto Cortés and Puerto Castilla, but there is still some activity in the city's port.

The close proximity to Pico Bonito National park, Cuero y Salado Wildlife Refuge and the Cayos Cochinos Marine Reserve gives the city the ambitious target of becoming an important hub for ecotourism. While the opportunities aren't immediately obvious, there is definitely a buzz about town – watch out for developments. The main plaza is worth walking around to see statues of various famous Hondurans including Lempira and a couple of ponds.

A **butterfly and insect museum** ⓘ *Col El Sauce, 2a Etapa Casa G-12, T2442-2874, http:// butterflywebsite.com, Mon-Fri 0800-1600, closed Wed afternoon, Sat and Sun for groups only with advance reservation, US$1.20, student reductions*, has a collection of over 10,000 butterflies, roughly 2000 other insects and snakes. It's good for all ages; there's a 25-minute video in both Spanish and English and Robert and Myriam Lehman guide visitors expertly through the life of the butterfly. There is also a **Butterfly Farm** ⓘ *daily 0800-1530, entry US$6*, on the grounds of **The Lodge** at Pico Bonito.

★Around La Ceiba

There are scores of small, rewarding attractions around La Ceiba. **Jutiapa** is a small dusty town with a pretty little colonial church. Contact Standard Fruit Company, Dole office in La Ceiba (off main plaza) to visit a local pineapple plantation. **Corozal** is an interesting Garífuna village near La Ceiba, at Km 209.5, with a beach, Playas de Sambrano and a hotel. **Sambo Creek**, another Garífuna village, has nice beaches, a few good hotels, a canopy tour and hot springs. It is an increasingly popular destination with foreign travellers and well worth checking out (see What to do, below). Near the towns of **Esparta** and **El Porvenir**, thousands of crabs come out of the sea in July and August and travel long distances inland. The **Catarata El Bejuco** is a waterfall 7 km along the old dirt road to **Olanchito** (11 km from La Ceiba). Follow a path signposted to Balneario Los Lobos to the waterfall about 1 km upriver through the jungle. There is good swimming from a pebbly beach where the river broadens. Along this road is **El Naranjo** near **Omega Tours Jungle Lodge and Adventure Company**.

Yaruca, 20 km down the old road to Olanchito, is easily reached by bus and offers good views of Pico Bonito. **Eco-Zona Río María**, 5 km along the Trujillo highway (signposted path up to the foothills of the Cordillera Nombre de Dios), is a beautiful walk through the lush countryside of a protected area. Just beyond Río María is **Balneario Los Chorros** (signposted), a series of small waterfalls through giant boulders into a deep rock pool that is great for swimming (with refreshments nearby). Upstream there is some beautiful scenery and you can continue walking through the forest and in the river, where there are more pools. Another bathing place, Agua Azul, with restaurant is a short distance away. The active can get on the **Río Cangrejal** for the exhilarating rush of Grade II, III and IV **whitewater rapids**, which can be combined with treks in to the wilderness of **Parque Nacional Pico Bonito** (see below).

La Ceiba

Where to stay	Rainbow Village 4	El Jardín de Susana 5
Casa de España 1		Expatriates Bar, Grill &
Casa de Nery 2	**Restaurants**	Cigar Emporium 2
El Estadio 3	Café Ki'Bok 1	La Palapa 6
Gran Hotel París 6	Cafetería Cobel 4	Paty's 7
Quinta Real 8	El Guapo's 3	Ponderosa 8

N
200 metres
200 yards

Beaches around La Ceiba

Beaches in and near La Ceiba include **Playa Miramar** (which is dirty and not recommended), **La Barra** (a better option), **Perú** (across the Río Cangrejal at Km 205.5, better still, quiet except at weekends, deserted tourist complex, restaurant, access by road to Tocoa, 10 km, then signposted side road 1.5 km, or along the beach 6 km from La Ceiba) and **La Ensenada** (close to Corozal).

The beaches near the fishing villages of Río Esteban and Balfate are very special and are near Cayos Cochinos (Hog Islands) where the snorkelling and diving is spectacular.

Cayos Cochinos

The Hog Islands, 17 km northeast of La Ceiba, constitute two small islands and 13 palm-fringed cayes. **Cochino Grande** is the larger island, rising to an altitude of just 143 m, and **Cochino Pequeño** is the smaller. Both have lush tropical vegetation with primeval hardwood forests and there are fewer biting insects than in the Bay Islands. As part of a National Marine Reserve, Cayos Cochinos and the surrounding waters are protected and filled with sealife. There is a fee to enter parts of the islands of US$10. There are Garífuna fishing villages of palm-thatched huts at Chachauate on Lower Monitor Cay, where you can organize basic accommodation, and East End Village on Cochino Grande.

Transport to the Hog Islands can be sought on the supply *cayuco* from Nueva Armenia, or by boat from La Ceiba, Sambo Creek or Roatán. However, for safety, it is recommended you use an insured tour operator with a good seaworthy vessel and life jackets; the extra cost is negligible. There is a small dirt airstrip and dug-out canoes are the local form of transport. The islands are privately owned and access to most of the cayes is limited, being occupied only by caretakers. Take whatever you need with you as there is almost nothing on the smaller cayes. However, the Garífuna are going to and fro all the time.

Parque Nacional Pico Bonito

Entrance US$7; children US$4. For further information on the park contact FUPNAPIB, on the La Ceiba–Tela highway, T2442-3044. Take care if you enter the forest: tracks are not yet developed, a compass is advisable.
Tour companies in La Ceiba arrange trips to the park.

Parque Nacional Pico Bonito (674 sq km) is the largest national park in Honduras and is home to Pico Bonito (2435 m). The Río Cangrejal, a mecca for whitewater rafting, marks the eastern border of the park. It has deep tropical hardwood forests that shelter, among other animals, jaguars and three species of monkey,

Cayos Cochinos (Hog Islands)

Cochino Grande
North East Cay
Cochino Pequeño
North West Cay
Lower Monitor
Timón
Pelon
Coral Reefs
Sandy Cays
N
2 km
2 miles

deep canyons and tumbling streams and waterfalls (including Las Gemelas, which fall vertically for some 200 m).

Parque Nacional Pico Bonito has two areas open for tourism. The first is the Río Zacate area, located past the community of El Pino, 10 km west of La Ceiba; the second is on the Río Cangrejal, near the community of El Naranjo, about 7.5 km from the paved highway.

Tip...
Go early in the morning for the best views, and to see birdlife and howler monkeys.

A hanging bridge over the Río Cangrejal provides access to the visitor centre and the **El Mapache Trail** up to the top of **El Bejuco** waterfall. Further up the road in **Las Mangas**, Guaruma (T2442-2693) there is a very nice trail with beautiful swimming holes in a pristine creek. The trail is well maintained and local guides are available.

For the Río Zacate area, access is just past the dry stream (*quebrada seca*) bridge on the main La Ceiba to Tela highway from where the road leads to the entrance through pineapple plantations to a steep trail leading up to the Río Zacate waterfall, about one hour 20 minutes' hiking. A good price range of accommodation is available in both areas.

Cuero y Salado Wildlife Reserve

Open 0600-1800, US$10 to enter the reserve, which you can pay at Fucsa; keep the receipt. It's an extra US$5 per person for accommodation. The reserve is managed by the Fundación Cuero y Salado (Fucsa) Refugio de Vida Silvestre, 1 block north and 3 blocks west of Parque Central to the left of the Standard Fruit Company, La Ceiba, T2443-0329, www.fucsa.blogspot.co.uk. The foundation is open to volunteers, preferably those who speak English and Spanish.

Encompassing 13,225 ha of rainforest and wetlands between the Cuero and Salado rivers, 27 km west of La Ceiba, is the Cuero y Salado Wildlife Reserve, which has a great variety of flora and fauna, including manatee, jaguar, monkeys and a large population of local and migratory birds.

Nilmo, a knowledgeable biologist who acts as a guide, takes morning and evening boat trips for those staying overnight, either through the canal dug by Standard Fruit, parallel to the beach between the palms and the mangroves, or down to the Salado lagoon. Five kayaks are available for visitors' use. In the reserve are spider and capuchin monkeys, iguanas, jaguar, tapirs, crocodiles, manatee, hummingbirds, toucans, ospreys, eagles and vultures. A five-hour trip will take you to Barra de Colorado to see the manatees. Fucsa's administration centre, on the banks of the Río Salado, has photos, charts, maps, radio and a two-room visitors' house. There is also a visitor centre, with a full-service cafeteria and bilingual guides.

Getting there Take a bus to La Unión (every hour, 0600 until 1500 from La Ceiba terminus, 1½ hours, ask to get off at the railway line, ferrocarril, or Km 17), an interesting journey through pineapple fields. There are several ways of getting into the park from La Unión. Walking takes 1½ hours. Groups usually

118•Honduras North coast

take a *motocarro*, a dilapidated train that also transports the coconut crop; there are definite departures at 0700 and 0800. From near Doña Tina's house (meals available), take a *burra*, a flat-bed railcar propelled by two men with poles (a great way to see the countryside) to the community on the banks of the Río Salado. To return to La Unión, it is another *burra* ride or a two-hour walk along the railway, then, either wait for a La Ceiba bus (last one at 1500), or ask for the short cut through grapefruit groves, 20 minutes, which leads to the main La Ceiba–Tela road, where there are many more buses back to town.

Listings La Ceiba and around *map p116*

Where to stay

La Ceiba

$$$ Casa de Nery
Primera Calle, Este Barrio La Isla, La Zona Viva, www.hotellacasadenery.com.
A good option for families, the green lawns of the resort-style Casa de Nery overlook the ocean and include a large pool, volleyball and basketball court. Amenities include Wi-Fi, a/c, cable TV and minibar. There are just 10 rooms and one smart little bungalow suitable for a couple.

$$$ Quinta Real
Zona Viva, on the beach, T2440-3311, www.quintarealhotel.com.
Popular place with big, well-furnished rooms that have a/c and cable TV. There's a pool, beach, restaurant and bars and free internet. (Taxi drivers sometimes confuse it with the **Hotel Quinta** opposite the Golf Club on the Tela–La Ceiba road, which is not as nice).

$$$-$$ Gran Hotel Paris
Parque Central, T2440-1414, www.granhotelparisonline.com.
Located in the heart of La Ceiba, this is the oldest hotel in town, established 1915. It has 84 comfortable if unadventurous rooms with a/c, cable

TV and Wi-Fi. The grounds include a pleasant pool, bar and a restaurant.

$$ Casa de España
Av 14 de Julio, entre Tercera y Cuarta Calle, T2454-0210, www.hotelcasadeespana.com.
Simple, reliable, neat, quiet and economical accommodation with a decent restaurant and roof terrace serving meat, seafood and tapas. Lovely, helpful, English-speaking owners and good reports.

$$ Hotel Rainbow Village
Colonia Confite, 2 mins from the airport, T2408-5696, www.hotel-rainbow-village.com.
This cute hotel is called the Rainbow Village for its multi-coloured bungalows. Amenities include a pleasant garden with hammocks, bar and pool. Barbara, the owner, is an excellent chef.

$ El Estadio
Calle Estero, next to the football stadium, T3187-6027.
Simple and basic, but all you need, this budget hotel would suit backpackers. The owner Peter is very friendly, helpful and English-speaking. Good Wi-Fi connections and there are cheap dorms too.

$ Tornabé Hostel
Bloque 4 #13, Colonia Monteverde, T9813-8998, www.tornabe.com.
Dorm beds at this jolly little backpacker hostel are just US$7 when you book a shuttle to/from Guatemala or Nicaragua. Facilities include Wi-Fi, movies and a/c. A new place, intimate, helpful and accommodating.

Around La Ceiba

$$$ Diving Pelican Inn
Sambo Creek, on Playa Helen, T3369-2208, www.divingpelicaninn.com.
Perched on the edge of the beach, Diving Pelican Inn is a villa-style B&B with 2 rooms and a detached apartment, all with lock boxes and private entrances, as well as a wealth of mod cons such as DVD player, coffee-maker, a/c and purified water. There's a pool with a waterfall, sun deck, honesty bar, fire pit and DVD library. Low-key and quiet, a good option for couples.

$$ Hotel Canadien
Sambo Creek, T2440-2099, www. hotelcanadien.com.
Long-standing and hospitable accommodation, including double suites. They can arrange trips to the Hog Islands for US$80 per boat.

$$ La Delphina Bed and Breakfast
Sambo Creek, T2405-1557, www. ladelphina.net.
A chilled out and intimate B&B option right on the edge of the beach. Rooms are simple but comfortable and amenities include bar, restaurant and pool. A variety of excursions and activities can be arranged. Attentive service and good reports.

$$ Paradise Found
Sambo Creek, Playa Helen, one block past the bus stop, near Hotel Canadian, T9808-8888, www.paradisefoundlaceiba.com.
Managed by Dante and Kristina, this down-to-earth B&B offers tidy, homely, no-frills lodgings with Wi-Fi and a/c; one room is wheelchair accessible. Good restaurant overlooking the waves (Dante is the chef), bike rentals and a variety of excursions are available. Good reports. Recommended.

$$ Villa Helen's Hotel
Sambo Creek, look for the signs from the main road, T2408-1137, www.villahelens.com.
Intimate and affordable, Villa Helen offers 4 beachfront rooms with cable TV and a/c, 2 suites with ocean views and 6 low-key cabins with a/c, hot water, living room and mountain views. Amenities include a leafy garden with a hexagonal jacuzzi, a poolside bar-restaurant, and massage services. Friendly and welcoming.

Cayos Cochinos

$$$ Turtle Bay Eco-Resort
Cochino Grande, T9842-3231, www. turtlebayecoresort.com.
Rustic cabins on the hillside, with hot water and fans. There's diving offshore, yacht moorings, and a music festival at the end of Jul, with local bands and dancers. For view over the cayes to the mainland, there's a good steep walk up to lighthouse.

Parque Nacional Pico Bonito
Río Cangrejo area

$$$$ Las Cascadas Lodge
El Naranjo, T9923-6237, www.lascascadaslodge.com.

Named after the 5 waterfalls cascading through the grounds, this luxurious jungle lodge was designed by award-winning architect David Sellon. It is a singularly beautiful property with boutique cabins and suites nestled on the banks of the Cangrejal river. A very special, romantic place.

$$$$-$$$ Villas Pico Bonito
7.5 km Carretera de Yaruca, T2416-5007, www.villaspicobonito.com.
An upscale jungle resort with a range of luxurious villas that would suit families or groups. Each unit is unique, some are more rustic and simple than others, but all enjoy tidy furnishings and forest views. The lovely landscaped grounds feature an infinity pool and restaurant.

$$$ Casa Cangrejal
Km 10 Río Cangrejal road, T2416-5046, www.casacangrejal.com.
This charming stone-built B&B backs onto verdant forests with restful patios and chill-out hammocks. Perfect for post-hike relaxation, a nearby creek has been channelled into small bathing pools, continually refreshed with highland water. All rooms have Wi-Fi and the usual mod cons. Natural and tranquil.

$$$ La Villa de Soledad
Look for the turn-off approximately 150m south of the visitor centre, T9967-4548, www.lavilladesoledad.com.
A lot of love and care has gone into the Villa de Soledad, the best B&B in the Pico Bonito area. Hosts John and Soledad are warm and attentive and know the surrounding countryside intimately; rafting, hiking and canopy tours can all be arranged. Steeped in verdant tropical gardens, accommodation includes tranquil, light, cosy and well-ventilated

rooms which open onto their own terraces, all with hammocks. Highly recommended.

$$-$ Jungle River Lodge
On Río Cangrejal overlooking Pico Bonito, T2440-1268, www.jungleriverlodge.com.
Private rooms and dorms, natural pools, restaurant and breathtaking views. Rafting, canopy tours, zip-wires, hiking and mountain biking tours available. Activities include a free night's accommodation. Take Yaruka bus from main bus terminal, get off at Km 7; a blue kayak marks the entrance on the river side of the road, call to arrange transport or join a tour.

$$-$ Omega Tours Jungle Lodge and Adventure Company
El Naranjo, T9631-0295, www.omegatours.info.
With wide range of options from simple rooms to comfortable *cabañas* and good food. Rafting and kayaking are available on the Río Cangrejal and trips to La Mosquitia (see page 135).

Río Zacate area

$$$$ The Lodge
Pico Bonito, 15 mins' drive west of La Ceiba, T2440-0388, T1-888-428-0221 (USA), www.picobonito.com.
Honduras' first world-class ecolodge at the base of Parque Nacional Pico Bonito. Luxury wooden cabins – with no TV, very peaceful – in 160 ha of grounds. There are forest trails, with lookout towers, natural swimming holes and waterfalls; nature guides and tours, very popular with birders; butterfly farm and serpentarium; swimming pool and gourmet restaurant. Highly recommended.

$ Natural View Ecotourism Center
In El Pino, T2386-9678.
Very rustic cabins with access to trails
in the vicinity. Cabins are built of adobe
walls and thatched room, with a private
bath, mosquito screens, but no power.
Set in the middle of a plant nursery with
a good restaurant on premises. Efraín
can help arrange several good trips
nearby including a boat trip down the
lower Río Zacate through mangroves
to a farm located next to the beach,
adjacent to Cuero y Salado.

$ Posada del Buen Pastor
T2950-3404.
Has 4 rustic rooms on the upper storey
of a private home with private bath,
cable TV and fan.

Cuero y Salado Wildlife Reserve

$ Refuge
T2443-0329, www.fucsa.blogspot.co.uk.
Fucsa's administration centre, on the
banks of the Río Salado. Has photos,
charts, maps, radio and a 2-room
visitor house, sleeping 4 in basic bunks,
electricity 1800-2100. There are no
mosquito nets, so avoid Sep and Oct
if you can. Don't wear open footwear
as snakes and yellow scorpions can be
found here. Food is available. There's also
tent space for camping at the refuge.
Book in advance.

Restaurants

La Ceiba

$$ Cafetería Cobel
*7 Calle between Av Atlántida and 14 de
Julio, 2 blocks from Parque Central.*
This could be the best *cafetería* in the
entire country; unmissable. Very popular
with locals, it's always crowded, and
serves good fresh food, with daily
specials. Highly recommended.

$$ El Guapo's
*Corner of 14 de Julio and 14 Calle. Open
daily for dinner.*
US-Honduran owned, good
combination of international and typical
Honduran cuisine.

$$ El Jardín de Susana
*Off Av Morazán and Calle 15, a bit
hidden, ask around.*
A new venture by Susana, the owner of
the locally revered Mango Tango (now
closed). They serve grilled fish, salads,
home-made breads, fresh fruit juices,
soups, pasta and other home-cooked
fare. As the name might suggest, it also
promises a pleasant garden setting. A bit
pricey for La Ceiba, but worth it.

$$ La Palapa
Av Víctor Hugo, next to Hotel Quinta Real.
Giant, palm-roofed, wood-beamed
palapa, serving juicy steaks, grills, fish,
seafood and burgers; also a sports
bar with half a dozen TV screens, and
serving ice-cold beer. Good value for
money though indifferent service.

$$ Ponderosa
*Av 14 de Julio, ½ a block from
Calle 17, www.restaurantela
ponderosalaceibahonduras.blogspot.
co.uk.*
A great rancho-style bar-restaurant with
authentic *comida típica*, rum and beer; all
served at plastic tables. They specialize
in grilled meats, all served with a side
of *frijoles* and fried *plátano*. Hearty
locals' joint with good prices, generous
portions and live music and dancing at
the weekends.

$$-$ Café Ki'Bok
4a Av, entre Calles 8a-9a.
This chilled-out bohemian café has a great stock of paperbacks to keep you entertained; take one, leave one behind. They serve coffee, cooked breakfasts and *comida típica*. Cosy, friendly and informal, with free Wi-Fi.

$ Expatriates Bar, Grill and Cigar Emporium
Final de Calle 12, above Refricón, 3 blocks south, 3 blocks east of Parque Central. Thu-Tue 1600-2400.
Honduran-American owners, very affordable food, including good steak and shrimps. Free internet. Also have a branch at the Cangrejal River, Km 9.

$ Paty's
Av 14 de Julio between 6 and 7 Calle.
Clean place offering milkshakes, wheatgerm, cereals, doughnuts, etc, and purified water. Opposite is an excellent pastry shop. There are 2 more **Paty's**, at 8 Calle E and the bus terminal.

Around La Ceiba

$$ Kabasa
Sambo Creek.
Seafood Garífuna-style, bar, in a delightful location.

$$ Paradise Found Bar and Grill
1 block past Sambo Creek bus stop, near Hotel Canadian, www. paradisefoundlaceiba.com.
A superb setting by the beach with an open-air veranda overlooking the waves. Offerings include massive hamburgers, homemade lasagne, brick-oven pizza, fresh seafood, and barbecue ribs, in addition to vegan and vegetarian options. You're in good hands as the chef is Italian.

La Ceiba
15-28 May San Isidro La Ceiba's patron saint's celebrations continue for 2 weeks, the highlight being the international carnival on the 3rd Sat in May, when La Ceiba parties long and hard to the Afro-Caribbean beat of *punta* rock.

Shopping

La Ceiba
Carrion Department Store (Av San Isidro with 7A Calle). **Deli Mart** late-night corner store on 14 de Julio, round the corner from the internet café, shuts at 2300. **El Regalito**, good-quality souvenirs at reasonable prices in small passage by large Carrión store. **T Boot**, store for hiking boots, Calle 1, east of Av San Isidro, T2443-2499. **Supermarket Super Ceibena** (2 on Av 14 de Julio and 6A Calle).

What to do

La Ceiba
Adventure tourism
Hiking, kayaking and whitewater rafting are all popular and many tour operators also maintain jungle lodges (see Where to stay, above). Ask around to find a tour that suits your needs and to verify credentials.
La Moskitia Eco Aventuras, *Av 14 de Julio at Parque Manuel Bonilla, T2442-0104, www.lamoskitia.hn.* Eco-adventure tours, run by Jorge Salaverri, an extremely knowledgeable nature guide, who is enthusiastic and flexible. Specializes in trips to Mosquitia, including week-long expeditions to Las Marias and hikes up Pico Baltimore and Pico Dama. Highly recommended.

Omega Tours, *T2440-0334, www.omega tours.info*. Runs rafting and kayaking trips on the Río Cangrejal, jungle hikes, and own hotel 30 mins upstream. Also tours to La Mosquitia ranging from easy adventure tours of 4 days to up to 13-day expeditions. Prices drop dramatically with more than 2 people.

Canopy tours

There are 2 modest canopy tours in La Ceiba, one in Pico Bonito National Park, US$40 per person; the other in Sambo Creek Spa, US$45 per person (see Spas below). Any tour operator in La Ceiba should be able to organize tickets and transport.

Diving

Pirate Islands Divers, *T3228-0009, www.pirateislandsdivers.com*. Pirate Islands Divers specializes in Cayos Cochinos diving with trips leaving Sambo Creek every day at 0700, weather permitting. They also offer PADI certification, from Open Water to Dive Master.

Language schools

It's best to do some research and look at the options. The following are worth considering:
Central America Spanish School, Av San Isidro No 110, Calle 12 y 13, next to Foto Indio, T2440-1707, www.ca-spanish.com. US$150 for the week, homestay also an option adding US$70, also have branches on Utila and Roatan.
Centro Internacional de Idiomas, T2440-1557, www.honduras spanish.com. Provides a range of classes 5 days for US$150, with hotel option US$290, with branches in Utila and Roatán.

Spas

Sambo Creek Canopy Tour and Spa, *main highway, 500 m east of the turn-off for Hotel Canadien, T3355-6481*. Services include a mud bath, massage and mineral-rich hot springs, all in a beautiful natural setting. Entrance US$25. Recommended.

Tour operators

Garífuna Tours, *Av San Isidro 1 Calle, T2440-3252, www.garifunatours.com*. Day trips into Pico Bonito National Park (US$34 per person), Cuero y Salado (US$49), rafting on the Cangrejal (US$34), trips out to Cayos Cochinos (US$49) and a shuttle service to Tela (US$1).
Reservaciones La Ceiba, *Col El Sauce, 4th floor, Block W, House 3, T2443-6536, www.reservacioneslaceiba.com*. A community-led tour operator, sustainable, co-operative and ecologically aware. They offer a broad range of natural and cultural tours including hiking in Pico Bonito, wildlife observation, visits to fincas, community tourism and rafting. Recommended.
Tourist Options, *Av La República, T9982-7534, www.hondurastouristoptions.com*. A wide range of regional and national tours, including birding trips, tours of Copán, Roatán, Cuero y Saldo Wildlife reserve and the Cayos Cochinos.

Cuero y Salado Wildlife Reserve

Although it is possible to go to the Salado and hire a villager and his boat, a qualified guide will show you much more. It is essential to bring a hat and sun lotion with you. Travel agencies in La Ceiba run tours there, but **Fucsa** arranges visits and owns the only accommodation in the reserve. Before going, check with **Fucsa** in La Ceiba. Although the office only has basic information, the people are helpful and there are displays and books about the flora and fauna to be found in the park. A guide and kayak for a 1-hr trip costs about US$10. Boatmen charge about US$20 for a 2-hr trip or US$40 for 5 hrs (6-7 persons maximum), US$6-7 for the guide.

Transport

Air For La Mosquitia see page 140.

Aeropuerto Internacional Golosón (LCE) is 10 km out of town. See Getting there, page 153, for international services. For details of flights to Bay Islands, see page 93. One-way fares to Roatán start at around US$50. At weekends there are some charter flights that may be better than scheduled flights. Taxi to town US$8 per person or walk 200 m to the main road and share for US$2 with other passengers, also buses from bus station near Cric Cric Burger at end 3 Av, US$0.15. Intercity buses pass by the entrance.

Boat Ferry schedules from the Muelle de Cabotaje as follows: Services to/from Utila with the Utila Princess, T2408-5163, www.utilaprincess.com, **La Ceiba–Utila** 0930 and 1600; **Utila–La Ceiba**, 0620 and 1400, US$25. Services to/from Roatán with Roatán Ferry, T2445-1795, www.roatanferry.com, **La Ceiba–Roatán**, 0930 and 1630, **Roatán–La Ceiba**, 0700 and 1400, US$31 regular class, US$36 first class. It is too far to walk to the pier, about 15-min taxi ride from town, US$2-3 per person if sharing with

4 people, buses available from centre of town.

Trips to the **Hog Islands** can be arranged, call T441-5987 or through **Garífuna Tours** (see What to do, page 114), US$65 for a boat load.

Bus Taxis from centre to bus terminal, which is a little way west of town (follow Blv 15 de Septiembre), cost US$1 per person, or there are buses from Parque Central. Most buses leave from here. **Traliasa**, **Etrusca** and **Cristina** bus service to **Tegucigalpa** via Tela several daily, US$6, avoiding San Pedro Sula (US$1 to Tela, 2 hrs); also hourly service to **San Pedro Sula**, US$2 (3-4 hrs). **Empresa Tupsa** direct to **San Pedro Sula** almost hourly from 0530 until 1800. Also 1st class with **Hedman Alas** – take taxi to separate terminal. To **Trujillo**, 3 hrs direct, 4½ hrs local (very slow), every 1½ hrs or so, US$3; daily bus La Ceiba– Trujillo–Santa Rosa de Aguán. To **Olanchito**, US$1, 3 hrs; also regular buses to **Sonaguera**, **Tocoa**, **Balfate**, **Isletas**, **San Esteban** and other regional locations.

Car Car rental Dino's Rent-a-Car, Hotel Partenon Beach, T2443-0404. **Maya Rent-a-Car**, Hotel La Quinta, T2443-3071. **Molinari** in Hotel París on Parque Central, T2443-0055.

Beaches around La Ceiba

Bus To **Nueva Armenia** from La Ceiba at 1100, US$0.75, 2½ hrs. At the bus stop is the office where boat trips are arranged to **Cayos Cochinos**, US$10, trips start at 0700.

★Once a major port and the former capital, Trujillo sits on the southern shore of the palm-fringed Bay of Trujillo. It is a quiet, pleasant town with clean beaches nearby and calm water that is ideal for swimming.

Christopher Columbus landed close to the area on his fourth voyage to the Americas and the town was later founded in 1525 by Juan de Medina, making it the oldest town in Honduras. Hernán Cortés arrived here after his famous march overland from Yucatán in pursuit of his usurping lieutenant, Olid. Filibuster William Walker was shot near here in 1860; a commemorative stone marks the spot in the rear garden of the hospital, one block east of the Parque Central, and the old cemetery (near Hotel Trujillo) is his final resting place.

Fortaleza Santa Bárbara ⓘ *US$1*, a ruined Spanish fortress overlooking the bay, is worth a visit. Most of the relics found there have been moved to the museum of Rufino Galán, but there are still a few rusty muskets and cannon balls. Twenty minutes' walk from Trujillo plaza is the **Museo y Piscina Rufino Galán Cáceres** ⓘ *US$1, US$0.50 to swim*, which has a swimming pool filled from the Río Cristales with changing rooms and picnic facilities. Close by, the wreckage of a US C-80 aircraft that crashed in 1985 forms part of Sr Galán's museum. The rest of the collection is a mass of curios, some very interesting. The cemetery is rather overgrown, with collapsed and open tombs, but it does give a feel of the origins of early residents. The **Fiesta de San Juan Bautista** is in June, with participation from surrounding Garífuna settlements.

West of Trujillo, just past the football field on the Santa Fe road, is the **Río Grande**, which has lovely pools and waterfalls for river bathing, best during the rainy season. Take the path on the far side of river, after about 10 minutes cut down to the rocks and follow the river upstream along the boulders.

Beaches

Good beaches are found both on the peninsula and around Trujillo Bay. Before setting out ask which beaches are safe. Take a bus from near the Parque Central towards Puerto Castilla and ask the driver to let you off at the path about 1 km beyond the bridge over the lagoon. Other beaches around Puerto Castilla are separated by mangroves, are littered and have sandflies. The beaches in town tend to be less clean. If you're tempted to walk to find a cleaner stretch of sand don't walk alone; tourists here have been assaulted and robbed.

West of Trujillo

There are interesting Garífuna villages west of Trujillo. The road is rough, often impassable in wet weather, and jeeps are needed even in the dry season. **Santa Fe**, 10 km west of Trujillo, is a friendly place with several good Garífuna restaurants; for example, **Comedor Caballero** and **Las Brisas de Santa Fe**, on the endless white sandy beach. The bus service continues to **San Antonio** (with a good restaurant behind the beach) and **Guadalupe**. Walk in the morning along the beach to Santa Fe and then get a bus back to Trujillo, taking plenty of water and sun block. This stretch of beach is outstanding, but watch out for *marea roja*, a sea organism that colours the water pink and can give irritating skin rashes to bathers. Also, be warned, local people consider this walk unsafe. It's best to go in a large group.

Santa Rosa de Aguán

One of the largest Garífuna communities, Santa Rosa de Aguán is an interesting coastal town, some 40 km east of Trujillo, with 7000 hospitable English- and Spanish-speaking inhabitants. The spreading settlement lies at the mouth of the Río Aguán, the greater part on the east of the bay. A white-sand beach stretches all the way to Limón, and the thundering surf is an impressive sight. Take drinking water, insect repellent, mosquito coils and high-factor sun screen.

If driving from Trujillo, turn left at Km 343, 20 km along the highway, where a good gravel road runs another 20 km to Santa Rosa. From where the road ends at the west bank, take a canoe ferry across to the east side.

Parque Nacional Capiro y Calentura

The Parque Nacional Capiro y Calentura encompasses these two mountains over looking Trujillo. The four- to six-hour walk to the summit gives spectacular views and on a clear day Isla Roatán can be seen in the distance. The walk is best done early in the morning when the forest is alive with the sounds of birds, monkeys and other wildlife. The path can be reached by walking (or taking a taxi) up the hill past the **Villa Brinkley Hotel**. The road to the summit is in poor condition from the entrance of the park and can only be driven in a 4WD. Insect repellent is needed if you pause. As with all walks in this area, it's safest to go in a group. The park is run by the **Fundación Capiro Calentura Guaimoreto (FUCAGUA)** ① *Parque Central, T434-429, Trujillo, open Mon-Fri*. They have information on all the reserves in the area and also on hiking and tours. Until a new office is built in the park, entry tickets must be bought here before going to Capiro y Calentura. They are opening up trails, improving old ones and organizing guided tours through parts of the forest. The hike along the Sendero de la Culebrina uses the remnants of a colonial stone road used to transport gold from the mines in the Valle de Aguán. Halfway up the **Cerro de las Cuevas**, 7 km beyond Cuyamel, are impressive caves showing traces of occupation by pre-Columbian Pech people.

Refugio de Vida Silvestre Laguna de Guaimoreto (RVSLG)

FUCAGUA, see above, also administers the Refugio de Vida Silvestre, Laguna de Guaimoreto (RVSLG), northeast of Trujillo, where there is a bird island (Isla de los Pájaros), monkeys and good fishing. To visit, either arrange a trip with Fucagua, a tour agency such as Turtle Tours, or take a bus from Trujillo towards Puerto Castilla, get off just after the bridge which crosses the lagoon, then walk away from the lagoon for about 200 m to a dirt track on the left. Follow this and cross a low bridge and on the left is the house of a man who rents dug-out canoes. The Isla de los Pájaros is about 3 km up the lagoon, a bit too far for a dug-out. Another alternative is to go down to the wharf and hire out a motorized canoe or launch (price depends on the number of passengers and length of trip). There are no roads, paths or facilities in the area.

Where to stay

$$$ Tranquility Bay Beach Retreat
5 km west of Trujillo next to the Campa Vista development, T9928-2095, www.tranquilitybayhonduras.com.
Managed by Larry and Linda from Vancouver, Tranquility Bay Beach Retreat is as relaxing as it promises to be. Their 5 *cabañas* are spacious and well-ventilated, have tropical views and sea breezes, and each one has a hammock too. The grounds are tidy, green and well-groomed.

$$$-$$ Christopher Columbus Beach Resort
Outside town along the beach, drive across airstrip, T2434-4966.
Has 72 rooms and suites, a/c, cable TV, pool, restaurant, watersports, tennis; it's painted bright turquoise.

$$ Hotel Casa Alemania
Barrio Río Negro, 20 mins from the centre of Trujillo, T2434-4466.
Managed by Gunter and Paula, this pleasant and hospitable B&B is a great place to chill out, especially in the bar in the evenings. Rooms are clean, cool, and comfortable. Good food and company.

$$ Hotel y Restaurante Campamento
4 km west of Trujillo on the road to Santa Fe.
This family-owned hotel-farm by the beach is a cosy, affordable, low-key spot and there are lots of nice animals on the property. Accommodation includes simple but well-kitted *cabañas*. A great local option, very welcoming and hospitable.

$$ O'Glynn
3 blocks south of the plaza, T2434-4592.
Smart, clean place, with good rooms and bathrooms, a/c, TV and fridge in some rooms. Highly recommended.

$ Mar de Plata
Up street west, T2434-4174.
Upstairs rooms are best, with a beautiful view, bath and fan. Friendly and helpful staff.

Restaurants

Don't miss the coconut bread, a speciality of the Garífuna.

$$ Chico's Place
On the beach.
Friendly and fun, Chico's Place is a typical open-air Caribbean beach restaurant with a thatched roof and ocean views. They serve whole fish and Salva Vida beer, so you can't go wrong. Take a walk through town to get there.

$$ El Delfín
On the beach.
Another good beachside option, El Delfín is a 3-storey structure that catches cool ocean breezes. They serve good chicken and seafood, including grilled shrimp, lobster and fish with a butter sauce.

$$ Oasis
Opposite HSBC.

Canadian-owned restaurant and bar serving good food with outdoor seating. A good meeting place, with an information board, local tours, English books for sale and a book exchange.

$ Bahía Bar
T2434-4770, on the beach by the landing strip next to Christopher Columbus.
Popular with expats, also Hondurans at weekends, serving vegetarian food. Also has showers and toilets.

Cafés

Ares Coffee
On the road to the beach, next to the national police just of the Parque Central, www.arescoffee.com.
A local coffee franchise with good strong brews, a/c and free Wi-Fi.

Head to **Rincón de los Amigos** or **Rogue's** if you're looking for drink at the end of the day. Also try the **Gringo Bar** and **Bahía Bar**. In **Barrio Cristales** at weekends there's *punta* music and lively atmosphere. Recommended.

The cinema shows current US releases (most in English with subtitles).

Garí-Arte Souvenir, *T2434-4207, daily.* In the centre of Barrio Cristales, is recommended for authentic Garífuna souvenirs. Owned by Ricardo Lacayo. **Tienda Souvenir Artesanía**, *next to Hotel Emperador*. Handicrafts, hand-painted toys. 3 supermarkets in the town centre.

Boat Cargo boats leave for **Mosquitia** (ask all captains at the dock, wait up to 3 days, see page 135), the **Bay Islands** (very difficult) and Honduran ports to the west. Ask at the jetty. The trip to **Puerta Lempira** costs about US$15.

Bus Trujillo can be reached by bus from **San Pedro Sula**, **Tela** and **La Ceiba** by a paved road through Savá, Tocoa and Corocito. From **La Ceiba** it is 3 hrs by direct bus, 4 hrs by local. 3 direct **Cotraibal** buses in early morning from Trujillo. Bus from **Tegucigalpa** (Comayagüela) with **Cotraibal**, 7 Av between 10 and 11 Calle, US$6, 9 hrs; some buses to the capital go via La Unión, which is not as safe a route as via San Pedro Sula. To **San Pedro Sula**, 5 daily 0200-0800, US$5. Public transport also to **San Esteban** and **Juticalpa** (leave from in front of church at 0400, but check locally, arriving 1130, US$5.20). Bus to **Santa Fe** at 0930, US$0.40, leaves from outside **Glenny's Super Tienda**. To **Santa Rosa de Aguán** and **Limón** daily.

El Progreso, an important but unattractive agricultural and commercial centre on the Río Ulúa, is 30 minutes' drive on the paved highway southeast of San Pedro Sula, en route to Tela. While most people make straight for the coast at Tela, heading east from El Progreso leads through mountain scenery up to the small town of Yoro, beyond to Olanchito and a link to La Ceiba. With everyone else rushing to the Bay Islands, you could well have the place to yourself.

Parque Nacional Pico Pijol
This park protects the 2282-m summit of primary cloudforest that is home to many quetzales. It is 32 km from the town of **Morazán** in the Yoro Department, which is 41 km from Progreso (bus from Progreso or Santa Rita). In Morazán are **Hospedaje El Corazón Sagrado**, several restaurants and a disco. The lower slopes of Pico Pijol have been heavily farmed. Access by vehicle is possible as far as Subirana. A guide is needed from there to a large cave nearby; access is difficult. Another trail to the summit (2282 m) starts at **Nueva Esperanza** village (bus from Morazán, Parque Central); ask for the correct trail. The first day is tough, all uphill with no shade; the second is tougher and requires a lot of clearing. Take a compass and topographical map. Also in the park is the waterfall at **Las Piratas** (bus Morazán–Los Murillos and then walk to El Ocotillo; ask for Las Piratas).

Yoro and around
The paved highway to the prosperous little town of Yoro passes through pleasant countryside surrounded by mountains and dotted with ranches and farms. The **Parque Nacional Montaña de Yoro** is 8 km to the southeast (access from Marale), comprising 257 sq km of cloudforest, home to the Tolupanes people, also known as Xicaques. The **Asociación Ecológica Amigos de la Montaña de Yoro** has an office in the Parque Central in Yoro. From Yoro a dirt road continues to **Olanchito** via **Jocón**, through attractive country as the road snakes along the pine-forested slopes of Montaña Piedra Blanca and Montaña de la Bellota, with fine views of the surrounding valleys and distant mountain ranges.

Listings El Progreso and east

Where to stay

Yoro and around

$ Aníbal
Corner of Parque Central, Yoro.
Excellent value and clean, pleasant rooms with private or shared bath and a wide balcony. There's also a restaurant.

$ Nelson
Yoro.
Comfortable rooms with bath, fan, modern, good restaurant/bar and good

outdoor swimming pool on 3rd floor, bar/disco on roof with marvellous views. Warmly recommended.

$ Valle Aguán y Chabelito
1 block north of Parque Central, Olanchito, T2446-6718 (same management as Hotel Olanchito).

Single rooms with a/c, doubles with fan, all rooms with cable TV. The best in town, with the best restaurant.

Transport

Yoro and around
Bus
Hourly bus service to **El Progreso**, several daily to **Sulaco**.

Tegucigalpa to the Mosquitia coast

a remote wilderness

Accessible only by air or sea, the Mosquitia coast is a vast expanse of rivers and swamps, coastal lagoons and tropical forests filled with wildlife but with few people.

From February to May you can taste the *vino de coyol*, which is extracted from a palm (a hole is made at the top of the trunk and the sap that flows out is drunk neat). With sugar added it ferments and becomes alcoholic (*chichi*); it is so strong it is called *patada de burro* (mule kick).

The Carretera de Olancho runs from the capital northeast to the Caribbean coast. It passes through Guaimaca and San Diego, Campamento, 127 km, a small, friendly village (with a few basic *hospedajes*) surrounded by pine forests, and on to the Río Guayape, 143 km.

By the river crossing at **Los Limones** is an unpaved road north to **La Unión** (56 km), deep in the northern moutains passing through beautiful forests and lush green countryside. To the north is the **Refugio de Vida Silvestre La Muralla-Los Higuerales** ⓘ *US$1*, where quetzales and emerald toucanettes can be seen between March and May in the cloud forest. For those that have made the effort to get to this spot, if you're camping you may experience the frissonic pleasure of jaguars 'screaming' during the night. The park comprises the three peaks of **La Muralla**, 1981 m, **Las Parras**, 2064 m, and **Los Higuerales**, 1985 m. Cohdefor has an office on the main plaza for information, closed weekends. You are now required to take a guide with you on the trail. Cost is US$4, arrange in La Unión. Four trails range from 1-10 km and are recommended. There are two campsites in the forest (contact Cohdefor on T2222-1027 for prior arrangements), or there is accommodation for one or two at the visitor centre.

Juticalpa
The main road continues another 50 km from Los Limones to Juticalpa (altitude 420 m), the capital of Olancho department, in a rich agricultural area for herding cattle and growing cereals and sugar cane. There is a paved road northeast through the cattle land of Catacamas, continuing to just beyond Dulce Nombre de Culmí.

Catacamas and around

Catacamas (altitude 400 m) lies at the foot of Agalta mountain in the Río Guayape valley in the Department of Olancho, 210 km from Tegucigalpa. The Río Guayape (named after an indigenous dress, *guayapis*) is famous for its gold nuggets.

The town was established by the Spaniards and the colonial church dates from the early 18th century. It is an agricultural and cattle-raising district. The National School of Agriculture (ENA) is based here; ask if you wish to visit their agricultural demonstration plots in the Guayape valley, 5 km south of the town.

Hiking in the mountains behind Catacamas is beautiful. From Murmullo there are trails to coffee farms. **Río Talgua**, 4 km east of Catacamas, is interesting with caves in which significant pre-Columbian remains have been found. The area and caves are worth a visit. Hiking to **El Boquerón**, stop off at the main road near Punuare, 17 km west of Catacamas, and walk up **Río Olancho**, which has nice limestone cliffs and a pretty river canyon. Through much of the canyon the stream flows underground.

Beyond Catacamas, a rough road continues northeast up the Río Tinto Valley to **Dulce Nombre de Culmí**. Further on is **Paya** where the road becomes a mule track but, in three to four days in the dry season, a route can be made over the divide (Cerro de Will) and down the Río Paulaya to Mosquitia (see below). Local police say that there is a path in the dry season from Dulce Nombre to San Esteban (about 30 km).

Juticalpa to Trujillo

There is a fine scenic road from Juticalpa to Trujillo. From Juticalpa head northeast and turn left where the paved road ends, to **San Francisco de la Paz**. Beyond San Francisco is **Gualaco**, which has an interesting colonial church (there are several places to stay; see Where to stay, below).

The town of **San Esteban** is 23 km from Gualaco. On the way you pass Agalta mountain, and some of the highest points in Honduras, as well as several waterfalls on the Río Babilonia.

After San Esteban the road continues to **Bonito Oriental** (via El Carbón, a mahogany collection point with the Paya communities in the vicinity). There are four hotels here. The final 38 km from Bonito Oriental to Trujillo are paved, through Corocito. There are many dirt roads between San Francisco and Trujillo. If driving, ask directions if in any doubt. Fuel is available in the larger villages but there is none between San Esteban and Bonito Oriental.

Parque Nacional Sierra de Agalta

Between the roads Juticalpa–Gualaco–San Esteban and Juticalpa–Catacamas–Dulce Nombre de Culmí lies the cloudforest of the Parque Nacional Sierra de Agalta, extending over 1200 ha and reaching a height of 2590 m at **Monte de Babilonia**, a massif with a number of interesting mountains. Several different ecosystems have been found with a wide variety of fauna and flora: 200 species of bird have been identified so far. There are several points of entry. Contact **Cohdefor** in Juticalpa, Culmí, Gualaco, San Esteban or Catacamas for information on access, maps, guides, mules and lodging. There is no infrastructure in the park, but a base camp is being built. A good trail leads to **La Picucha** mountain (2354 m). Access is from El Pacayal, 750 m, a short distance towards San Esteban from Gualaco (bus at 0700 which goes on to Tocoa). There are two campsites on the trail; the first at 1060 m is just short of **La Chorrera** waterfall, which has a colony of white-collared swifts that nest in the cave behind the falls. Four to six hours' walk above is the second campsite at 1900 m. The final section is mainly dwarf forest with low undergrowth on the summit. There is much wildlife to be seen and a good viewpoint 1 km beyond at the site of two abandoned radio towers. Hiking time is two days.

Listings Tegucigalpa to the northeast coast

Where to stay

$ Hospedaje San Carlos
La Unión.
Serves good vegetarian food.

$ Hotel
On plaza, Guaimaca, above restaurant Las Cascadas.
Good value, clean rooms, and friendly staff.

Juticalpa

$ El Paso
1 Av NE y 6 Calle NO, 6 blocks south of Parque (on way to highway), T2885-2311.
Quiet place offering clean rooms with bath and fan. Laundry facilities. Highly recommended.

$ Familiar
1 Calle NO between Parque and Antúñez.
Basic but clean rooms with bath. Recommended.

Catacamas and around

$ Juan Carlos
Barrio José Trinidad Reyes, T2899-4212.
Good restaurant. Recommended.

$ La Colina
T2899-4488.
Rooms with bath, hot water, fan and TV. Parking.

Juticalpa to Trujillo

$ Calle Real
Gualaco, near Parque Central.
Friendly place with basic rooms, will store luggage.

$ Centro
San Esteban.
The best place to stay, with spotless rooms and run by a nice family.

Restaurants

Juticalpa

$ Casa Blanca
1 Calle SE.
Quite a smart restaurant with a good cheap menu; try the paella.

$ El Rancho
2 Av NE.
Pleasant place which specializes in meat dishes and has lots of choice on its menu.

Cafés

La Galera
2 Av NE.
Specializes in *pinchos*.

Tropical Juices
Blv de los Poetas.
Good fruit juices.

Catacamas and around
In **Dulce Nombre de Culmí**, there are
several *comedores* on the main plaza.

$ As de Oro
Catacamas.
Good beef dishes, served in Wild West–
style surroundings.

$ Continental
Catacamas.
Chicken dishes and pizza, which you can
wash down with a US beer.

Juticalpa to Trujillo
There are 3 nice *comedores* in **San
Esteban** near the Hotel San Esteban.

Bars and clubs

Catacamas and around
Fernandos and Extasis Montefresco
are bars outside town towards
Tegucigalpa, with pool (US$1.20) and live
music 2 evenings a week.

Entertainment

Catacamas and around
Cine Maya, Barrio El Centro, cinema.

Shopping

Juticalpa
From 0600 on Sat, the market in Parque
Central has a good selection of food,
fruit, vegetables and souvenirs, said to
be the best outdoor market in Olancho.

Transport

Bus From **Comayagüela** to La Unión,
daily, take 4 hrs. To get to the park, hire
a truck from La Unión for about US$18.
There's little traffic so it's difficult to
hitchhike. If driving from **San Pedro
Sula**, take the road east through Yoro
and Mangulile; from **La Ceiba**, take the
Savá– Olanchito road and turn south 13
km before Olanchito.

Juticalpa
Bus Bus station is on 1 Av NE, 1 km
southeast of Parque Central, taxis
US$0.50. Hourly to **Tegucigalpa** from
0330 to 1800; to **San Esteban** from
opposite Aurora bus terminal at 0800,
6 hrs, US$2.25. To **Trujillo** 0400, 9 hrs,
US$5.20. To **Tocoa** at 0500.

Catcamas and around
Bus From **Tegucigalpa** to Juticalpa/
Catacamas, **Empresa Aurora**, 8 Calle
6-7 Av, Comayagüela, T237-3647, hourly
0400-1700, 3¼ hrs, US$2 to Juticalpa, 4
hrs US$2.75 to Catacamas. **Juticalpa**–
Catacamas, 40 mins, US$0.60. To **Dulce
Nombre de Culmí** (see above), 3 hrs,
US$1.35, several daily.

Juticalpa to Trujillo
Bus To Juticalpa and to the north coast
(Tocoa and Trujillo) buses are fairly
frequent.

★Forested, swampy and almost uninhabited, Mosquitia is well worth visiting if you have the time and energy. In the the Central American Little Amazon, you can hope to see rainforest wildlife including monkeys and incredible birdlife as you drift through the varied habitat that includes lowland tropical rainforest, coastal lagoons, undisturbed beaches, mangroves, grasslands and patches of pine savannah. Home to members of the Miskito and Pech tribes as well as the Garífuna ethnic group who live in small communities on the coast and along the major rivers. The Río Plátano Biosphere Reserve, a UNESCO World Heritage Site, covers an area over 5200 sq km, one of the largest protected areas in Central America.

Coastal villages

A narrow strand of land divides the inland waterway and Ibans lagoon from the Caribbean. Along this pleasant setting lie a number of small native villages starting with the Garífuna village of Plaplaya and continuing through the Miskito villages of Ibans, Cocobila, Raistá, Belén, Nueva Jerusalem and Kuri. Trails connect all of these villages making exploration easy with vast expanses of unspoiled, white-sand beaches providing an easy route for getting from place to place, with the sea providing a wonderful way to cool off during the heat of the day.

Apart from generally relaxing in the slow-paced life along the coast there are several interesting things to do in the area. In **Plaplaya**, a community-run Sea Turtle Project aims to protect the leatherback and loggerhead turtles that nest along the coast. Each night during the breeding season (March-June) members of the village patrol the beaches to find nesting turtles, carefully gathering the eggs and re-burying them in a guarded area where they are watched over until they hatch. The newborn turtles are then released into the sea. Visitors can accompany the beach patrols for a small donation to the program. There are two traditional dance groups in Plaplaya that can provide an interesting evening's entertainment for visitors.

The Miskito village of **Kuri**, 1½ hours along the beach from Belén, is worth a visit. Here the traditional wooden and thatch houses sit behind the beach, sheltered from the sea breezes by the 'Beach Grape' and palm trees along the sand dunes.

Reserva de la Biósfera Río Plátano

The reserve was established by the Honduran government in 1980 to protect the outstanding natural and cultural resources of the Río Plátano valley and its environs. In 1982 UNESCO declared the reserve a World Heritage Site. The tropical jungles here shelter a number of endangered birds, mammals and fish, among them **scarlet macaws** and **harpy eagles**, **jaguars** and **tapirs**, and the **cuyamel**, a prized food fish fast becoming extinct throughout

Tip...
Several commercial guides organize trips into the Río Plátano Biosphere Reserve and may be a good option for those with limited Spanish.

Essential La Mosquitia

Access

While certainly a challenging environment, many backpackers visit the reserve either alone or with professional guides. For those travelling alone, as long as you have basic Spanish and are a reasonably confident traveller this is the cheapest option.

Tourist information

Mosquitia Pawisa (MOPAWI), head office in Puerto Lempira, T898-7460, www.mopawi.org, another office in Tegucigalpa, Residencias Tres Caminos 4b, lote 67, T235-8659, plus offices in several other villages, is the best source of information about the indigenous communities in Mosquitia. It is a non-profit-making, non-sectarian organization dedicated to the development of the region and the conservation of the biodiversity of its flora and fauna; volunteer opportunities are available.

MOPAWI is concerned with the protection of natural and human resources throughout Mosquitia and the Department of Gracias a Dios. Among its programmes is the conservation of marine turtles and the green iguana. The Reserva Biósfera Río Plátano (525,100 ha) with the Reserva Antropólogica Tawahka, the Reserva Nacional Patuca and together with Mosquitia Nicaragüense, constitute one of the largest forest reserves north of the Amazon.

What to take

It's a tough environment and you should go prepared. Take a mosquito net and repellent, clothing for rain and also for cooler temperatures at night, good walking shoes and a first aid kit. Also enough cash in small denominations for your stay (there are no banks in the area) and plastic bags to keep things dry.

Medical services

Alas de Socorro operates from Ahuas to collect sick people from villages to take them to Ahuas hospital. Contact the Moravian church (in Puerto Lempira Reverend Stanley Goff, otherwise local pastors will help).

When to go

With access by air, sea and road, you can visit any time of the year but it is usually best to avoid the heavy rains from November to January. The driest months are March to May and August to October.

Honduras. In addition, there are a number of **archaeological sites** about which little is known, although archaeologists finally managed to locate the fabled lost White City of the Maya in 2015, hidden in an isolated valley, in an undisclosed location, deep in the thick jungles of the Plátano headwaters.

The Miskito and the Pech living along the lower Plátano cultivate yuca, bananas, rice, corn and beans, and also feed themselves by hunting and fishing. The upper (southern) portion of the Plátano watershed is being quickly populated by mestizo immigrants from the poverty-stricken south of Honduras. These new settlers are cutting down the forest to plant crops and raise cattle, hunting wildlife mercilessly and dynamite-fishing. The government's intention officially to allow settlers into the Sico and Paulaya valleys, on the western edge of the reserve, was roundly criticized. It was feared that the agrarian reform programme would lead to the desertification of the Río Plátano. Added to the damage being done by the settlers, there are now disturbing reports that drug smugglers are cutting landing strips deep in the jungle. Given the pressure the reserve is under, it is recommended to visit it sooner rather than later.

Along the Río Plátano

For those in search of a little more rugged adventure you should find a boat to take you up the Río Plátano to Las Marías, a small Miskito and Pech village that is the last outpost of civilization in this part of the reserve. Local boatman are trying to organize themselves with a view to regulating minimum standards, a fair price for the passage and a rotation system to ensure the work is shared more evenly between them.

Most people stay the night in Raistá before and after visiting Las Marías. Fuel is very expensive in La Mosquitia and this is reflected in the high cost of transportation. The ride to Las Marías costs about US$130 so put together a group of four or five people to share the cost. That price should get you a boat and boatman for three days to take you on the round trip (four to six hours each way) from the coast with a day in Las Marías to look around. If you stay longer you should negotiate a fair price with the boatman to cover his extra time. Bring food and water for the trip as well as other jungle gear. The journey upstream to Las Marías, although beautiful, can become very tedious and uncomfortable. Birdwatching can provide a diversion; there are three species of toucan as well as several species of parrot, tanagers, herons, kingfishers, vultures, hawk eagles and oropendolas. If you are lucky you might see crocodiles, turtles or iguanas. On arrival in Las Marías, arrange return at once.

An alternative route to Las Marías is by boat across Ibans Lagoon, 45 minutes by tuk-tuk, then 6½ hours' walk through jungle (rough path, hot, mosquitoes, take lots of water and insect repellent, and wear good hiking boots). This is only recommended for fit walkers in drier weather. Expect to pay around US$30 for the guide, and if returning from Las Marías by boat you'll probably still have to pay the return fare even if you're only travelling one way.

Las Marías

This Miskito-Pech village is the furthest limit of upstream settlement. Once in Las Marías you're normally met by a member of the *saca guía*, a representative of the Las Marías Ecotourism Committee who will let you know what trips are available in the area and help make arrangements on a rotation system that shares the work among the community. This group was set up with the help of MOPAWI and Peace Corps with the aim of developing and coordinating a system of ecotourism that benefits the local people, protects the reserve and also offers extraordinary experiences to tourists. A number of guides have been trained in Las Marías to deal with international visitors. They are coordinated by the Committee, have a set price structure with prices and rules posted on the walls of all the *hospedajes*.

Typical guided trips include day hiking on trails around the village, a three-day hike to scenic **Pico Dama** (very strenuous), a day trip by *pipante* upriver to see the **petroglyphs** at **Walpulbansirpi** left by the ancestors of the Pech or multi-day trips upriver to visit other petroglyph sites and view wildlife in the heart of the reserve. Note that it's harder to advance upriver during the rainy season from June to December.

Brus Laguna

It is a 15-minute scenic flight from Puerto Lempira (see below) above Caratasca Lagoon and grassy, pine-covered savannahs to **Ahuas**, one-hour walk from the Patuca River (fabled for gold). There is a hospital here, four missions, some basic accommodation and a generally improving atmosphere. Irregular *cayucos* sail down to Brus Laguna for US$2.50, at the mouth of the Río Patuca, or US$12.50 (15 minutes) scenic flight in the mission plane. The airstrip is 4 km from the village; take a lift for US$1. There is a disco at the riverside to the left of the bridge. The village is plagued by mosquitoes throughout summer and autumn.

Puerto Lempira

Puerto Lempira is on the large Caratasca Lagoon. The main office of MOPAWI (see page 136) is here. The airstrip is only five minutes' walk from town. Regular tuk-tuks (motorized canoes) cross the lagoon to **Kaukira**, US$1.20 (a nice place, but there's nothing there), **Yagurabila** and **Palkaka**. The tuk-tuks leave Kaukira daily except Sunday at 0500, returning during the morning. In the afternoon the lagoon is usually too rough to cross.

Inland by road from Puerto Lempira are **Mocorón** and **Rus Rus**, which may be visited with difficulty (there is no public transport but any vehicle will give a lift) and is a beautiful, quiet village (accommodation at Friends of America hospital's house; meals from Capi's next door, ask Friends about transport out). A branch off this road leads southeast to **Leimus** on the Río Coco and the border with Nicaragua. Ask for Evaristo López (at whose house you can get breakfast) who can arrange transport to Leimus, most days, three to four hours for about US$3.50. He is also knowledgeable about area safety.

The road continues south to the small town of **Ahuashbila** on the upper river of the Río Coco, which marks the border with Nicaragua.

Where to stay

Coastal villages
Plaplaya

$ Basilia
15 mins west of centre.
Traditional and the cheapest.

$ Doña Sede
East of village centre.
Good meals.

Raistá and Belén
Choose between **Eddie and Elma Bodden** ($) on the lagoon and **Doña Cecilia Bodden** ($), just up from the lagoon towards the sea. Try the food at **Elma's Kitchen** ($) in Raistá, thought by some to be the best on the coast. Near the lagoon between Raistá and Belén is **Doña Exe** ($), and in Belén there is **Doña Mendilia** ($), near the grass airstrip.

Las Marías
Balancing the benefits of tourism is difficult in such a sensitive area. Sharing the benefits is one way of offsetting the negative impact of tourism and, whenever possible, the Ecotourism Committee tries to share tourists between the 4 basic but clean *hospedajes* (all $) of **Ovidio**, **Justa**, **Tinglas** or **Diana**, with meals available for US$3. Very friendly and with wonderful community atmosphere, highly recommended (no electricity after about 1900, so bring a torch).

Brus Laguna

$ Estancia and Paradise
T2433-8043 and T2433-8039.

Rooms with a fan and optional private bath.

Puerto Lempira

$ Gran Hotel Flores
Some rooms with bath. Recommended.

$ Pensión Moderno
Good, friendly place, with electricity from 1800-2230.

$ Villas Caratascas
Huts with bath. There is also a restaurant and a disco here.

Restaurants

Puerto Lempira

$ Delmy
3 blocks north of main street.
Noisy restaurant serving chicken and other dishes.

$ Doña Aida
North side of main road to landing bridge.
Fresh orange juice.

$ La Mosquitia
Centro Comercial Segovia in main street.
Breakfasts and cheap fish.

What to do

All-inclusive packages range from 3-14 days and cost about US$100 per day. In order to support ecotourism in the reserve you are encouraged to check the tour operator you are considering works with local people. For other options, see under What to do, Tela (page 114) and La Ceiba (page 123).

Bob 'The Butterfly, Bird and Bug Guy' Gallardo, *based in Copán Ruinas, rgallardo32@hotmail.com.* Highly regarded birding and other specialized nature trips to La Mosquitia.

La Moskitia Eco Aventuras, *with Jorge Salaverri, office in La Ceiba, T2442-0104, www.lamoskitia.hn.* Specializing in trips to La Mosquitia, this excellent company is possibly the best and most knowledgeable wildlife guide in all Central America.

Mesoamerica Travel (Col Juan Lindo, No 709, 8 Calle and 32 Av NO, San Pedro Sula, T2558-6447, www.mesoamerica-travel.com) and **Fundación Patuca** (Hauke Hoops) (T236-9910), also specialize in travel in this region. **Mesoamerica** is the only company to run tours to the Zona Arriba of the Río Patuca (5 or 10 days).

Las Marías

The services of the *saca guía* are US$3.50. Guides are required even for day hikes due to the possibility of getting lost or injured on the faint jungle trails. The cost for a guide is US$6 per day for groups up to 5. Overnight hikes require 2 guides. River trips in a *pipante*, a shallow dug-out canoe manoeuvered with poles (*palancas*) and paddles (*canaletes*), require 3 guides plus US$4.20 for the canoe. 2 visitors and their gear will fit in each boat with the guides.

Transport

La Mosquitia

Air Alas de Socorro fly to **Ahuas**, T2233-7025. This company charters planes for US$565, but per person it is US$60 1 way to Ahuas. **SAMi** flies to various villages from Puerto Lempira, eg **Ahuas, Brus Laguna, Belén**. There are

expensive express flights to places like **Auka, Raya, Kaukira**.

Boat Coastal supply vessels run between **La Ceiba** and the coastal villages of La Mosquitia. The *Corazón* and *Mr Jim* make the trip weekly and their captains can be found at the harbour east of La Ceiba. Prices vary (US$10-20); be prepared for basic conditions. There are no passenger facilities such as beds or toilets on board and the journey takes a good 24 hrs.

Rivers, lagoons and inland waterways are the highways in the reserve and dug-out canoes provide the public transportation. Once in Palacios, you can catch *colectivo* boat transport at the landing near the **Río Tinto Hotel** to travel along the inland passage to coastal villages in the reserve such as Plaplaya, Raistá and Belén (about US$3.50 for a 1 or 2-hr trip). There is usually a boat to meet the planes that arrive in the morning and information on prices to different locations is posted in the airline offices. If you miss the *colectivo* you will usually have to pay extra for a special trip (about US$20).

Road An upgraded road is the cheapest and most favoured route by locals. Take a bus from **La Ceiba** to Tocoa (US$2). From the market in Tocoa take a series of pickups (US$16 per person) along the beach to Batalla, crossing the various creeks that block the way in launches that wait to meet the cars. The journey to **Batalla** takes about 5½ hrs. From Batalla cross the lagoon in a boat to **Palacios** (US$0.70) and continue from there. The trip is not possible in the wetter months of the year (Jul, Oct and Nov).

Note Some may suggest the possibility of catching a truck from Limón to Sangrilaya then walking along the beach and wading across rivers for 1-2 days to get to Batalla. While this is possible it is not recommended because of the heat, bugs and general safety issues.

Background
Honduras

Regional history

Arrival of the American people

While controversy continues to surround the precise date humans arrived in the Americas, the current prevailing view suggests the first wave of emigrants travelled between Siberia and Alaska across the Bering Strait ice bridge created in the last Ice Age, approximately 15,000 years ago. Small hunter-gatherer groups quickly moved through the region, and in fertile lands they developed agriculture and settled. By 1500 BC sedentary villages were widespread in many parts of the Americas, including Central America, where stone-built cities and complex civilizations also began to emerge.

Pre-Columbian civilizations

Despite the wide variety of climates and terrains that fall within Central America's boundaries, the so-called Mesoamerican civilizations were interdependent, sharing the same agriculture based on maize, beans and squash, as well as many sociological traits. These included an enormous pantheon of gods, pyramid-building, a trade in valuable objects, hieroglyphic writing, astronomy, mathematics and a complex calendar system. Historians divide Mesoamerican civilizations into three broad periods, the **pre-Classic**, which lasted until about AD 300, the **Classic**, until AD 900, and the **post-Classic**, from AD 900 until the Spanish conquest.

Olmecs
Who precisely the Olmecs were, where they came from and why they disappeared is a matter of debate. It is known that they flourished from about **1400-400 BC**, lived in the **Mexican Gulf coast** region between Veracruz and Tabasco, and that all later civilizations have their roots in Olmec culture. They are particularly renowned for their carved **colossal heads**, jade figures and altar. They gave great importance to the jaguar and the serpent in their imagery and built large ceremonial centres such as **San Lorenzo** and **La Venta**. The progression from the Olmec to the Maya civilization seems to have taken place at Izapa on the Pacific border of present-day Mexico and Guatemala.

Maya
The best known of the pre-Conquest civilizations were the Maya, thought to have evolved in a formative period in the **Pacific highlands** of Guatemala and El Salvador between **1500 BC** and about **AD 100**. After 200 years of growth it entered what is known today as its Classic period, when the civilization flourished in Guatemala, El Salvador, Belize, Honduras and southern Mexico. The height of the Classic period lasted until AD 900, after which the Maya resettled in the Yucatán, possibly after a devastating famine, drought or peasant uprising. They then came

under the influence of the central Mexican Toltecs, who were highly militaristic, until the Spanish conquest in the 16th century.

Throughout its evolution, Mayan civilization was based on independent city states that were governed by a theocratic elite of priests, nobles and warriors. Recent research has revealed that these cities, far from being the peaceful ceremonial centres once imagined, were **warring adversaries** striving to capture victims for sacrifice. This change in perception of the Maya was largely due to a greater understanding of Mayan **hieroglyphic writing**, which appears both on paper codices and on stone monuments. Aside from a gory preoccupation with sacrifice, Mayan culture was rich in **ceremony, art, science, folklore** and **dance**. Their cities were all meticulously designed according to strict and highly symbolic geometric rules: columns, figures, faces, animals, friezes, stairways and temples often expressed a date, a time or a specific astronomical relationship. Impressively, the Mayan calendar was so advanced that it was a nearer approximation to sidereal time than either the Julian or the Gregorian calendars of Europe; it was only .000069 of a day out of true in a year. The Maya also formulated the concept of 'zero' centuries in advance of the Old World, plotted the movements of the sun, moon, Venus and other planets, and conceived a time cycle of more than 1800 million days.

Conquest

It was only during his fourth voyage, in 1502, that **Columbus** reached the mainland of Central America. He landed in **Costa Rica** and Panama, which he called **Veragua**, and founded the town of Santa María de Belén. In 1508 Alonso de Ojeda received a grant of land on the Pearl coast east of Panama, and in 1509 he founded the town of San Sebastián, later moved to a new site called Santa María la Antigua del Darién (now in Colombia). In 1513 the governor of the colony at Darién was **Vasco Núñez de Balboa**. Taking 190 men he crossed the isthmus in 18 days and caught the first glimpse of the Pacific; he claimed it and all neighbouring lands in the name of the King of Spain. But from the following year, when **Pedrarias de Avila** replaced him as Governor, Núñez de Balboa fell on evil days, and he was executed by Pedrarias in 1519. That same year Pedrarias crossed the isthmus and founded the town of Panamá on the Pacific side. It was in April 1519, too, that **Cortés** began his conquest of Mexico. Central America was explored from these two nodal points of Panama and Mexico.

Settlement

The groups of Spanish settlers were few and widely scattered, a fundamental point in explaining the **political fragmentation** of Central America today. Panama was ruled from Bogotá, but the rest of Central America was subordinate to the Viceroyalty at Mexico City, with Antigua, Guatemala, as an Audiencia for the area until 1773, and thereafter Guatemala City. Panama was of paramount importance for colonial Spanish America for its strategic position, and for the trade passing across the isthmus to and from the southern colonies. The other provinces were of comparatively little value.

The small number of **Spaniards intermarried** freely with the locals, accounting for the predominance of mestizos in present-day Central America. But the picture has regional variations. In Guatemala, where there was the highest native population density, intermarriage affected fewer of the natives, and over half the population today is still purely *indígena* (**indigenous**). On the Meseta Central of Costa Rica, the natives were all but wiped out by disease and, as a consequence of this great disaster, there is a community of over two million whites, with little *indígena* admixture. **Blacks** predominate along the Caribbean coast of Central America. Most were brought in as cheap labour to work as railway builders and banana planters in the 19th century and canal cutters in the 20th. The **Garífuna** people, living between southern Belize and Nicaragua, arrived in the area as free people after African slaves and indigenous Caribbean people intermingled following a shipwreck off St Vincent.

Independence and after

On 5 November 1811, **José Matías Delgado**, a priest and jurist born in San Salvador, organized a revolt with another priest, Manuel José Arce. They proclaimed the Independence of El Salvador, but the Audiencia at Guatemala City suppressed the revolt and took Delgado prisoner. Eleven years later, in 1820, the revolution of Spain itself precipitated the Independence of Central America. On 24 February 1821, the Mexican **General Agustín de Iturbide** announced his **Plan de Iguala** for an independent Mexico. Several months later, the Central American *criollos* followed his example and announced their own **Declaration of Independence** in Guatemala City on 15 September 1821. Iturbide invited the provinces of Central America to join with him and, on 5 January 1822, Central America was annexed to Mexico. Delgado, however, refused to accept this decree and Iturbide, who had now assumed the title of **Emperor Agustín I**, sent an army south under Vicente Filísola to enforce it. Filísola had completed his task when he heard of Iturbide's abdication, and at once convened a general congress of the Central American provinces. It met on 24 June 1823, and thereafter established the **Provincias Unidas del Centro de América**. The Mexican Republic acknowledged their Independence on 1 August 1824, and Filísola's soldiers were withdrawn.

The United Provinces of Central America
In 1824, the first congress, presided over by Delgado, appointed a provisional governing *junta* which promulgated a constitution modelled on that of the United States. The Province of Chiapas was not included in the Federation, as it had already adhered to Mexico in 1821. Guatemala City, by force of tradition, soon became the seat of government.

The first president under the new constitution was **Manuel José Arce**, a liberal. One of his first acts was to **abolish slavery**. El Salvador, protesting that he had exceeded his powers, rose in December 1826. Honduras, Nicaragua and Costa Rica joined the revolt, and in 1828 **General Francisco Morazán**, in charge of the army of Honduras, defeated the federal forces, entered San Salvador and marched against Guatemala City. He captured the city on 13 April 1829, and established that contradiction in terms: a liberal dictatorship. Many conservative leaders were expelled and church and monastic properties confiscated. Morazán himself became President of the Federation in 1830. He was a man of considerable ability; he ruled with a strong hand, encouraged education, fostered trade and industry, opened the country to immigrants, and reorganized the administration. In 1835 the capital was moved to San Salvador.

These reforms antagonized the conservatives and there were several uprisings. The most serious revolt was among the *indígenas* of Guatemala, led by Rafael Carrera, an illiterate mestizo conservative and a born leader. Years of continuous warfare followed, during the course of which the Federation withered away. As a result, the federal congress passed an act which allowed each province to assume the government it chose, but the idea of a federation was not quite dead. Morazán became President of El Salvador. Carrera, who was by then in control of Guatemala, defeated Morazán in battle and forced him to leave the country. But in 1842, Morazán overthrew Braulio Carrillo, then dictator of Costa Rica, and became president himself. At once he set about rebuilding the Federation, but a popular uprising soon led to his capture. He was shot on 15 September 1842 and with him perished any practical hope of Central American political union.

The separate states

The history of **Guatemala**, **El Salvador**, **Honduras** and **Nicaragua** since the breakdown of federation has been tempestuous in the extreme (**Costa Rica**, with its mainly white population and limited economic value at the time, is a country apart, and **Panama** was Colombian territory until 1903). In each, the ruling class was divided into pro-clerical conservatives and anti-clerical liberals, with constant changes of power. Each was weak, and tried repeatedly to buttress its weakness by alliances with others, which invariably broke up because one of the allies sought a position of mastery. The wars were mainly ideological wars between conservatives and liberals, or wars motivated by inflamed nationalism. Nicaragua was riven internally by the mutual hatreds of the Conservatives of Granada and the Liberals of León, and there were repeated conflicts between the Caribbean and interior parts of Honduras. Despite the permutations and combinations of external and civil war there has been a recurrent desire to re-establish some form of **La Gran Patria Centroamericana**. Throughout the 19th century, and far into the 20th, there have been ambitious projects for political federation, usually involving El Salvador, Honduras and Nicaragua; none of them lasted more than a few years.

Honduras

Honduras was largely neglected by Spain and its colonists, who concentrated on their trading partners further north or south. The resulting disparity in levels of development between Honduras and its regional neighbours caused problems after Independence in 1821. Harsh partisan battles among provincial leaders resulted in the collapse of the Central American Federation in 1838. The national hero, **General Francisco Morazán** was a leader in unsuccessful attempts to maintain the Federation and the restoration of Central American unity was the main aim of foreign policy until 1922.

Banana Republic

Honduras has had a succession of military and civilian rulers and there have been 300 internal rebellions, civil wars and changes of government since Independence, most of them in the 20th century. Political instability in the past led to a lack of investment in economic infrastructure and socio-political integration, making Honduras one of the poorest countries in the Western Hemisphere. It earned its nickname of the 'Banana Republic' in the first part of the 20th century following the founding of a company in 1899, by the Vaccaro brothers of New Orleans, which eventually became the Standard Fruit Company and which was to make bananas the major export crop of Honduras. The United Fruit Company of Boston was also founded in 1899 and, 30 years later, was merged with the Cuyamel Fruit Company of Samuel Zemurray, who controlled the largest fruit interests in Honduras. United Fruit (UFCo), known as El Pulpo (the octopus), emerged as a major political influence in the region with strong links with several dictatorships.

The Great Depression

The 1929 Great Depression caused great hardship in the export-oriented economies of the region, and in Honduras it brought the rise of another authoritarian regime. **Tiburcio Carías Andino** was elected in 1932 and, through his ties with foreign companies and other neighbouring dictators, he was able to hold on to power until renewed turbulence began in 1948, and he voluntarily withdrew from power a year later. The two political parties, the Liberals and the Nationals, came under the control of provincial military leaders and, after two more authoritarian Nationalist governments and a general strike in 1954 by radical labour unions on the north coast, young military reformists staged a palace coup in 1955. They installed a provisional junta and allowed elections for a constituent assembly in 1957. The assembly was led by the Liberal Party, which appointed **Dr Ramón Villeda Morales** as president, and transformed itself into a national legislature for six years. A newly created military academy graduated its first class in 1960, and the armed forces began to professionalize their leadership in conjunction with the civilian economic establishment. Conservative officers, nervous of a Cuban-style revolution, pre-empted elections in 1963 in a bloody coup which deposed Dr Villeda, exiled Liberal Party members and took control of the national police, which they organized into special security forces.

Football War

In 1969, Honduras and El Salvador were drawn into a bizarre episode known as the 'Football War', which took its name from its origin in a disputed decision in the third qualifying round of the World Cup. Its root cause, however, was the social tension aroused by migrating workers from overcrowded El Salvador to Honduras. In 13 days, 2000 people were killed before a ceasefire was arranged by the Organization of American States. A peace treaty was not signed until 1980, and the dispute provoked Honduras to withdraw from the Central American Common Market (CACM), which helped to hasten its demise.

Tensions between the two countries can still easily rise. Disputes over the border and fishing rights in the Gulf of Fonseca are a cause of friction, and in August 2001, Honduras expelled two Salvadoreans on spying charges. Honduras also has disputed land claims with Nicaragua to the east. However, regional cooperation is sufficiently well developed for regional conferences to tackle the problems with commitments to non-aggressive solutions.

Transition to democracy

The armed forces, led chiefly by **General López Arellano** and his protégés in the National Party, dominated government until 1982. López initiated land reform but, despite liberal policies, his regime was brought down in the mid-1970s by corruption scandals involving misuse of hurricane aid funds and bribes from the United Brands Company. His successors increased the size and power of the security forces and created the largest air force in Central America, while slowly preparing for a return to civilian rule. A constituent assembly was elected in 1980 and general elections held in 1981. A constitution was promulgated in 1982 and **President Roberto Suazo Córdoba** of the Liberal Party assumed power. During this period, Honduras cooperated closely with the USA on political and military issues, particularly in covert moves to destabilize Nicaragua's Sandanista government, and became host to some 12,000 right-wing Nicaraguan contra rebels. It was less willing to take a similar stand against the FMLN left-wing guerrillas in El Salvador for fear of renewing border tensions. In 1986 the first peaceful transfer of power between civilian presidents for 30 years took place when **José Azcona del Hoyo** (Liberal) won the elections. Close relations with the USA were maintained in the 1980s, Honduras had the largest Peace Corps Mission in the world, non-governmental and international voluntary agencies proliferated as the government became increasingly dependent upon US aid to finance its budget.

In 1989, the general elections were won by the right-wing **Rafael Leonardo Callejas Romero** of the National Party, which won a 14-seat majority in the National Assembly. Under the terms of the Central American Peace Plan, the contra forces were demobilized and disarmed by June 1990. The Honduran armed forces have come under greater pressure for reform as a result of US and domestic criticism of human rights abuses. A report published in April 1993 recommended a series of institutional reforms in the judiciary and security services, including the resolution by the Supreme Court of all cases of jurisdictional conflict between civilian and military courts. This and other measures led to some, but by no means all, improvements in respect of human rights.

Liberal government since 1993

In the campaign leading up to the 1993 general elections, the Liberal candidate, **Carlos Roberto Reina Idiáquez**, pledged to provide every citizen *"techo, trabajo, tierra y tortilla"* (roof, work, land and food), arguing for a more socially conscious face to the economic adjustment programme inaugurated by President Callejas. Although many of his economic policies were unpopular, and he was unable to alleviate widespread poverty in the short term, President Reina received approval for his handling of the military and investigations of human rights' abuses.

The 1997 presidential elections were again won by the Liberal candidate, **Carlos Flores Facusse**. He had the support of the business community, who believed he would control public spending and reduce the government deficit in line with IMF targets, but he also campaigned against economic austerity and in favour of bridging the gap between rich and poor. The passage of Hurricane Mitch over Honduras in October 1998 forced the Flores administration to refocus all its attention on rebuilding the country at all levels, social, economic and infrastructural.

Ricardo Maduro of the National Party was sworn in as president in January 2002. Elections in November 2005 were won by the Liberal Party's **Manuel Zelaya**, with a majority of just 75,000 votes. Zelaya had served in the government of Carlos Flores. On taking office he vowed to continue the fight against gang violence along with tackling corruption in government, creation of hundreds of thousands of badly needed jobs and support for CAFTA free trade agreement with the US.

But despite the determination, violence continues to dominate the political agenda, with prison riots and occasional ransoms of high-profile individuals undermining the rule of law. In 2007, Zelaya ordered national media outlets to carry government propaganda for two hours a day for 10 days to counteract a campaign of misinformation.

The Coup

In 2009, President Manuel Zelaya was ousted in a military coup. Troops seized the president early in the morning and sent him – still wearing his pyjamas – into exile in Costa Rica. The move followed the president's proposal to hold a referendum on changing the law to allow him to stand for a second term of office. When the head of the armed forces opposed the plan, Zelaya fired him, which triggered the coup. Zelaya now lives in the Dominican Republic. Meanwhile, recent presidential elections were won by **Porfirio 'Pepe' Lobo Sosa** of the right-wing National Party, with the largest number of votes ever recorded in Honduras' history. He took office in January, 2010. Since then, the country has seen a sharp upturn in violent crime, an escalation of the war on drugs and a general deterioration in infrastructure, along with a marked strengthening of oligarch families, bluntly backed by the police and military. A series of ugly land disputes resulted in a spate of political assassinations, mostly of young peasant activists, and against the backdrop of a human rights crisis, elections were held in 2013. Juan Orlando Hernández of the ruling National Party was voted to office. There has been no significant improvement for the vast majority of everyday Hondurans.

Culture

People
Estimates put the population at about 8.5 million. The pure indigenous population is only an estimated 7% of the total population, and the percentage of pure Spanish or other European ancestry is even smaller. The two largest indigenous groups are the Chortis from Santa Rosa de Copán westwards to the border with Guatemala, and the Lencas in the departments of Lempira, Intibucá and, above all, in the highlands of La Paz. There are also about 45,000 Miskito people who live on the Caribbean coast, alongside several communities of Garífunas (black Caribs). The population is 90% mestizo. Some 53% are peasant farmers or agricultural labourers, with a low standard of living.

Religion and education
Education is compulsory, but not all the rural children go to school 33% of the population over the age of 10 have had no formal schooling. According to UNESCO 27.1% of people over 15 are illiterate. The Universidad Nacional, based in Tegucigalpa, has departments in Comayagua, San Pedro Sula and La Ceiba. Also in Tegucigalpa are the Universidad José Cecilio del Valle, Universidad Católica (with campuses in San Pedro Sula and Choluteca), Universidad Tecnológica Centro Americana and Universidad Pedagógica Nacional; there is also the Universidad de San Pedro Sula, Universidad Pedagógica Francisco Morazán and Universidad Tecnológica Centroamericana. The majority of the population is Catholic.

Music
The visitor seeking specifically Honduran native music will find little to satisfy him or her. Honduras shares with Belize and Guatemala the presence of Garífuna or black Caribs on the Caribbean coast. These descendants of indigenous Caribs and escaped black slaves were deported to the area from St Vincent in the late 18th century and continue to maintain a very separate identity, including their own religious observances, music and dances, profoundly African in spirit and style.

Land and environment

With a territory of 112,100 sq km, Honduras is larger than all the other Central American republics except Nicaragua. Bordered by Nicaragua, Guatemala and El

Salvador, it has a narrow Pacific coastal strip, 124 km long on the Gulf of Fonseca, and a northern coast on the Caribbean of 640 km.

Inland, much of the country is mountainous: a rough plateau covered with volcanic ash and lava in the south, rising to peaks such as Cerro de las Minas in the Celaque range (2849 m), but with some intermont basins at between 900 and 1800 m. The volcanic detritus disappears to the north, revealing saw-toothed ranges which approach the coast at an angle; the one in the extreme northwest, along the border with Guatemala, disappears under the sea and shows itself again in the Bay Islands. At most places in the north there is only a narrow shelf of lowland between the sea and the sharp upthrust of the mountains, but along two rivers (the Aguán in the northeast, and the Ulúa in the northwest) long fingers of marshy lowland stretch inland between the ranges. The Ulúa lowland is particularly important; it is about 40 km wide and stretches southwards for 100 km where the city of San Pedro Sula is located. From its southern limit a deep gash continues across the highland to the Gulf of Fonseca on the Pacific. The distance between the Caribbean and the Pacific along this trough is 280 km; the altitude at the divide between the Río Comayagua, running into the Ulúa and the Caribbean, and the streams flowing into the Pacific, is only 950 m. In this trough lies Comayagua, the old colonial capital. The lowlands along the Gulf of Fonseca are narrower than they are along the Caribbean; there is no major thrust inland as there is along the Ulúa.

The prevailing winds are from the east, consequently the Caribbean coast has a high rainfall and is covered with deep tropical forest. The intermont basins, the valleys and the slopes sheltered from the prevailing winds bear oak and pine down to as low as 600 m. Timber is almost the only fuel available. In the drier areas, north and south of Tegucigalpa, there are extensive treeless savannahs.

Today, land under some form of cultivation is only 18% of the total, while meadows and pastures make up 14% of total land use. Rugged terrain makes large areas unsuitable for any kind of agriculture. Nevertheless, there is undeveloped agricultural potential in the flat and almost unpopulated lands of the coastal plain east of Tela to Trujillo and Puerto Castilla, in the Aguán valley southward and in the region northeast of Juticalpa. The area to the northeast, known as the Mosquitia plain, is largely unexploited and little is known of its potential.

Climate

Rain is frequent on the Caribbean coast year-round; the heaviest occurs from September to February inclusive. In Tegucigalpa the dry season is normally from November to April inclusive. The coolest months are December and January, but this is when heavy rains fall on the north coast, which could impede travel. The driest months for this area are April and May, though they are very hot. However, weather predictions in this area have become more difficult in recent years, whether because of the *El Niño* phenomenon or for other reasons. Rain, when it comes, is usually heavy, but of short duration.

Practicalities
Honduras

Getting there

All countries in Latin America (in fact across the world) officially require travellers entering their territory to have an onward or return ticket and may at times ask to see that ticket. Although rarely enforced at airports, this regulation can create problems at border crossings. In lieu of an onward ticket out of the country you are entering, any ticket out of another Latin American country may sometimes suffice, or proof that you have sufficient funds to buy a ticket (a credit card will do).

Fares from Europe and North America to Latin American destinations vary and it is worth shopping around. An indication of cost is difficult to give due to the large number of variables, not least fluctuations in currency and oil prices. The main factors are frequency and popularity of a destination at a particular time of a year. Peak periods and higher prices correspond to holiday season in the northern hemisphere. The very busy seasons are as follows: 7 December to 15 January and July to Mid-September. If you intend travelling during those times, book as far ahead as possible. Check with an agency for the best deal.

Fares fall into three groups, and are all on scheduled services. **Excursion (return) fares**: these have restricted validity on either to seven or 90 days, or seven to 180 days, depending on the airline. They are fixed-date tickets where the dates of travel cannot be changed after issue without incurring a penalty. **Yearly fares**: these may be bought on a one-way or return basis, and usually the returns can be issued with the return date left open. You must, however, fix the route. **Student** (or under-26) **fares**: one way and returns available, or 'open jaws' for people intending to travel a linear route and return from a different point from that which they entered.

Tegucigalpa, La Ceiba, San Pedro Sula and Roatán all have international airports.

From Europe There are no direct flights to Tegucigalpa from Europe, all traffic is routed via the US (see below). There are flights to Roatán from Milan-Malpensa with **Air Italy**. **Note** All travellers to the US (including those in transit) who are eligible for a visa waiver must submit to the Electronic System for Travel Authorization (ESTA), www.esta.cbp.dhs.gov. It is best to do this well in advance of travel; keep a printed copy of your receipt for presentation at check-in. The authorization costs US$14 and is valid for two years.

From USA and Canada There are flights to Tegucigalpa from Miami with **American Airlines**; from Atlanta with **Delta Airlines**; and from Houston-Intercontinental with **United**. There are flights to Roatán from Miami and Dallas/Fort Worth with **American Airlines**; from Atlanta with **Delta Airlines**; from Montreal-Trudeau and Toronto-Pearson with **Air Transat** and **Sunwing Airlines** (seasonal); and from

Houston-Intercontinental with **United Airlines**. There are flights to San Pedro Sula from Miami and New York-JFK with **Avianca**; from Atlanta with Delta; from Fort Lauderdale and Houston-Intercontinental with **Spirit Airlines**; from Houston-Intercontinental and Newark with **United Airlines**.

From Latin America There are flights to Tegucigalpa from Guatemala City with **Aerolíneas Sosa**; from Guatemala City, San José, and San Salvador with **Avianca**; from Guatemala City with **CM Airlines**; from Managua with La Costeña; from Panama City and San José with **Copa**; from Guatemala City with **Transportes Aeros Guatemaltecos**. There are flights to Roatán from San Salvador with Avianca; from Guatemala City with **Transportes Aeros Guatemaltecos**, and from Belize City with **Tropic Air**. There are flights to San Pedro Sula from Guatemala City with **Aerolineas Sosa**; from México City with **Aeroméxico** connect; from Guatemala City, San Salvador, and San José with **Avianca**; from Guatemala City with **CM Airlines**; from Panama City and San José with **Copa Airlines**; from Belize City with **Tropic Air**; from Guatemala City with **Transportes Aéreos Guatemaltecos**. There are flights to La Ceiba from Grand Cayman with **Aerolíneas Sosa** and **Cayman Airways**.

Road

There are numerous border crossings. With **Guatemala** to the west you can cross near Copán Ruinas at El Florido, on the Caribbean coast at Corinto or to the south at Agua Caliente. For **El Salvador** there are crossings at El Poy, leading to Suchitoto in the west, and Perquín leading to San Miguel and the east. For **Nicaragua**, the border post town of Guasale in the south leads 116 km on a very bad road to the Nicaraguan town of León, while the inland routes at Las Manos and El Espino guide you to Estelí and Matagalpa, in the northern hills. Crossing to Nicaragua through the Mosquitia coast is not possible – officially at least. See also boxes, pages 155, 156, 157 and 158.

Taxes are charged on entry and exit at land borders, but the amount varies, despite notices asking you to denounce corruption. Entry is 60 lempiras and exit

BORDER CROSSING

Honduras–Belize

Puerto Cortés– Placencia
There is a weekly boat service from Puerto Cortés to Placencia, via Mango Creek, every Monday; in good weather the crossing takes two hours. Obtain all necessary exit stamps and visas before sailing; see page 110.

Puerto Cortés– Dangriga
Subject to good weather, boat services to Dangriga depart from Puerto Cortés every Monday at 1100 and continue to Belize City; see page 110.

is 30 lempiras. Double is charged on Sunday. If officials make an excess charge for entry or exit, ask for a receipt. Do not attempt to enter Honduras at an unstaffed border. When it is discovered that you have no entry stamp you will either be fined US$60 or escorted to the border, and you will have to pay the guard's food and lodging; or you can spend a night in jail.

Sea

See box, above, for boat services from Belize to Honduras.

BORDER CROSSING
Honduras–Guatemala

El Salvador and Honduras are covered under the CA-4 border control agreement (see box, page 154), but you must still submit to immigration formalities before proceeding.

El Florido

This is a popular and busy crossing, but straightforward for pedestrians. If entering Honduras just to visit Copán ruins, you can get a temporary 72-hour exit pass, but you must return on time. There are numerous money-changers, but you'll find better rates in Copán. Immigration on both sides of the border is open 0700-1900. Get a receipt for 'extra charges'. On the Guatemalan side there are numerous minibus services to Guatemala City and Antigua. In Honduras minibuses run all day until 1700 to Copán ruins.

Entre Ríos–Corinto

This Caribbean coast crossing has a road connecting Puerto Barrios (Guatemala) and Puerto Cortés (Honduras) with a bridge over the Motagua river. If you arrive in Guatemala from Honduras by boat, go straight to either of the immigration office in Puerto Barrios or Lívingston. If.leaving Guatemala by boat to Honduras, make sure you get your exit stamp at one of these two offices first. Honduran immigration is at Corinto if crossing from Puerto Barrios in Guatemala. Once in Guatemala, there's highway access to Guatemala City and Santa Elena/Flores. On the Honduran side there are connections to the northern coast. Buses leave Corinto for Omoa and Puerto Cortés every hour or so.

Agua Caliente

This is a busy crossing, but it's quicker, cheaper and more efficient than the one at El Florido. There are banks, a tourist office, *comedor* and *hospedaje* on the Honduran side. If you're leaving Honduras, keep some lempiras for the ride from Agua Caliente to Esquipulas. Guatemalan immigration is open 0600-1900, Honduran immigration 0700-1800. On the Guatemalan side, minibuses go to Esquipulas with connections to Guatemala City, Chiquimula and the highway to Flores. In Honduras, there are several buses daily from Agua Caliente to San Pedro Sula, six to seven hours, and also frequent services to Nueva Ocotepeque.

Getting around

Air

There are airstrips in all large towns and many of the remote smaller ones. For the Bay Islands, there are domestic flights to **Roatán** from Tegucigalpa with **Aerolíneas Sosa**, **Avianca**, **CM Airlines**, and **Easy Sky**; from La Ceiba with **AeroCaribe**, **Aerolíneas Sosa**, **Easy Sky**, and **Lanhsa**. The small carrier **Island Air**

BORDER CROSSING
Honduras–El Salvador

El Salvador and Honduras are covered under the CA-4 border control agreement (see box, page 154), but you must still submit to immigration formalities before proceeding.

El Poy
This crossing between northern El Salvador and southwestern Honduras is straightforward, but it's better to arrive early if you have a long journey ahead. If changing currency, bargain hard with the money-changers. Travelling onwards to Honduras, shuttles carry passengers to Nueva Ocotopeque, 15-20 minutes, where you can catch highway connections north to Santa Rosa de Copán. On the El Salvador side, buses to San Salvador depart hourly, three to four hours, passing La Palma en route, 30 minutes.

El Amatillo
The Río Goascarán forms the border at El Amatillo. If driving, you will be hounded by *tramitadores*, some of them are unethical, but their services aren't really required here anyway. Expect thorough car searches. Both Salvadorean and Honduran immigration are open 0600-1700 with a break for lunch. In Honduras, there are hourly services to Tegucigalpa, four hours; and to Choluteca, every 30 minutes, three hours. In El Salvador, there are regular bus services (No 330) to San Miguel, 1½ hours.

Sabanetas–Perquín
The international boundary here has been variously disputed throughout history. A treaty resolved the disagreement in 2006 and the border now lies 3 km north of Perquín in El Salvador, though it may be impassable after heavy rains. Travel early morning for the best chance of transport connections. There is a Honduran immigration office 5 km inside the country. Note that this is not a major crossing and motorists with international plates are being turned away. Irregular onward bus services go to Marcala in Honduras and San Miguel in El Salvador.

flies between Utila and Roatán. As well as connecting with the Bay Islands, flights from La Ceiba also operate to Guanaja and Puerto Lempira. Schedules and fares are always changing; most tour operators in Honduras can help with ticketing. Airport departure tax is US$38 (not charged if in transit less than nine hours). There is a 10% tax on all tickets sold for domestic and international journeys.

Road

Until relatively recently, Honduras had some of the best roads in Central America. However, since the political crisis in 2009 many sections have become neglected

BORDER CROSSING
Honduras–Nicaragua

Nicaragua and Honduras are covered under the CA-4 border control agreement (see box, page 154), but you must still submit to immigration formalities before proceeding.

Guasaule
There are good roads at this crossing, the preferred route of international buses. If you're driving, it might be worth hiring a 'helper' to steer you through the formalities. There is a bank by Nicaraguan immigration and lots of money-changers (beware children trying to distract you while you make the transaction). Both Honduran and Nicaraguan immigration are open 0800-1600. On the Nicaraguan side, there are buses to Chinandega and León every 30 minutes, one to two hours, along with a few direct services to Managua. In Honduras, there are regular buses to Choluteca, 45 minutes.

Las Manos–Ocotal
This is recommended as the best route if travelling between the capital cities of Managua and Tegucigalpa. If driving, *tramitadores* will help you through the paperwork (for a US$5 tip). Both Honduran and Nicaraguan immigration are open 0800-1600. Exchange rates are better on the Nicaraguan side. Buses to run Ocotal in Nicaragua every 30 minutes, from there you can connect to Estelí or Managua. In Honduras, there are direct connections to Tegucigalpa.

El Espino–Somoto
Border formalities are reportedly very tedious at this crossing. There are places to eat, but no hotels at the border itself. In Nicaragua, buses run from the border to Somoto every 30 minutes; taxis also run, but beware of overcharging. There are roughly six daily buses to Managua, 3½ hours. In Honduras, taxis and minibuses shuttle passengers from the border to Choluteca.

Leimus–Waspam
This is a hardcore crossing in the heart of the Mosquitia and not for fainthearted. You are strongly advised to seek up-to-date advice from immigration officials before attempting the crossing as it may be impossible to travel between border posts on the same day, requiring additional paperwork. There are no banks or ATMs in the region so bring all the cash you need. Shop owners in Waspam may change currency. In Honduras, obtain your stamps in Puerto Lempira. There is no known immigration office in Waspam, the nearest may be in Bilwi (Puerto Cabezas), a gruelling six hours away on rough dirt roads, which may be impassable in wet season. In Honduras, Leimus has road connections with Puerto Lempira.

and pitted with huge potholes, particularly between San Pedro Sula and Copán. Traffic tends to travel fast on the main roads and accidents are second only to Costa Rica in Latin America. If driving, take care and look out for speed bumps (*túmulos*), which are usually unmarked. Avoid driving at night; farm animals grazing along the verges often wander across the road. Total road length is now 14742 km, of which 3367 km are paved, 11357 km are all-weather roads and the remainder are passable in the dry season.

Bus

There are essentially three types of service: local (*servicio a escala*), direct (*servicio directo*) and luxury (*servicio de lujo*). Using school buses, a *servicio a escala* is very slow, with frequent stops and detours and is uncomfortable for long periods. *Servicio directo* is faster, slightly more expensive and more comfortable. *Servicio de lujo* has air-conditioned European and Brazilian buses with videos. For safety, it is highly recommended you use direct or luxury services where possible, such as **Hedman Alas**, www.hedmanalas.com, and **Viana Transportes**, www.vianatransportes.com. If you intend to do a lot of bus travel in Honduras, consider buying a discount card from Hedman Alas' sister company, **Promodias**, www.promodias.com, available at bus terminals; it offers deals on hotels, restaurants and other tourist services.

Buses set out early in the day, with a few night buses running between major urban centres. Try to avoid bus journeys after dark as there are many more accidents and even occasional robberies.

If you suffer from motion sickness, the twisty roads can become unbearable. Avoid sitting at the back of the bus, take some water and sit by a window that will open. Minibuses are faster than buses, so the journey can be quite hair-raising. Pickups that serve out-of-the-way communities will leave you covered in dust (or soaked) – sit in or near the cab if possible.

Car

Regular gasoline/petrol costs around US$3.60 per US gallon for regular, US$3.87 per gallon for special, and US$3.09 for diesel. On entering with a car (from El Salvador at least), customs and the transit police give a 30-day permit for the vehicle. This must be renewed in Tegucigalpa (anywhere else authorization is valid for only one department). Charges for motorists appear to be: on entry, US$30 in total for a vehicle with two passengers, including provisional permission from the police to drive in Honduras, US$1 (official minimum) for car papers, fumigation and baggage inspection; on exit, US$2.30 in total. Motorcyclists face similar charges. These charges are changing all the time and differ significantly from one post to another (up to US$40 sometimes). They are also substantially higher on weekends and holidays. You will have to pass through Migración, Registro, Tránsito, Cuarentena, Administración, Secretaría and then a police vehicle check. At each stage you will be asked for money, for which you will not always get a receipt. On arriving or leaving with a vehicle there are so many checks that it pays to hire a *tramitador* to steer you to the correct officials in the correct order (US$1-2 for the guide). No fresh food is allowed to cross the border. The easiest border crossing is at Las Manos. The **Pan-American Highway** in Honduras is in bad condition in parts. One reader warns to "beware of potholes that can take a car. They suddenly appear after 20 km of good road without warning." If hiring a car, make sure it has all the correct papers and emergency triangles, which are required by law.

Cycling
Bicycles are regarded as vehicles but are not officially subject to entrance taxes. Bicycle repair shops are difficult to find, and parts for anything other than mountain bikes may be very hard to come by. Some buses and most local flights will take bicycles. Most main roads have hard shoulders and most drivers respect cyclists. It is common for cars to blow their horn to signal their approach.

Hitchhiking
Hitchhiking is relatively easy. Travel is still on foot and by mule in many rural areas.

Taxi
Taxis are widely available. Tuk-tuks have become very popular in Honduras, and are a quick and cheap way to move around in towns and cities.

Maps

The Instituto Geográfico Nacional produces two 1:1,000,000 maps (1995) of the country: one is a tourist map which includes city maps of Tegucigalpa, San Pedro Sula and La Ceiba, and the other is a good road map although it does not show all the roads. Both maps are widely available in bookshops in major cities and some hotels. International Travel Maps (ITM) has a 1:750,000 map of Honduras.

Essentials A-Z

Customs and duty free

There are no customs duties on personal effects. You are allowed to bring in 200 cigarettes or 100 cigars, or 500 g of tobacco, and 2 quarts of spirit.

Electricity

Generally 110 volts but, increasingly, 220 volts is being installed. US-style plugs.

Embassies and consulates

For all Honduran embassies and consulates abroad and for all foreign embassies and consulates in Honduras, see http://embassy.goabroad.com.

Health

See your GP or travel clinic at least 6 weeks before departure for general advice on travel risks and vaccinations. Try a specialist travel clinic if your own GP is unfamiliar with health conditions in Honduras. Make sure you have sufficient medical travel insurance (see below), get a dental check, know your own blood group and if you suffer a long-term condition such as diabetes or epilepsy, obtain a Medic Alert bracelet/ necklace (www.medicalert.co.uk). If you wear glasses, take a copy of your prescription.

Vaccinations

Vaccinations for tetanus, hepatitis A and typhoid are commonly recommended for Honduras. In addition, yellow fever vaccination is required if entering from an infected area (ie parts of South America). Vaccinations may also be advised against tuberculosis, hepatitis B, rabies, diphtheria and cholera. The final decision, however, should be based on a consultation with your GP or travel clinic. In all cases you should confirm your primary courses and boosters are up to date.

Health risks

Gastroenteritic diseases are most common. Visitors should take care over what they eat during the first few weeks, and should drink *agua cristal* (purified bottled water).

Dengue fever is carried by mosquitos in urban areas, but it is rare for travellers to contract it; use repellent, sleep under a fan (the mosquitos cannot fly against it) and take all the usual sensible precautions. **Chikungunya virus** is a new and rapidly spreading disease in Central America, also carried by mosquitos. **Malaria** is relatively rare and confined to remote rural settings.

For **diarrhoea**, mild dysentery, amoebas and parasitic infections get Nodik tablets from any chemist or large supermarket, around US$14 for a 3-day cure. You can test for parasites at laboratories, which are widespread. Note that due to amoebic life cycles it can sometimes take 3-5 consecutive days of testing for results to show positive.

There is **cholera**, so eating on the street or at market stalls is not recommended.

If you get sick

Contact your embassy or consulate for a list of doctors and dentists who speak your language, or at least some

English. Good-quality healthcare is available in the larger centres but it can be expensive, especially hospitalization. There are hospitals and private clinics in Tegucigalpa, San Pedro Sula and larger towns.

Useful websites
www.btha.org British Travel Health Association.
www.cdc.gov US government site that gives excellent advice on travel health and details of disease outbreaks.
www.fco.gov.uk British Foreign and Commonwealth Office travel site has useful information on each country, people, climate and a list of UK embassies/consulates.
www.fitfortravel.scot.nhs.uk A-Z of vaccine/health advice for each country.
www.numberonehealth.co.uk Travel screening services, vaccine and travel health advice, email/SMS text vaccine reminders and screens returned travellers for tropical diseases.

Identification

It is advisable to carry some form of identification at all times, because spot checks have increased, especially when entering or leaving major towns and near to international borders.

Internet

Internet cafés are widely available in the capital and in popular locations. Prices and connections vary greatly; in cities good speeds are at about US$1 per hour. On the islands, prices are a bit higher.

Language

Spanish is the main language, but English is often spoken in the north, in

the Bay Islands, by West Indian settlers on the Caribbean coast, and in business communities.

Media

The principal newspapers in Tegucigalpa are *El Heraldo* and *La Tribuna*. In San Pedro Sula they are *El Tiempo* and *La Prensa*. Links on the net at www.honduras.com. The English weekly paper *Honduras This Week*, is now mainly online at www.hondurasthisweek.com. They're frequently looking for student interns.

There are 6 television channels and 167 broadcasting stations. Cable TV is available in large towns and cities.

Money

US$1 = Lps 21.95. €1 = Lps 24.35. £1 = Lps 34.15 (Jul 2015).

The unit of currency is the lempira (written Lps and referred to as lemps) named after a famous indigenous chief who lost his life while fighting the invasion of the Spanish. It is reasonably stable against the US dollar. Divided into 100 centavos, there are nickel coins of 5, 10, 20 and 50 centavos. Bank notes are for 1, 2, 5, 10, 20, 50, 100 and 500 lempiras. No one has change for larger notes, especially the 500. Any amount of any currency can be taken in or out of the country.

Credit cards and currency cards
Acceptance of credit cards is widespread but commissions can be as high as 6%. Some businesses may try to tack on a service charge to credit card purchases, which is illegal. Ask the manager to call **BAC** and check if the charge is permitted. It is advisable to have US$ cash, in smaller denominations, US$10-50.

MasterCard and Visa are accepted in

major hotels and most restaurants in cities and larger towns. Amex is accepted in more expensive establishments. Cash advances are available from **BAC**, **Banco Atlántida**, **Aval Card** and **Honducard** throughout the country. BAC represents Amex and issues and services Amex credit cards.

If you don't want to carry lots of cash, prepaid currency cards allow you to preload money from your bank account, fixed at the day's exchange rate. They look like a credit or debit card and are issued by specialist money-changing companies, such as **Travelex** and **Caxton FX**, and the **Post Office**. You can top up and check your balance by phone, online and sometimes by text.

Cost of living and travelling

Honduras is not expensive: 2 people can travel together in reasonable comfort for US$40 per person per day (less if on a tight budget), but prices for tourists fluctuate greatly. Transport, including domestic flights, is still the cheapest in Central America. Diving will set you back a bit, but at US$280 or so for a PADI course, it is still the cheapest in Central America.

Opening hours

Banks In Tegucigalpa Mon-Fri 0900-1500; on the north coast Sat 0800-1100.
Post offices Mon-Fri 0700-2000; Sat 0800-1200.
Shops Mon-Fri 0900-1200, 1400-1800; Sat 0800-1200.

Post

Airmail takes 4-7 days to Europe and the same for the USA. It's expensive for parcels and is probably worth using a courier. 20 g letter to USA US$0.80, Europe US$1.30, rest of the world US$1.75. Parcel up to 1 kg to the USA US$18, Europe US$29, rest of the world US$35.

Safety

There are serious domestic social problems in Tegucigalpa and San Pedro Sula, including muggings and theft, but there is a Tourist Police service in place in Copán Ruinas, Roatán, La Ceiba, Tela and San Pedro Sula that has reduced the problem. Take local advice and be cautious when travelling alone or off the beaten track. It is considered unsafe for tourists to use public transport within the cities of Tegucigalpa and San Pedro Sula; use licensed taxis only. Armed robberies on intercity buses are not unheard of, especially on the routes between Tegucigalpa, San Pedro Sula and La Ceiba, where it is best to use one of the direct services; Hedman Alas and Viana Transportes are highly recommended for their strict security measures. Contrary to the bad press, the vast majority of Hondurans are honest, friendly, warm and welcoming, and the general perception is that tourists are not targeted by criminals. You can check the latest security news at the UK Foreign Office, www.gov.uk/foreign-travel-advice/honduras.

Telephone

Country code T+504.

Local operator T192; General information T193; International operator T197.
Hondutel provides international telephone services from stations throughout the country. The system has improved dramatically in recent years due to competition, with an increasing majority of Hondurans owning a cell phone. You can buy a cell

phone for about US$10 from Tigo, Claro and Digicel, with phone cards from US$2 upwards.

Time

-6 hrs GMT.

Tipping

Normally 10% of the bill but more expensive places add a service charge.

Tourist information

Instituto Hondureño de Turismo, main office is at Edificio Europa, Av Ramón E Cruz and Calle República de México, Col San Carlos, Tegucigalpa, T2222-2124. Also an office at Toncontín Airport and several regional offices.

Useful websites

www.hondurastips.hn A reliable favourite with lots of information about Honduras and hotel, restaurant and transport listings (Spanish only). The biannual publication, *HONDURAS Tips*, edited by John Dupuis in La Ceiba, Edificio Gómez, Local No 2, 4 Calle, T2440-3383, is full of interesting and useful tourist information, in English and Spanish, free (available in Tegucigalpa from Instituto Hondureño de Turismo, and widely distributed around the country in major hotels).
www.hondurasweekly.com News, cultural features, travel tips, listings and links.
www.letsgohonduras.com The official Tourist Office (IHT) guide on the internet, with basic highlights.
www.netsys.hn Good business directory and useful links (in English).

Several regional guides are being developed – these are mentioned within the text.

Visas and immigration

Neither a visa nor tourist card is required for nationals of Western European countries, USA, Canada, Australia, New Zealand, Japan, Argentina, Chile, Guatemala, Costa Rica, Nicaragua, El Salvador, Panama and Uruguay. Citizens of other countries need either a tourist card, which can be bought from Honduran consulates for US$2-3, or a visa, and they should enquire at a Honduran consulate in advance to see which they need. The price of a visa seems to vary depending on nationality and where it is bought. Extensions of 30 days are easy to obtain (up to a maximum of 6 months' stay, cost US$5). There are immigration offices for extensions at Tela, La Ceiba, San Pedro Sula, Santa Rosa de Copán, Siguatepeque, La Paz and Comayagua, and all are more helpful than the Tegucigalpa office.

In 2006 Guatemala, El Salvador, Honduras and Nicaragua signed a Central America-4 (CA-4) Border Control Agreement; see box, page 154. You will have to visit a country outside of these countries to re-enter and gain 90 days. These rules have been introduced to stop people leaving the country for 72 hrs (which is the legal requirement) every 6 months and returning, effectively making them permanent residents.

Weights and measures

The metric system is official.

Index

Entries in bold refer to maps

Credits

Footprint credits
Editor: Jo Williams
Production and layout: Patrick Dawson
Maps: Kevin Feeney
Colour section: Angus Dawson

Publisher: Patrick Dawson
Managing Editor: Felicity Laughton
Administration: Elizabeth Taylor
Advertising sales and marketing:
John Sadler, Kirsty Holmes
Business Development: Debbie Wylde

Photography credits
Front cover: Henner Damke/
Shutterstock.com.
Back cover: Top: soft_light/
Shutterstock.com. **Bottom**: Dennis
Sabo/Shutterstock.com.

Colour section
Inside front cover: Stubblefield
Photography/Shutterstock.com,
Christian Kober/SuperStock, Animals
Animals/SuperStock, Brendan van
Son/Shutterstock.com. **Page 1**:
Wolfgang Kaehler/SuperStock. **Page 2**:
Stubblefield Photography/Shutterstock.
com. **Page 4**: Presse750/Dreamstime.
com, Christian Kober/SuperStock,
Lspencer/Shutterstock.com. **Page 5**:
age fotostock/SuperStock, Barna Tanko/
Shutterstock.com. **Page 7**: Martin Battiti/
Dreamstime.com, Hemis.fr/SuperStock.
Page 8: Minden Pictures/SuperStock.
Duotone Page 18: Brendan van Son/
Shutterstock.com.

Printed in Spain by GraphyCems

Publishing information
Footprint Honduras
2nd edition
© Footprint Handbooks Ltd
September 2015

ISBN: 978 1 910120 35 4
CIP DATA: A catalogue record for this
book is available from the British Library

® Footprint Handbooks and the
Footprint mark are a registered
trademark of Footprint Handbooks Ltd

Published by Footprint
6 Riverside Court
Lower Bristol Road
Bath BA2 3DZ, UK
T +44 (0)1225 469141
F +44 (0)1225 469461
footprinttravelguides.com

Distributed in the USA by
National Book Network, Inc.

Every effort has been made to ensure
that the facts in this guidebook are
accurate. However, travellers should still
obtain advice from consulates, airlines,
etc about travel and visa requirements
before travelling.The authors and
publishers cannotaccept responsibility
for any loss, injury or inconvenience
however caused.